D1511721

STEVENSON • WATTERS • ALLEN • LAIHO

LUMBERJANES™

OUT OF TIME

BOOM! BOX™

BOOM! BOX™

LUMBERJANES Volume Four, July 2016. Published by BOOM! Box, a division of Boom Entertainment, Inc. Lumberjanes is ™ & © 2016 Shannon Watters, Grace Ellis, Noelle Stevenson & Brooke Allen. Originally published in single magazine form as LUMBERJANES No. 14-17. ™ & © 2015 Shannon Watters, Grace Ellis, Noelle Stevenson & Brooke Allen. All rights reserved. BOOM! Box™ and the BOOM! Box logo are trademarks of Boom Entertainment, Inc., registered in various countries and categories. All characters, events, and institutions depicted herein are fictional. Any similarity between any of the names, characters, persons, events, and/or institutions in this publication to actual names, characters, and persons, whether living or dead, events, and/or institutions is unintended and purely coincidental. BOOM! Box does not read or accept unsolicited submissions of ideas, stories, or artwork.

A catalog record of this book is available from OCLC and from the BOOM! Studios website, www.boom-studios.com, on the Librarians Page.

BOOM! Studios, 5670 Wilshire Boulevard, Suite 450, Los Angeles, CA 90036-5679. Printed in China. First Printing.

ISBN: 978-1-60886-860-5, eISBN: 978-1-61398-531-1

THIS LUMBERJANES FIELD MANUAL BELONGS TO:

NAME:_____

TROOP:_____

DATE INVESTED:_____

FIELD MANUAL TABLE OF CONTENTS

LUMBERJANES
FIELD MANUAL

For the Intermediate Program

Tenth Edition • April 1984

Prepared for the

**Miss Qiunzella Thiskwin
Penniquiqul Thistle Crumpet's**

CAMP FOR  HARDCORE LADY-TYPES

"Friendship to the Max!"

A MESSAGE FROM THE LUMBERJANES HIGH COUNCIL

miss Quinzella Thiskwin Penniquiqul Thistle Crumpet's
Camp for
HARDCORE LADY TYPES
FRIENDSHIP to the MAX!

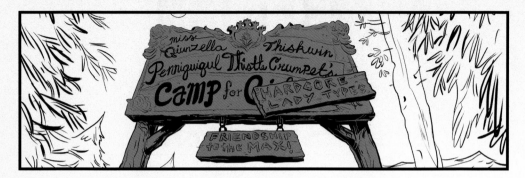

Close your eyes and think of the happiest moment of your life. Really think about the details of that moment, where you were, the smell of the air, or if there were people with you. It's this moment that you truly felt joy, that you felt like you were part of something bigger than yourself in just a breath of time. It's these moments that we strive for with our Lumberjanes camp. Imagine a world in which you were not only motivated to succeed in any aspect of life, had any path available in front of you, and could also choose the stones in which the path was made. Personally, my path would by have been made of flagstone.

This volume of the Lumberjanes guide is meant to help any who hold it, anybody can take the lessons that are explained here and bring them to fruition in their everyday life, and the not so everyday life. The biggest lesson that we can teach you today is that time is fluid. It runs between our fingers quickly but it can also stand still, as if frozen in a moment. Time will never be controlled but that doesn't mean that it won't work for you when need most.

As you get older, you'll look at the past and wonder about all the things that could have been. About all the things you should have done, or maybe even the things you would have avoided if you had the same knowledge that you do today. You will think about the friendships that you created when you were young and innocent of the ways of the world and how those friendships grew into something amazing, or maybe they grew apart. At our camp we hope that you will be able to create friendships that will last with you until the very end of time, that will triumph over any obstacle and only grow stronger. And if these friendships should wane, then we hope it's a natural process of growing older and wiser, for we are all very different in our own ways and sometimes that means we have to take different paths on this crazy life.

THE LUMBERJANES PLEDGE

I solemnly swear to do my best
Every day, and in all that I do,
To be brave and strong,
To be truthful and compassionate,
To be interesting and interested,
To pay attention and question
The world around me,
To think of others first,
To always help and protect my friends,
[redacted]
And to make the world a better place
For Lumberjane scouts
And for everyone else.

THEN THERE'S A LINE ABOUT GOD, OR WHATEVER

OUT OF TIME

Written by
Noelle Stevenson
& Shannon Watters

Illustrated by
Brooke Allen

Colors by
Maarta Laiho

Letters by
Aubrey Aiese

Cover by
Noelle Stevenson

Badges and Design by
Scott Newman

Associate Editor
Whitney Leopard

Editor
Dafna Pleban

*Special thanks to **Kelsey Pate** for giving the Lumberjanes their name.*

Created by **Shannon Watters, Grace Ellis, Noelle Stevenson & Brooke Allen**

LUMBERJANES FIELD MANUAL

CHAPTER THIRTEEN

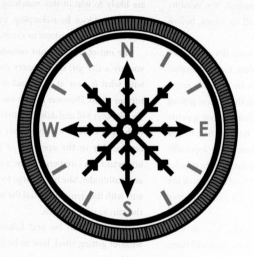

Lumberjanes "Out-of-Doors" Program Field

SNOW-GLOBE TROTTER BADGE

"There's snow stopping us now!"

Traveling the world is just one of the many enjoyments of life, and being a Lumberjane is, for a large part, about enjoyment. Every Lumberjane should leave camp with the basic understanding of survival when it comes to any form of travel. Whether it be a sleeping party with just a blanket and the stars for company or a grand excursion through the tallest mountains she is able to find. A Lumberjane encounters many problems through life, but she will survive and thrive through them all. One of the many goals of the Lumberjanes is to make sure every young lady leaves with the tools to succeed. And some of these tools are taught as the Lumberjanes earns her *Snow-Globe Trotter* badge.

Traveling is a fine pass time, as well as a great career that any Lumberjane could find herself enjoying. It is the tendency for a Lumberjane to want to learn everything there is to know about the world at large. She will want

to learn, and she will want to discover and explore all the places that haven't yet been touched by civilization. There are so many amazing worlds out there and this camp is only the beginning. There are many exercises the Lumberjanes will find at this camp that will help them find the tools and training they need to make all of this possible for them.

To obtain the *Snow-Globe Trotter* badge, a Lumberjane must keep a journal of her discoveries as she travels through the camp. With the help of her cabin, she will connect with the nature around her and create a map of the area. She will gain basic survival skills of what to do in the wilderness, and she will learn the amazing art of mapmaking. She will be able to be identify plants from all over the globe, as well as know the traits of poisonous plants, so that she should come across something unknown she will be able to ensure that none of her

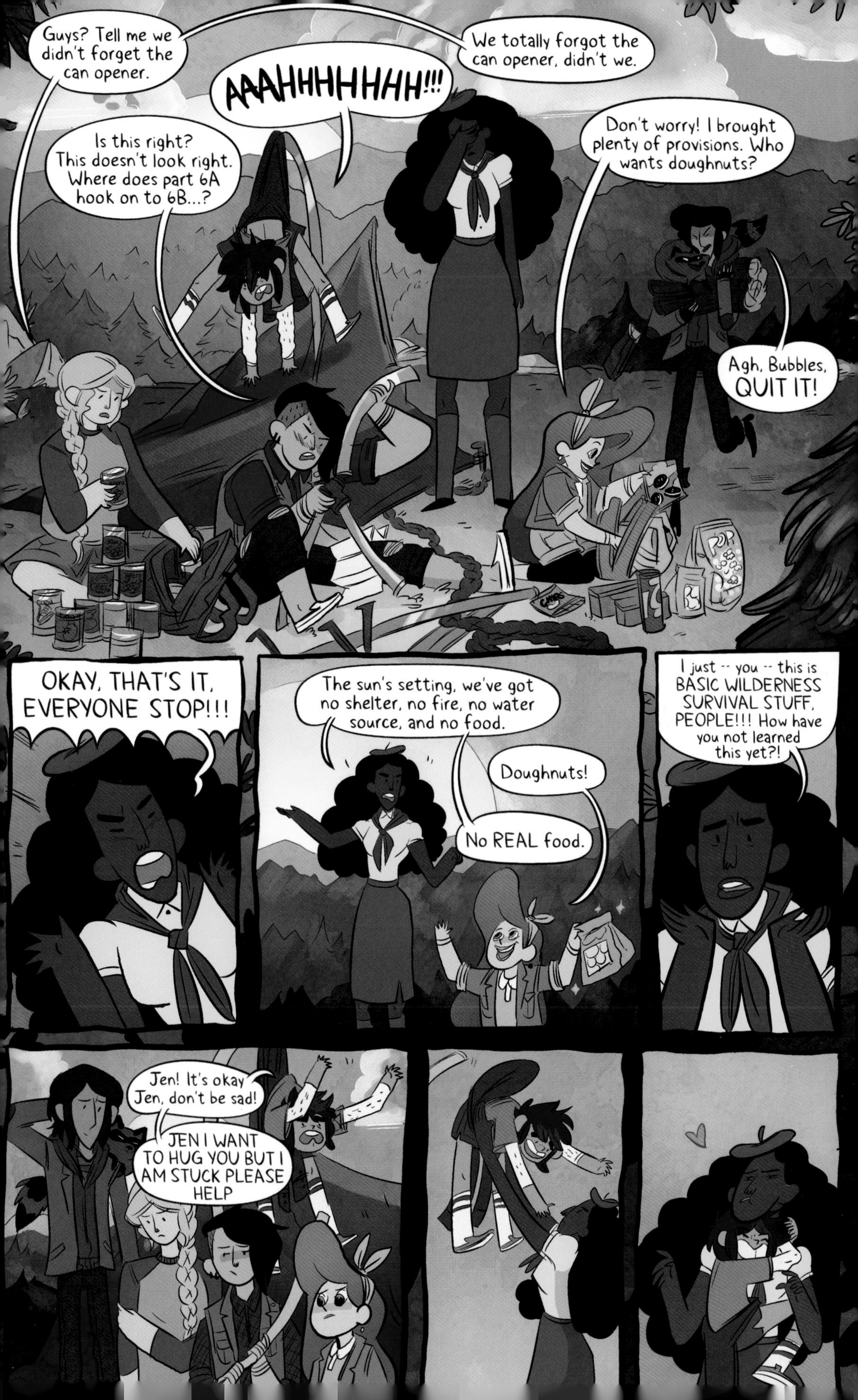

Guys? Tell me we didn't forget the can opener.
We totally forgot the can opener, didn't we.
AAAHHHHHHH!!!
Is this right? This doesn't look right. Where does part 6A hook on to 6B...?
Don't worry! I brought plenty of provisions. Who wants doughnuts?
Agh, Bubbles, QUIT IT!
POP
CHIPS
OKAY, THAT'S IT, EVERYONE STOP!!!
The sun's setting, we've got no shelter, no fire, no water source, and no food.
Doughnuts!
No REAL food.
I just -- you -- this is BASIC WILDERNESS SURVIVAL STUFF, PEOPLE!!! How have you not learned this yet?!
Jen! It's okay Jen, don't be sad!
JEN I WANT TO HUG YOU BUT I AM STUCK PLEASE HELP

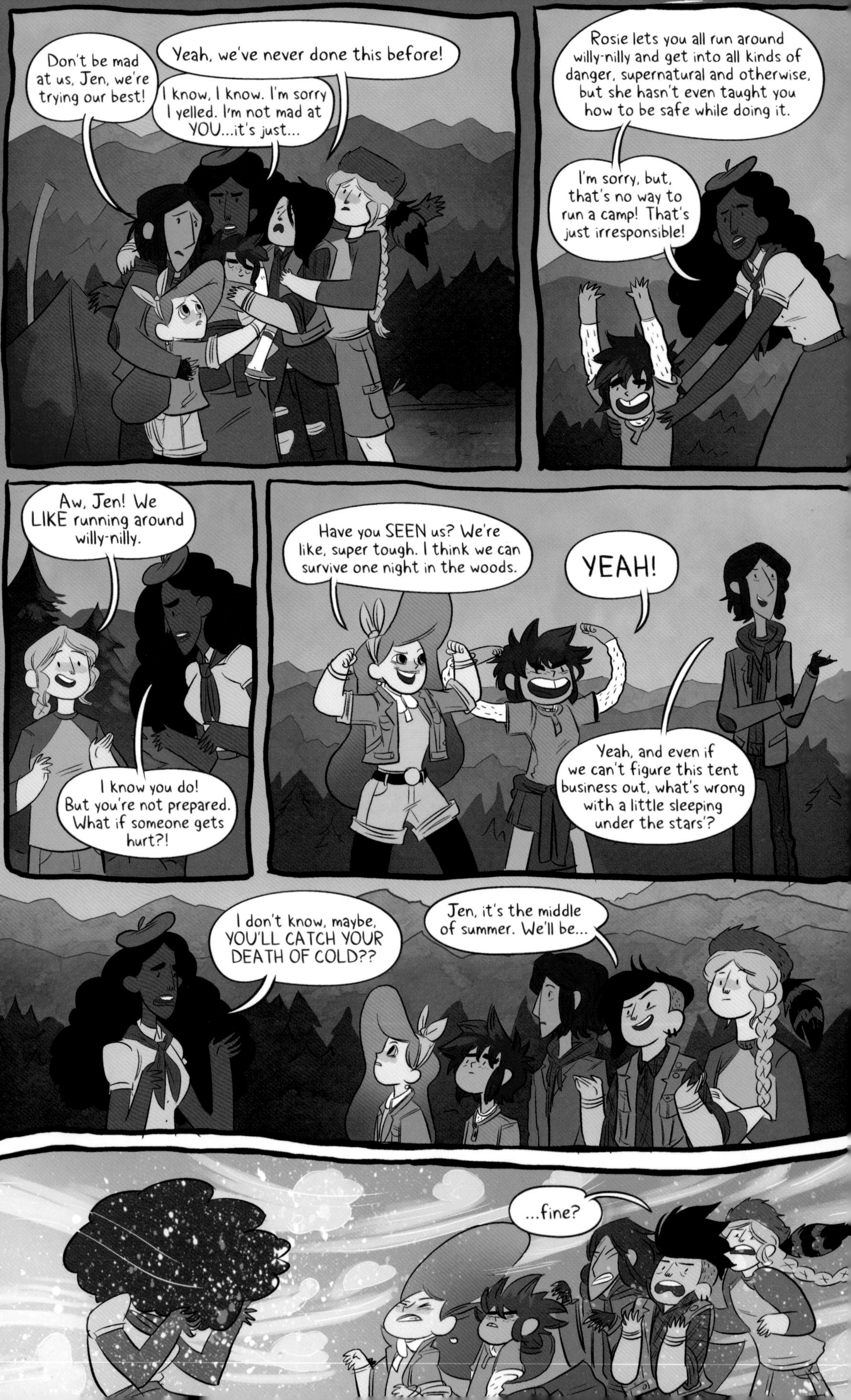
Don't be mad at us, Jen, we're trying our best!
Yeah, we've never done this before!
I know, I know. I'm sorry I yelled. I'm not mad at YOU...it's just...
Rosie lets you all run around willy-nilly and get into all kinds of danger, supernatural and otherwise, but she hasn't even taught you how to be safe while doing it.
I'm sorry, but, that's no way to run a camp! That's just irresponsible!
Aw, Jen! We LIKE running around willy-nilly.
I know you do! But you're not prepared. What if someone gets hurt?!
Have you SEEN us? We're like, super tough. I think we can survive one night in the woods.
YEAH!
Yeah, and even if we can't figure this tent business out, what's wrong with a little sleeping under the stars?
I don't know, maybe, YOU'LL CATCH YOUR DEATH OF COLD??
Jen, it's the middle of summer. We'll be...
...fine?

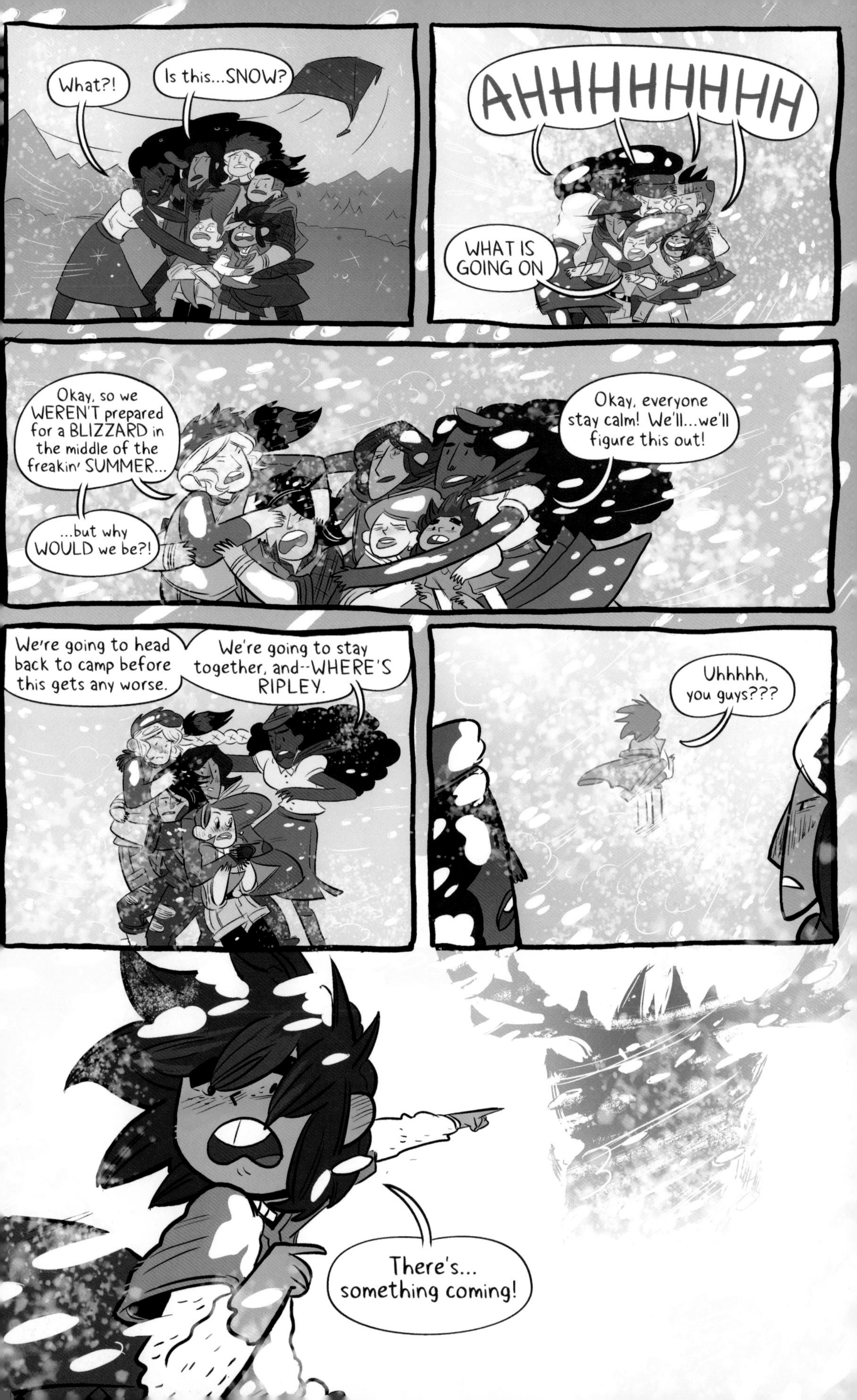
What?!
Is this...SNOW?
AHHHHHHHHH
WHAT IS GOING ON
Okay, so we WEREN'T prepared for a BLIZZARD in the middle of the freakin' SUMMER...
...but why WOULD we be?!
Okay, everyone stay calm! We'll...we'll figure this out!
We're going to head back to camp before this gets any worse.
We're going to stay together, and--WHERE'S RIPLEY.
Uhhhhh, you guys???
There's... something coming!

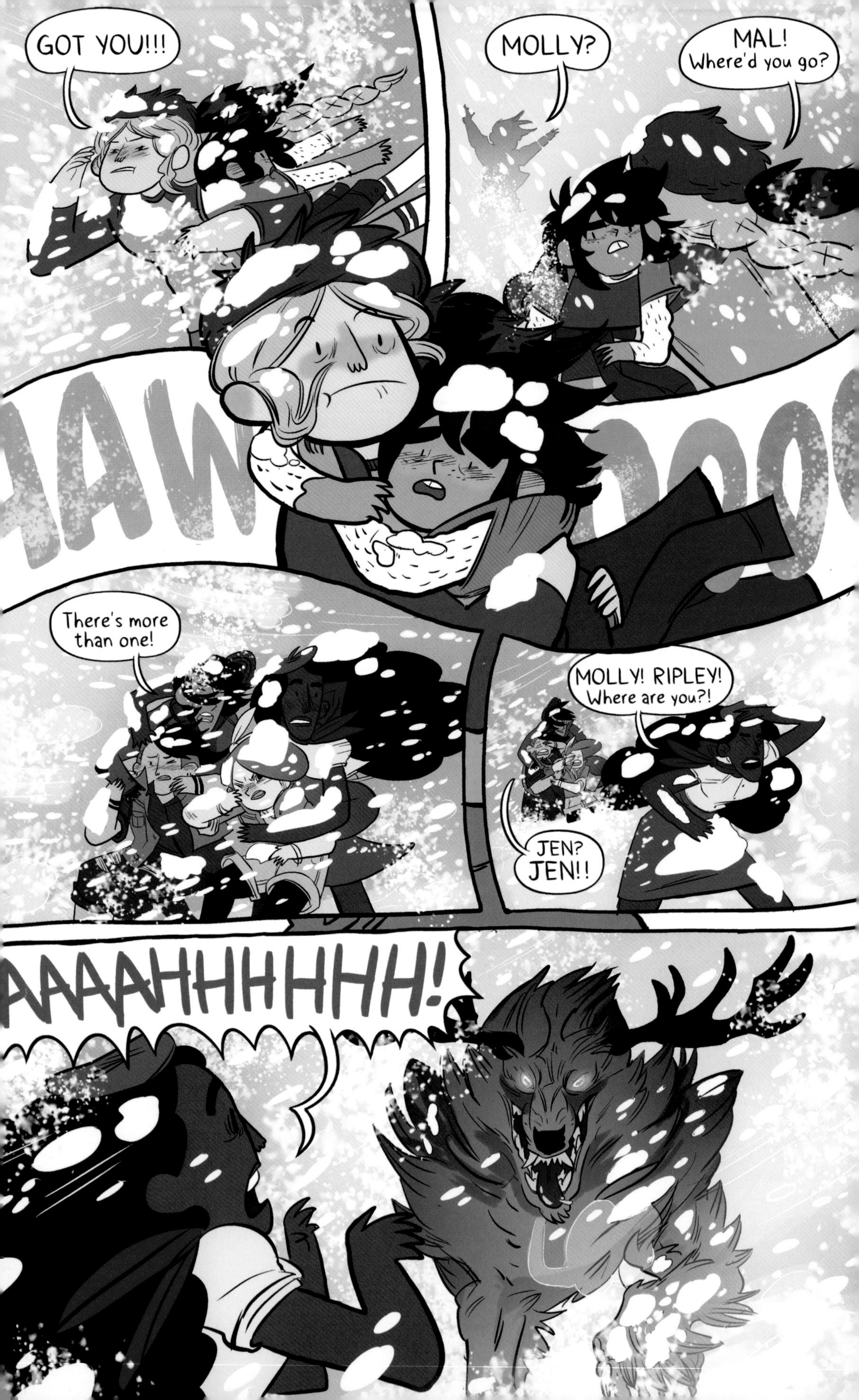
GOT YOU!!!
MOLLY?
MAL!
Where'd you go?
There's more than one!
MOLLY! RIPLEY!
Where are you?!
JEN?
JEN!!
AAAAHHHHHH!

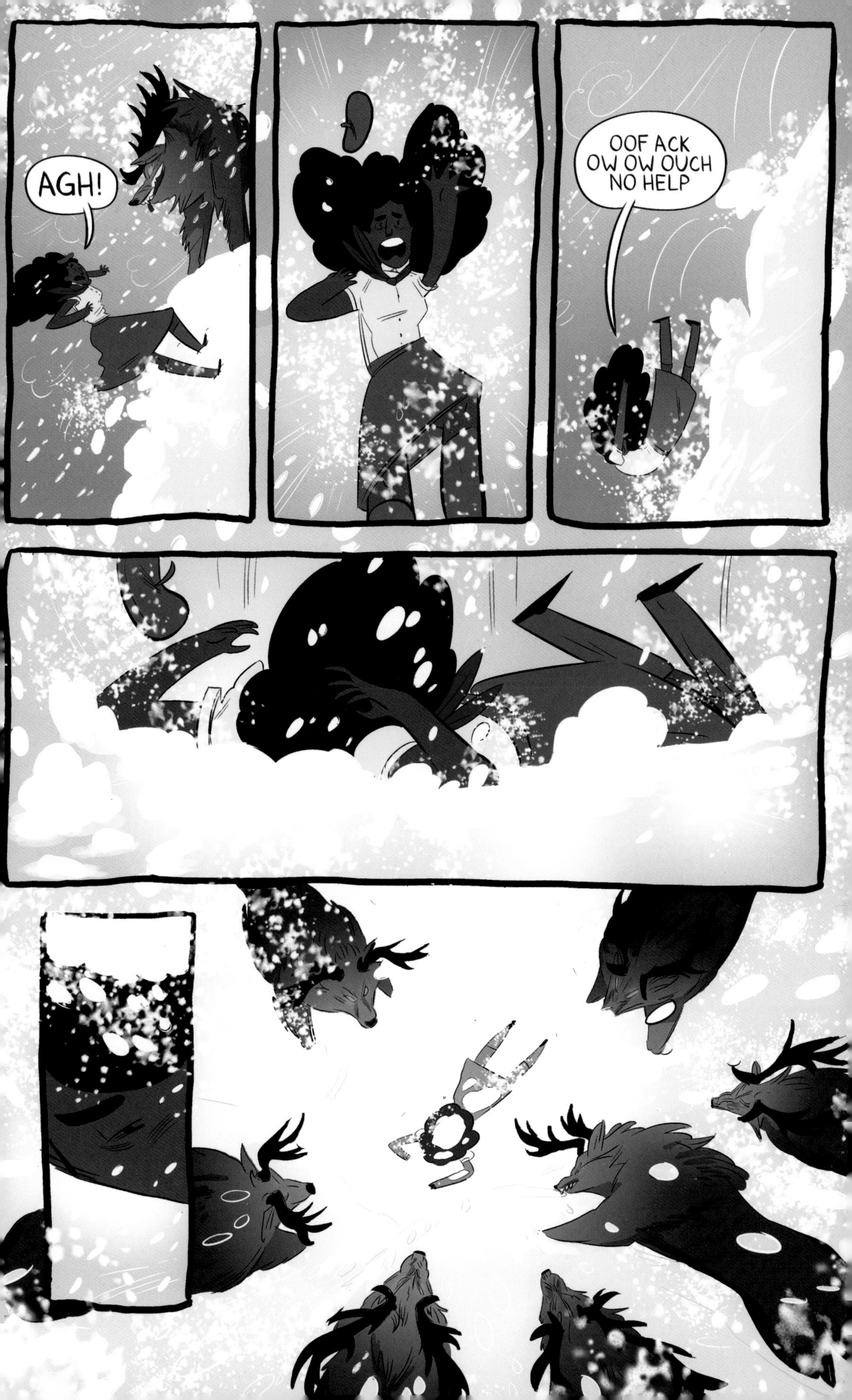
AGH!
OOF ACK
OW OW OUCH
NO HELP

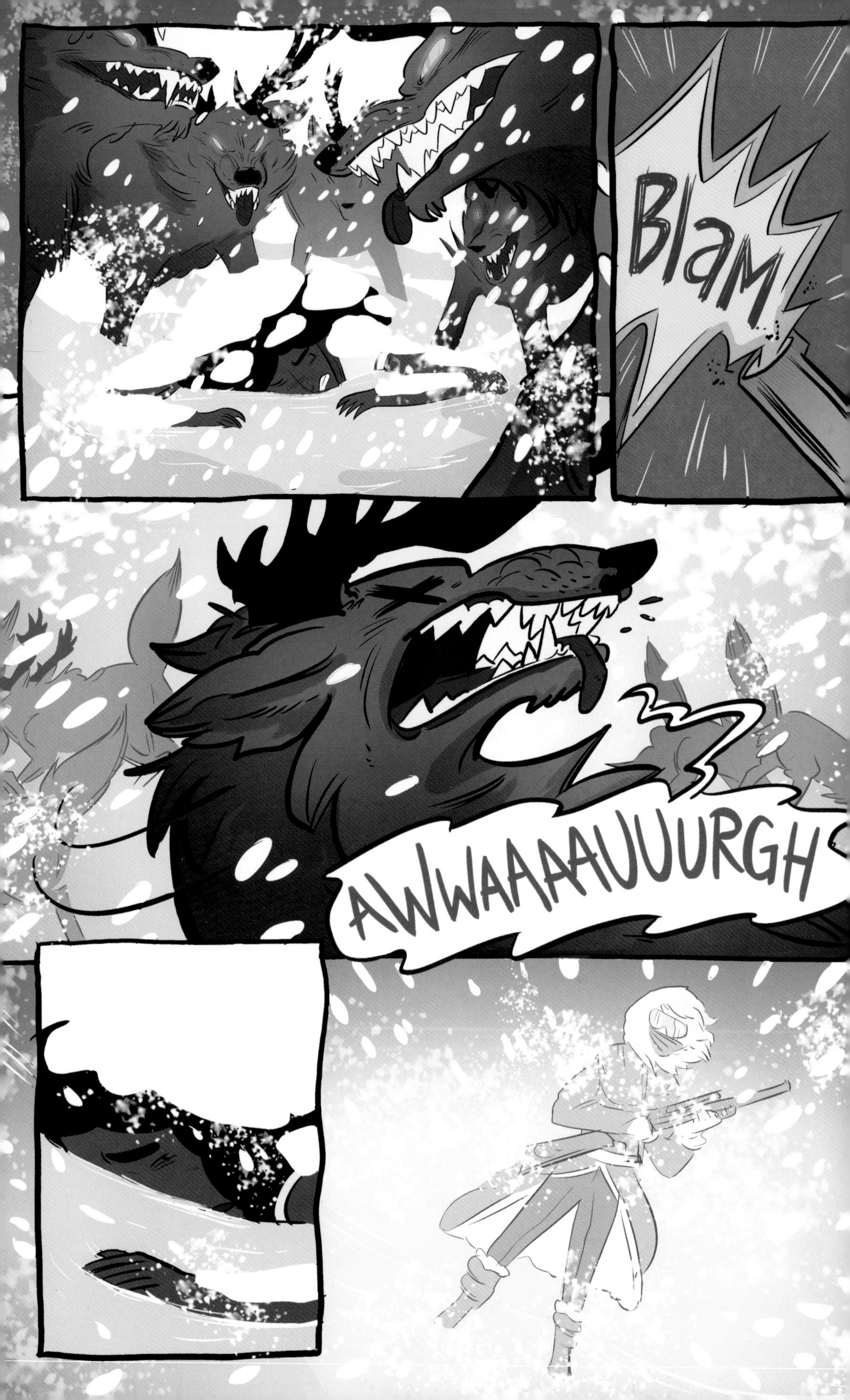
BLAM
AWWAAAAUUURGH

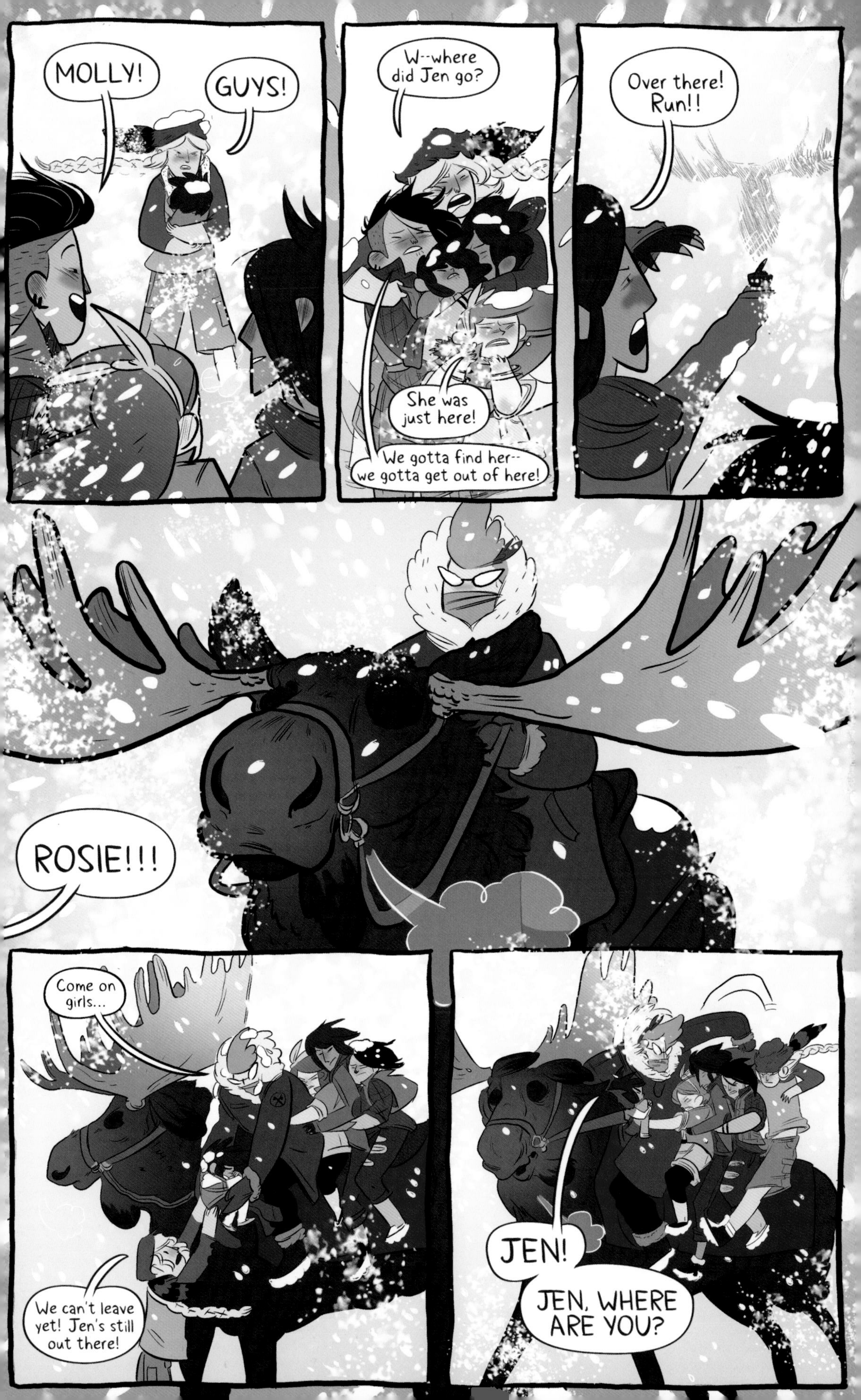
MOLLY!
GUYS!
W--where did Jen go?
She was just here!
We gotta find her-- we gotta get out of here!
Over there! Run!!
ROSIE!!!
Come on girls...
We can't leave yet! Jen's still out there!
JEN!
JEN, WHERE ARE YOU?

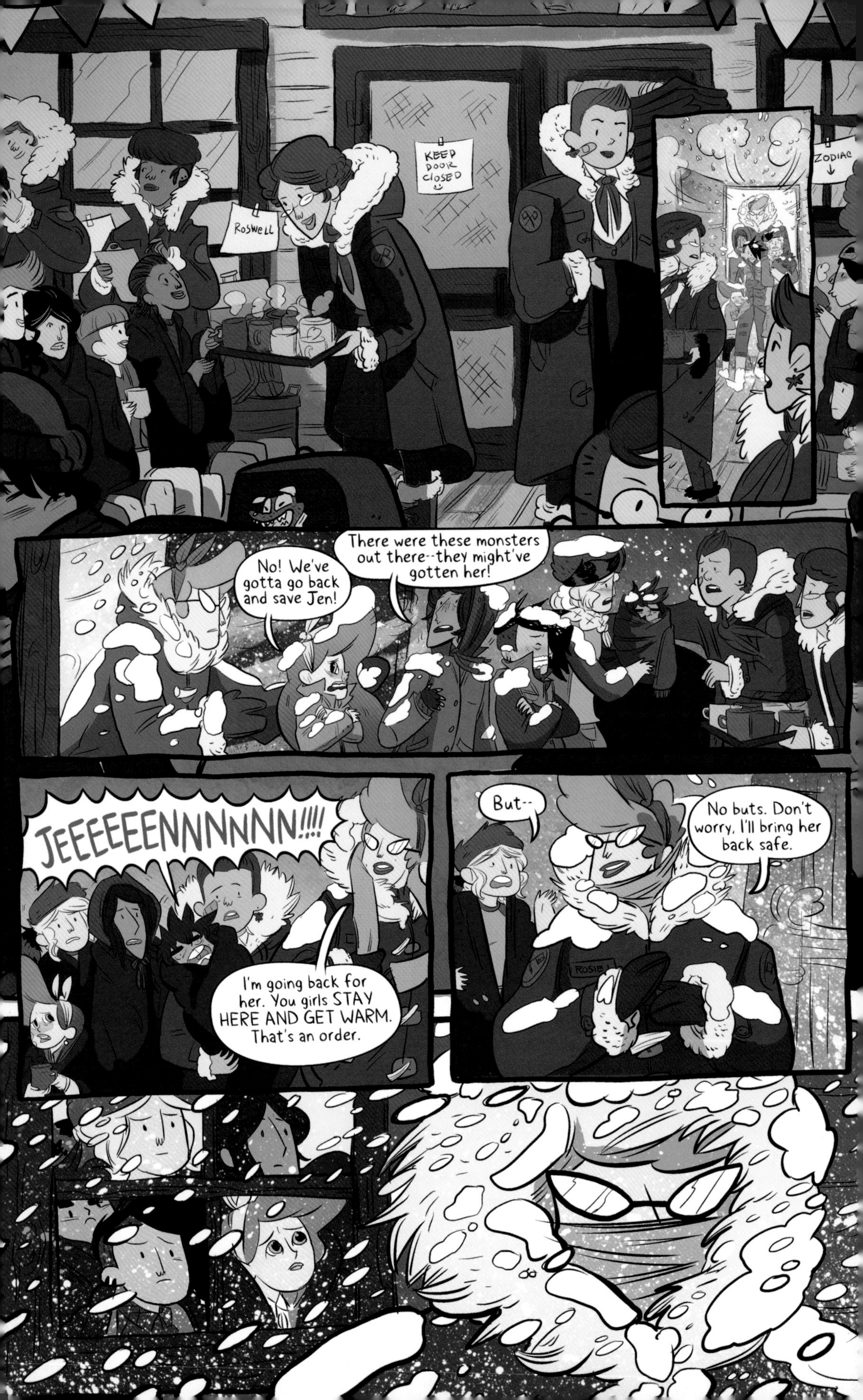
KEEP DOOR CLOSED
ROSWELL
ZODIAC
No! We've gotta go back and save Jen!
There were these monsters out there--they might've gotten her!
JEEEEEENNNNNN!!!!
I'm going back for her. You girls STAY HERE AND GET WARM. That's an order.
But--
No buts. Don't worry, I'll bring her back safe.
ROSIE

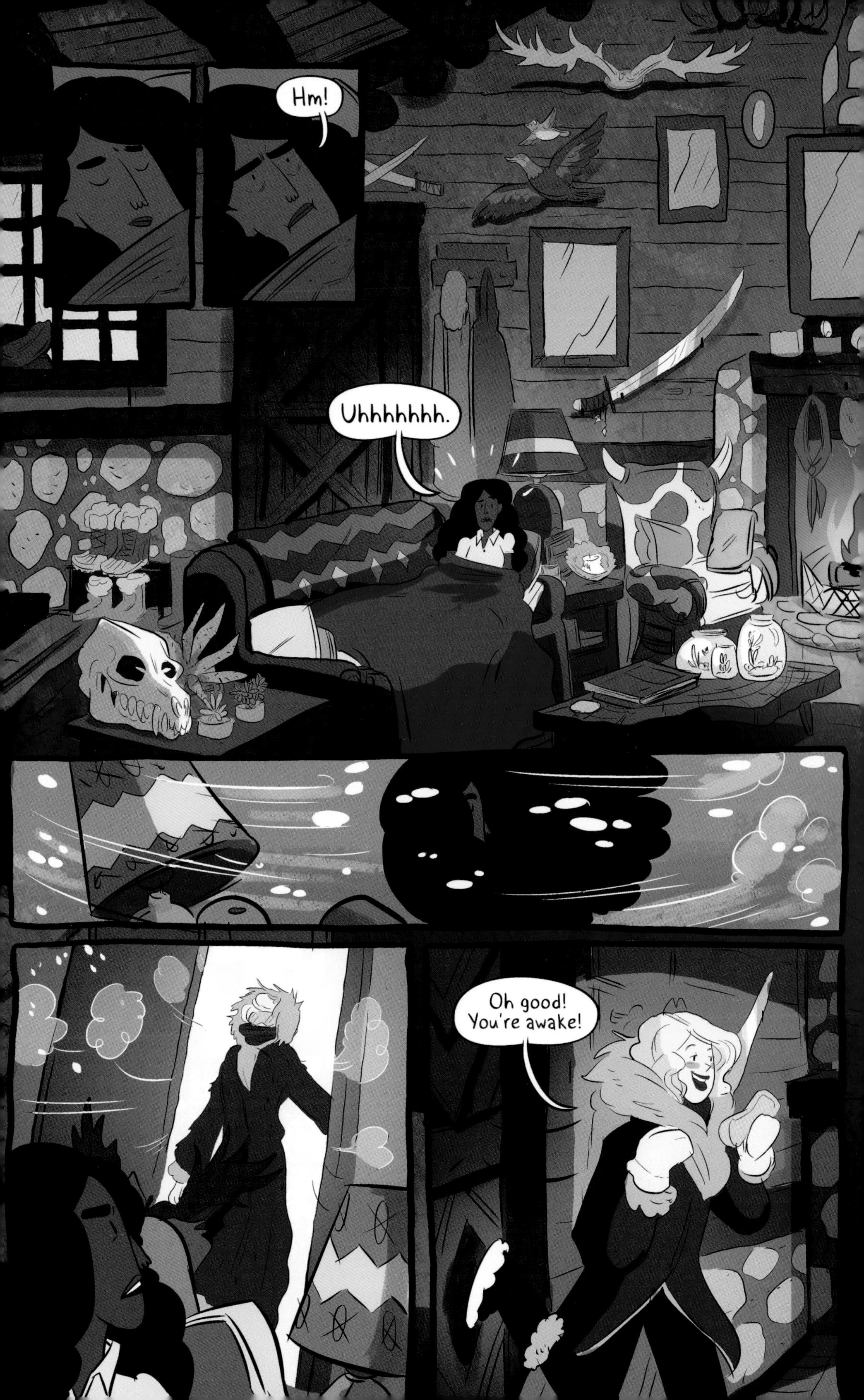
Hm!
Uhhhhhhh.
Oh good!
You're awake!

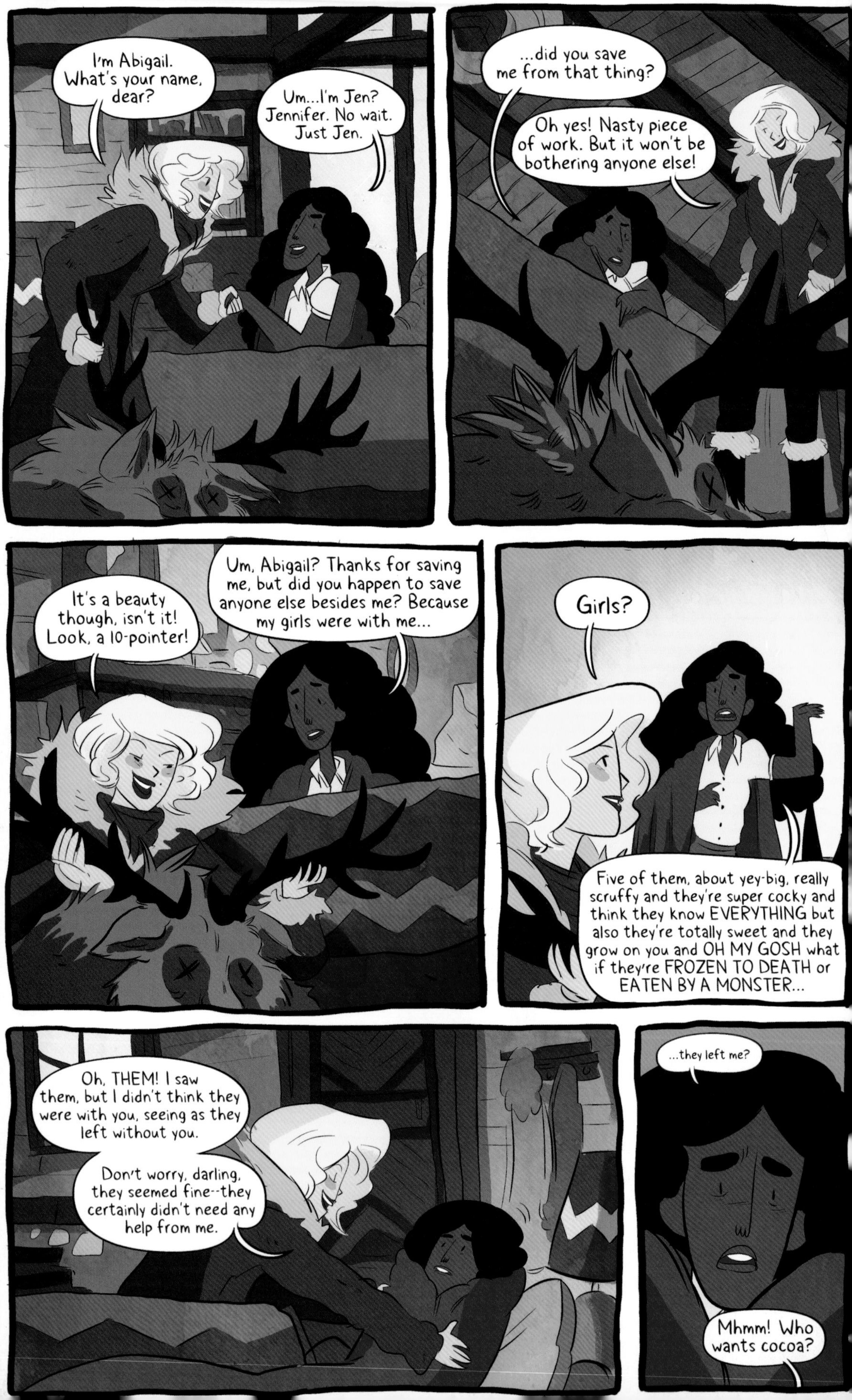
I'm Abigail. What's your name, dear?
Um...I'm Jen? Jennifer. No wait. Just Jen.
...did you save me from that thing?
Oh yes! Nasty piece of work. But it won't be bothering anyone else!
It's a beauty though, isn't it! Look, a 10-pointer!
Um, Abigail? Thanks for saving me, but did you happen to save anyone else besides me? Because my girls were with me...
Girls?
Five of them, about yey-big, really scruffy and they're super cocky and think they know EVERYTHING but also they're totally sweet and they grow on you and OH MY GOSH what if they're FROZEN TO DEATH or EATEN BY A MONSTER...
Oh, THEM! I saw them, but I didn't think they were with you, seeing as they left without you.
Don't worry, darling, they seemed fine--they certainly didn't need any help from me.
...they left me?
Mhmm! Who wants cocoa?

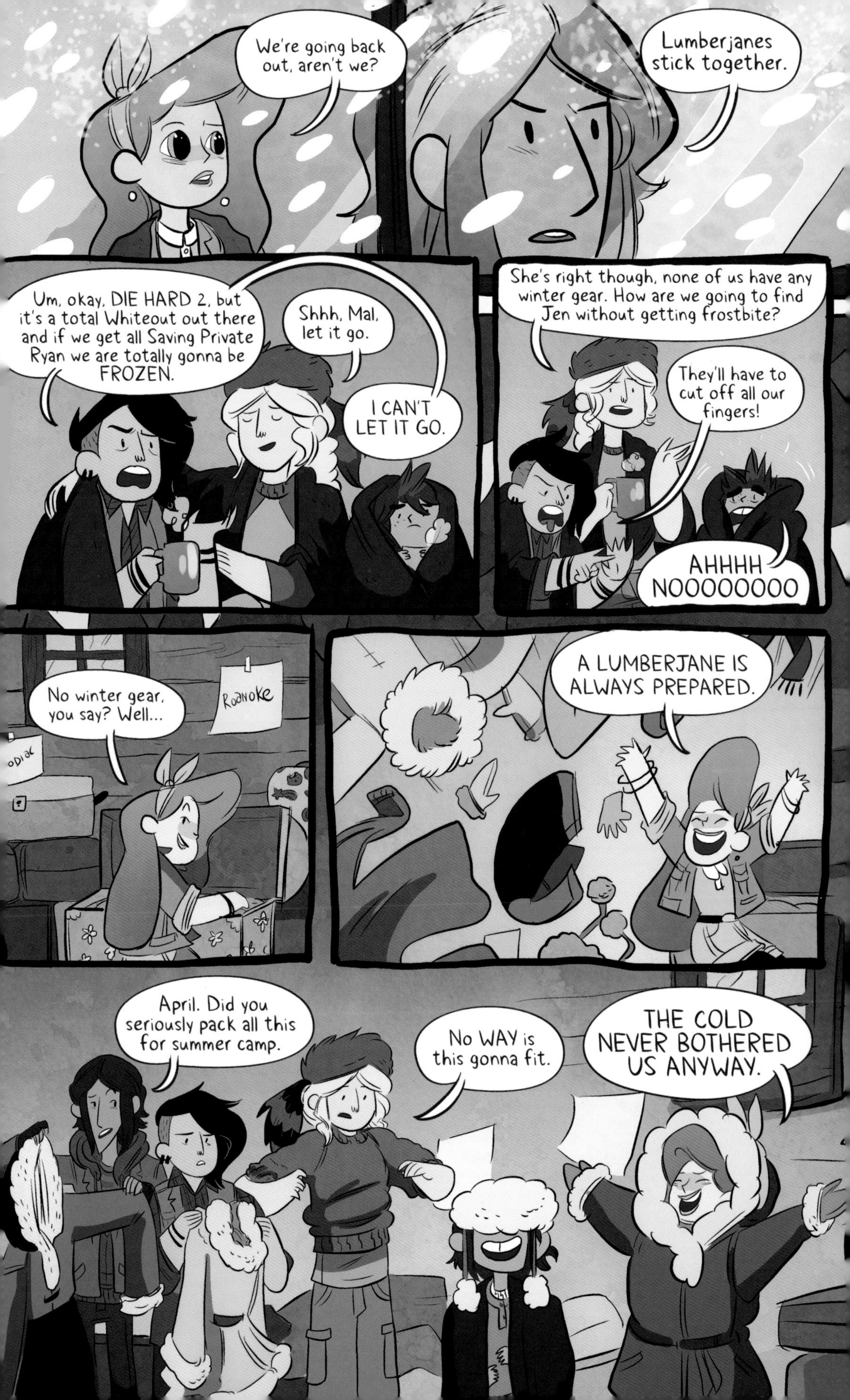
We're going back out, aren't we?
Lumberjanes stick together.
Um, okay, DIE HARD 2, but it's a total Whiteout out there and if we get all Saving Private Ryan we are totally gonna be FROZEN.
Shhh, Mal, let it go.
I CAN'T LET IT GO.
She's right though, none of us have any winter gear. How are we going to find Jen without getting frostbite?
They'll have to cut off all our fingers!
AHHHH NOOOOOOOO
No winter gear, you say? Well...
Roanoke
A LUMBERJANE IS ALWAYS PREPARED.
April. Did you seriously pack all this for summer camp.
No WAY is this gonna fit.
THE COLD NEVER BOTHERED US ANYWAY.

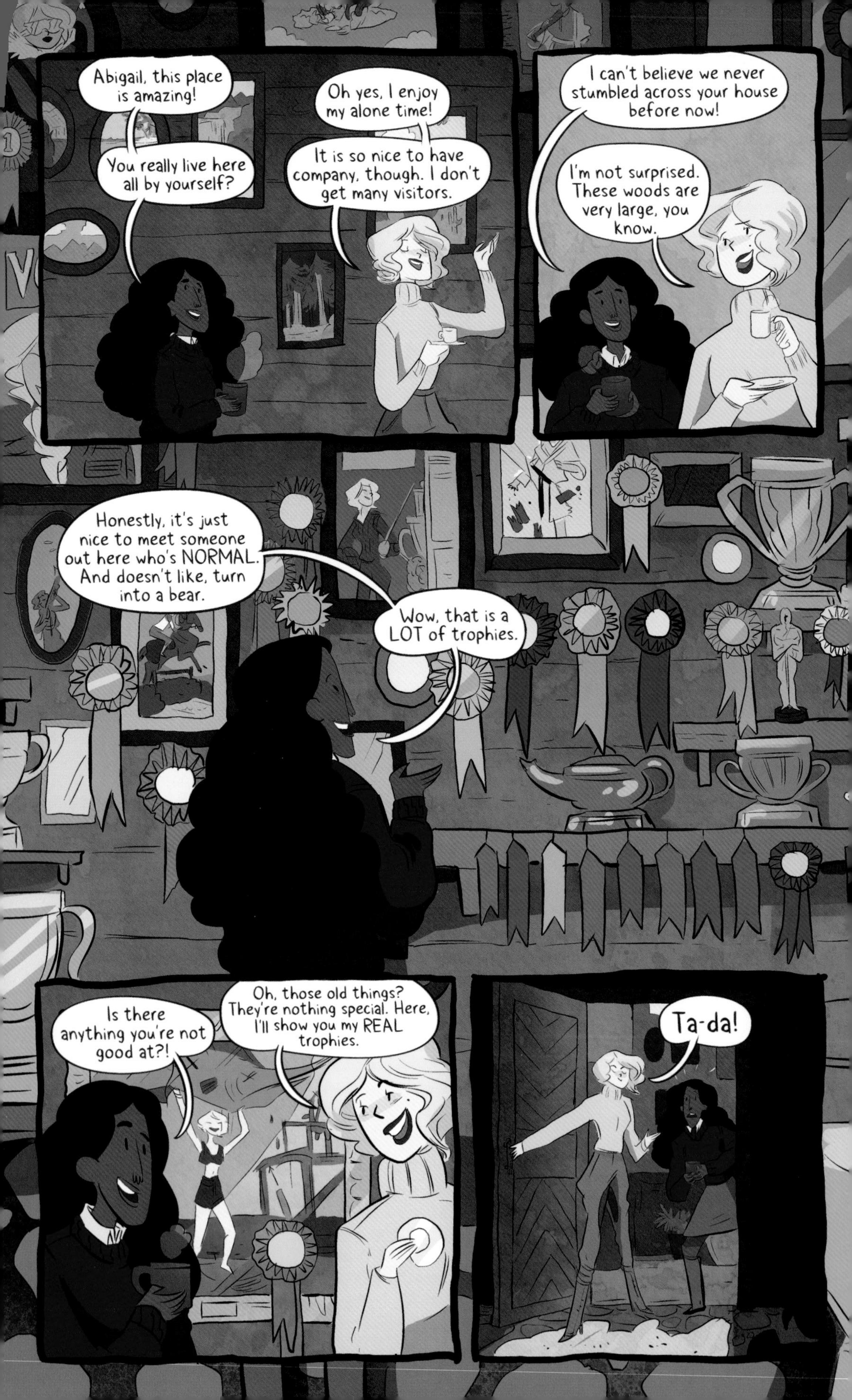
Abigail, this place is amazing!
You really live here all by yourself?
Oh yes, I enjoy my alone time!
It is so nice to have company, though. I don't get many visitors.
I can't believe we never stumbled across your house before now!
I'm not surprised. These woods are very large, you know.
Honestly, it's just nice to meet someone out here who's NORMAL. And doesn't like, turn into a bear.
Wow, that is a LOT of trophies.
Is there anything you're not good at?!
Oh, those old things? They're nothing special. Here, I'll show you my REAL trophies.
Ta-da!

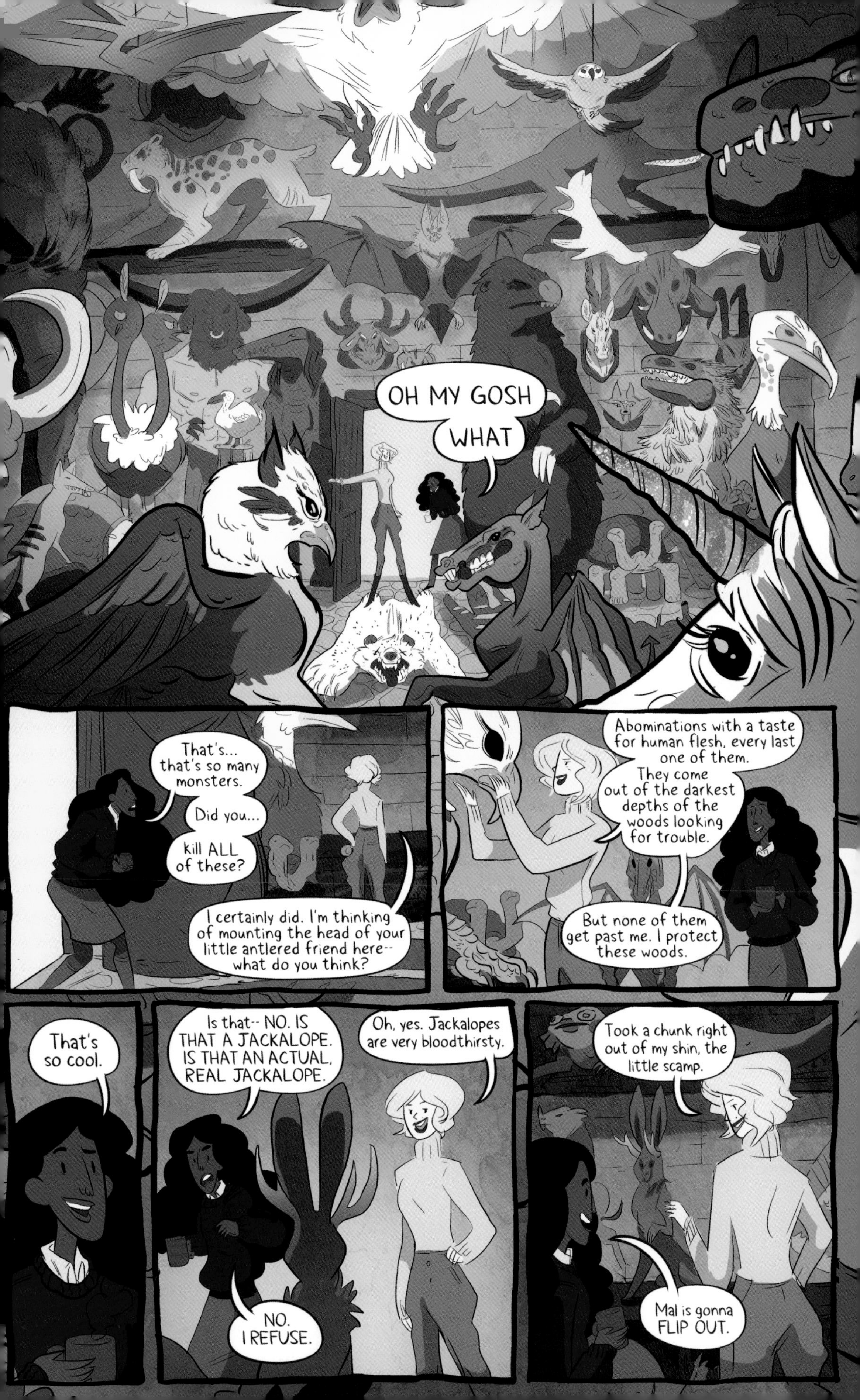
OH MY GOSH
WHAT
That's... that's so many monsters.
Did you...
kill ALL of these?
I certainly did. I'm thinking of mounting the head of your little antlered friend here-- what do you think?
Abominations with a taste for human flesh, every last one of them.
They come out of the darkest depths of the woods looking for trouble.
But none of them get past me. I protect these woods.
That's so cool.
Is that-- NO. IS THAT A JACKALOPE. IS THAT AN ACTUAL, REAL JACKALOPE.
Oh, yes. Jackalopes are very bloodthirsty.
NO. I REFUSE.
Took a chunk right out of my shin, the little scamp.
Mal is gonna FLIP OUT.

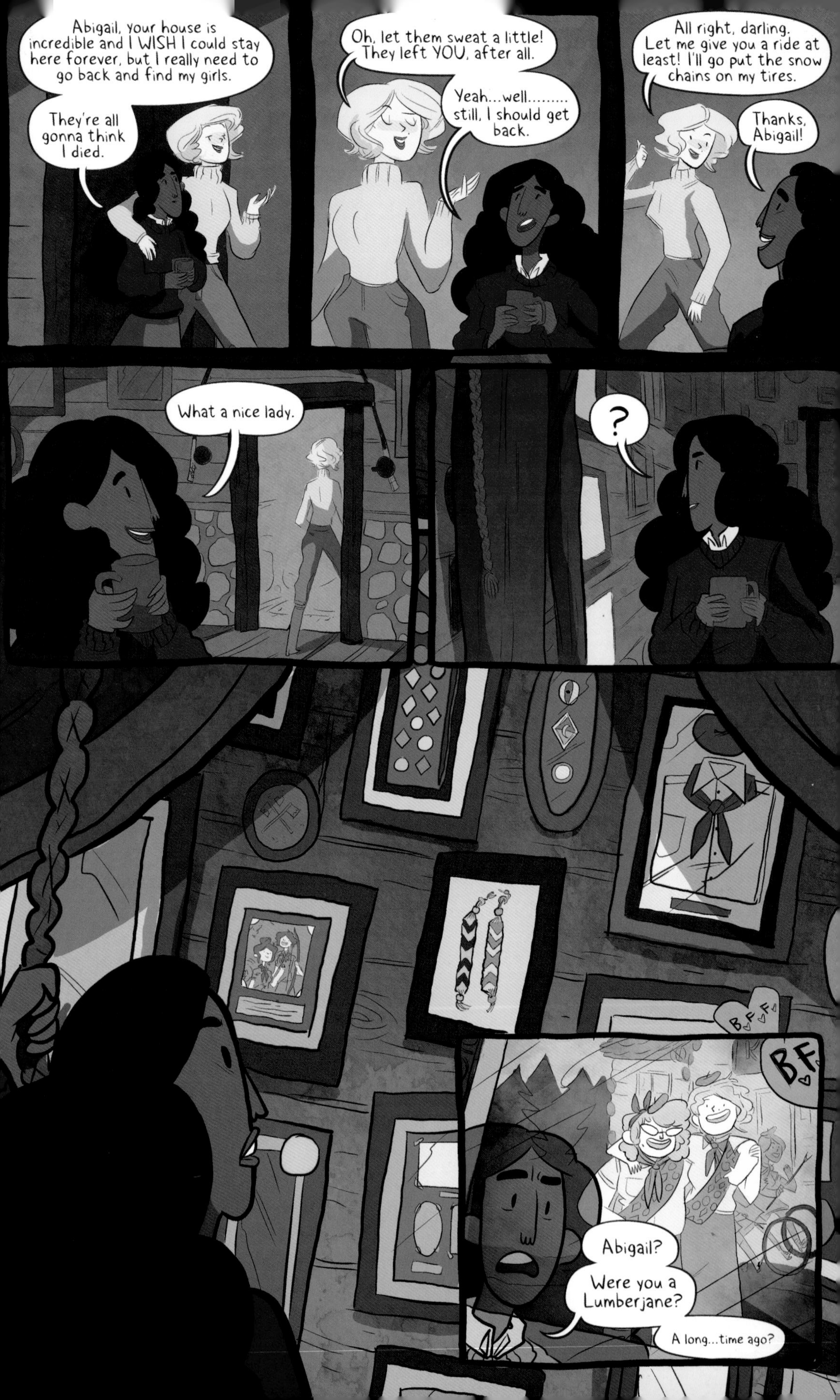
Abigail, your house is incredible and I WISH I could stay here forever, but I really need to go back and find my girls.
They're all gonna think I died.
Oh, let them sweat a little! They left YOU, after all.
Yeah...well......... still, I should get back.
All right, darling. Let me give you a ride at least! I'll go put the snow chains on my tires.
Thanks, Abigail!
What a nice lady.
?
BFF
BF
Abigail?
Were you a Lumberjane?
A long...time ago?

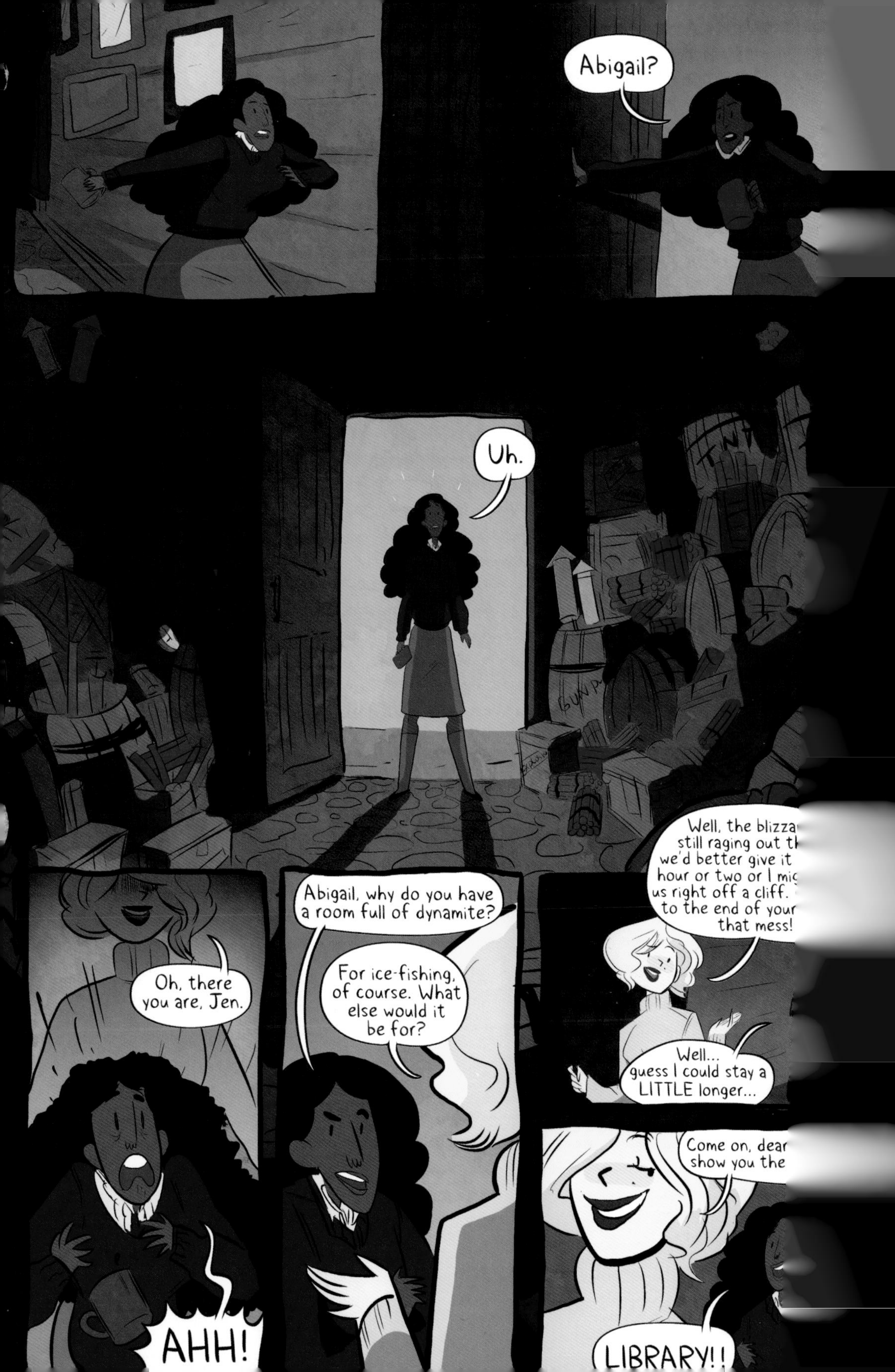
Abigail?
Uh.
TNT
Oh, there you are, Jen.
AHH!
Abigail, why do you have a room full of dynamite?
For ice-fishing, of course. What else would it be for?
Well, the blizza still raging out t we'd better give it hour or two or I mig us right off a cliff. to the end of your that mess!
Well... guess I could stay a LITTLE longer...
Come on, dear show you the
LIBRARY!!

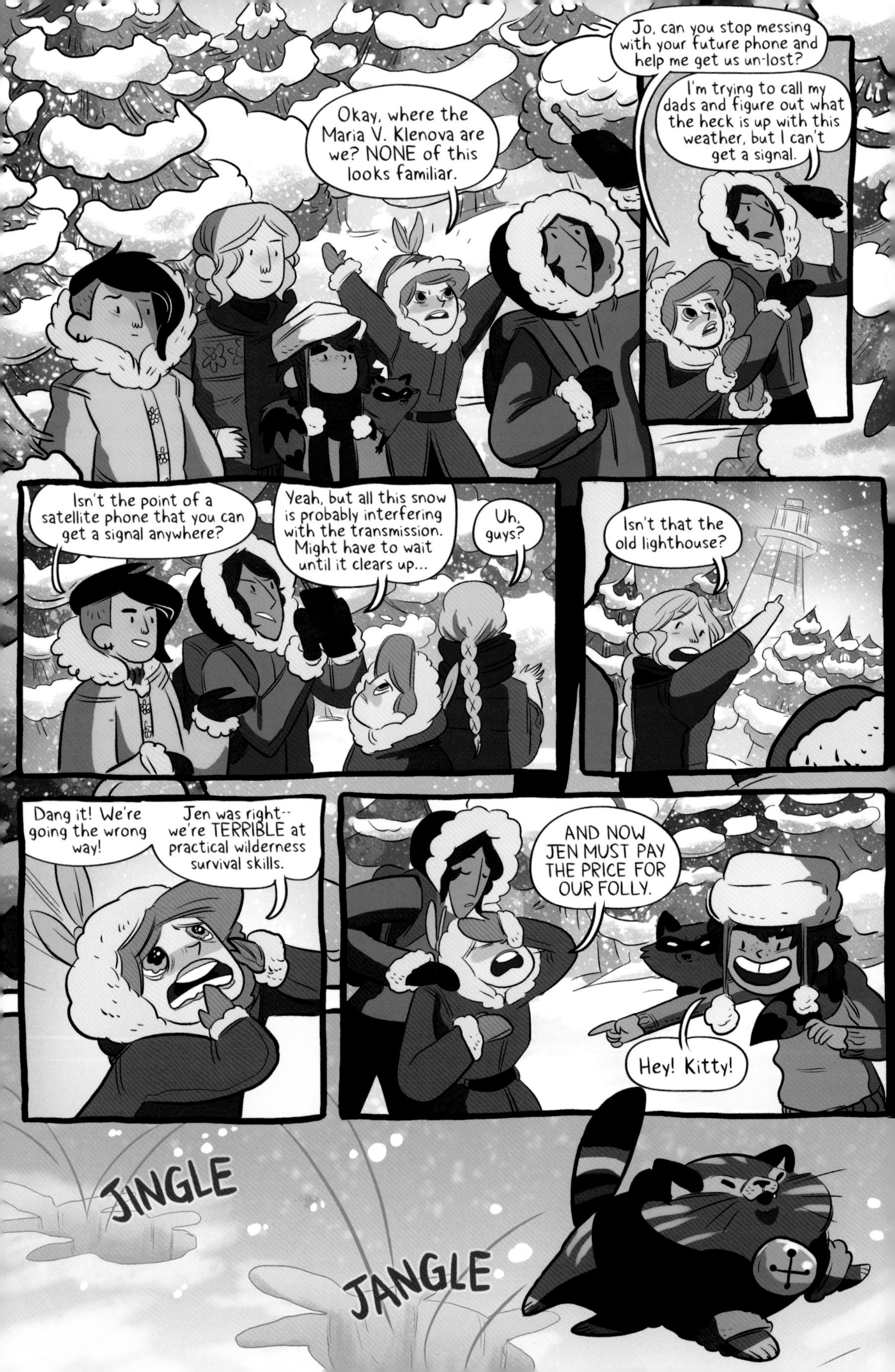
Okay, where the Maria V. Klenova are we? NONE of this looks familiar.
Jo, can you stop messing with your future phone and help me get us un-lost?
I'm trying to call my dads and figure out what the heck is up with this weather, but I can't get a signal.
Isn't the point of a satellite phone that you can get a signal anywhere?
Yeah, but all this snow is probably interfering with the transmission. Might have to wait until it clears up...
Uh, guys?
Isn't that the old lighthouse?
Dang it! We're going the wrong way!
Jen was right-- we're TERRIBLE at practical wilderness survival skills.
AND NOW JEN MUST PAY THE PRICE FOR OUR FOLLY.
Hey! Kitty!
JINGLE
JANGLE

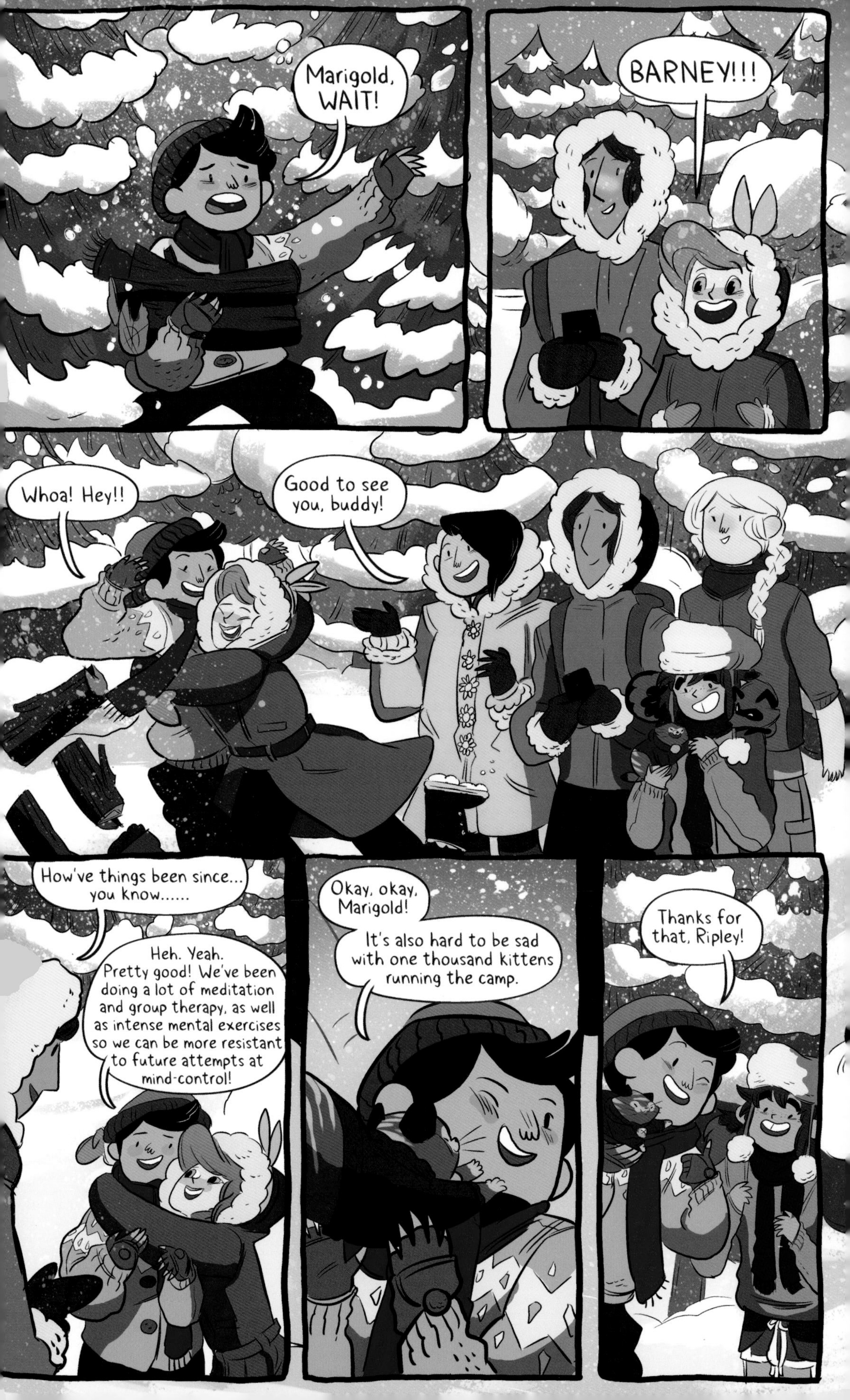

Marigold, WAIT!
BARNEY!!!
Whoa! Hey!!
Good to see you, buddy!
How've things been since... you know......
Heh. Yeah. Pretty good! We've been doing a lot of meditation and group therapy, as well as intense mental exercises so we can be more resistant to future attempts at mind-control!
Okay, okay, Marigold!
It's also hard to be sad with one thousand kittens running the camp.
Thanks for that, Ripley!

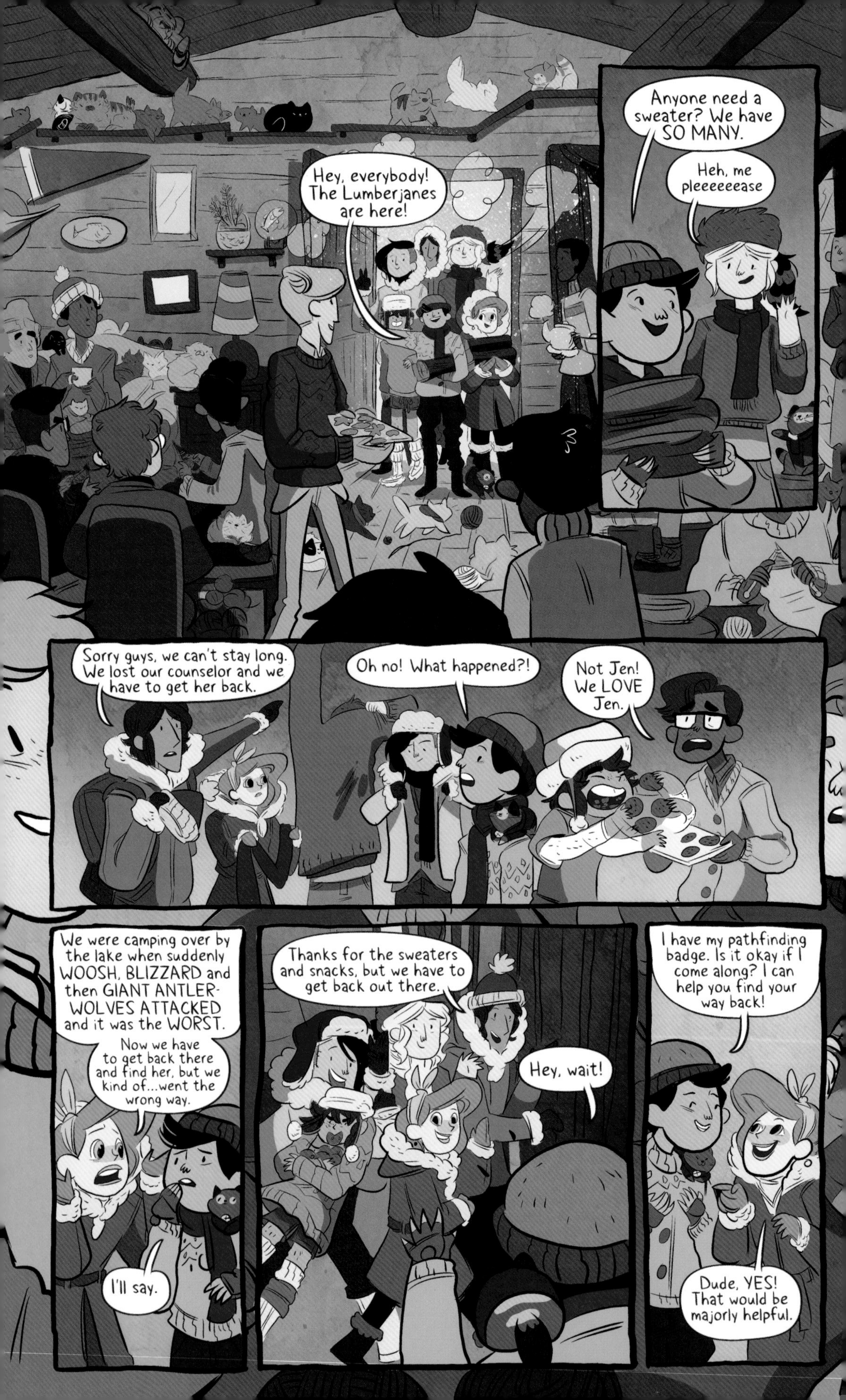
Hey, everybody! The Lumberjanes are here!
Anyone need a sweater? We have SO MANY.
Heh, me pleeeeeease
Sorry guys, we can't stay long. We lost our counselor and we have to get her back.
Oh no! What happened?!
Not Jen! We LOVE Jen.
We were camping over by the lake when suddenly WOOSH, BLIZZARD and then GIANT ANTLER-WOLVES ATTACKED and it was the WORST.
Now we have to get back there and find her, but we kind of...went the wrong way.
I'll say.
Thanks for the sweaters and snacks, but we have to get back out there.
Hey, wait!
I have my pathfinding badge. Is it okay if I come along? I can help you find your way back!
Dude, YES! That would be majorly helpful.

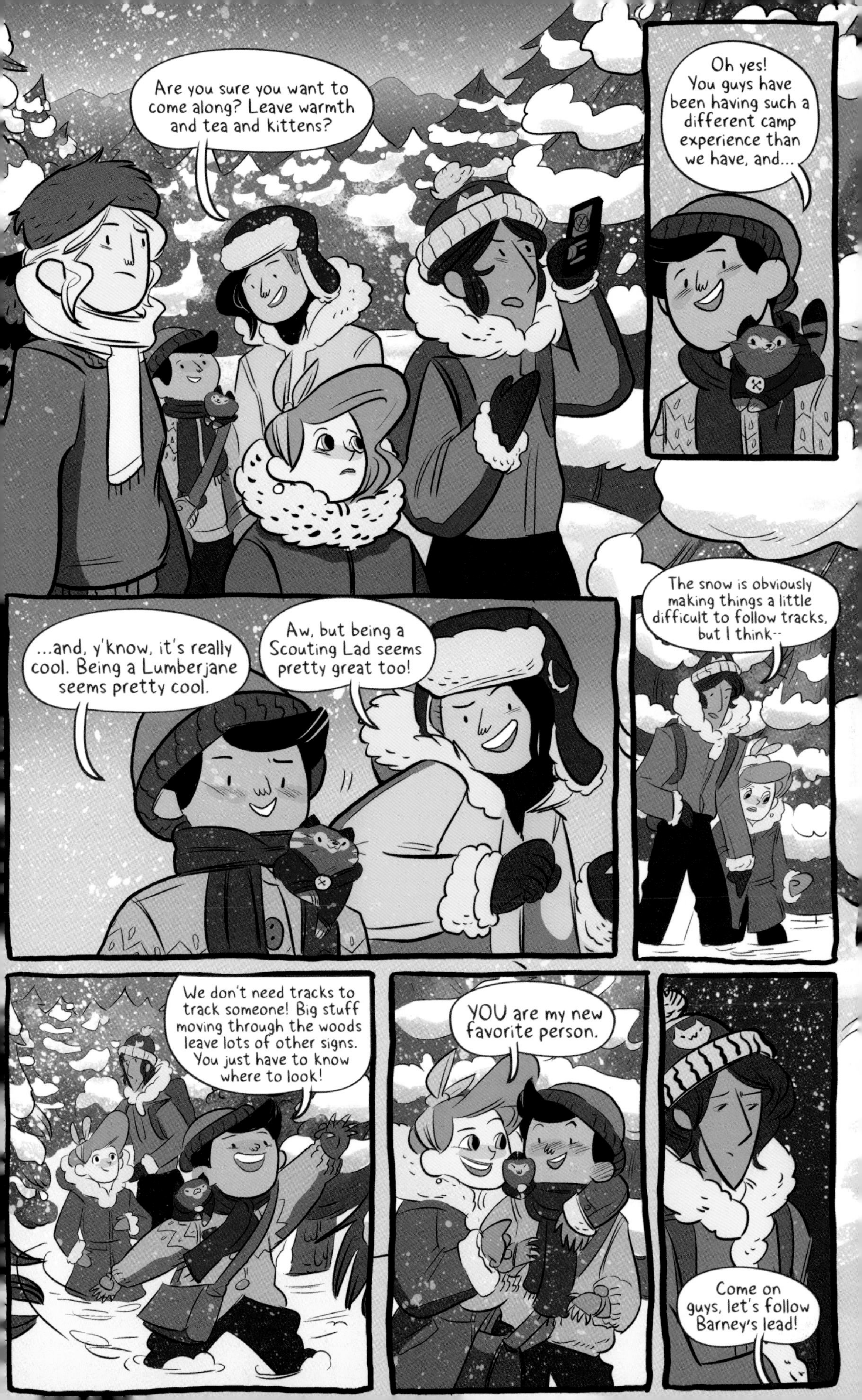
Are you sure you want to come along? Leave warmth and tea and kittens?
Oh yes! You guys have been having such a different camp experience than we have, and...
...and, y'know, it's really cool. Being a Lumberjane seems pretty cool.
Aw, but being a Scouting Lad seems pretty great too!
The snow is obviously making things a little difficult to follow tracks, but I think--
We don't need tracks to track someone! Big stuff moving through the woods leave lots of other signs. You just have to know where to look!
YOU are my new favorite person.
Come on guys, let's follow Barney's lead!

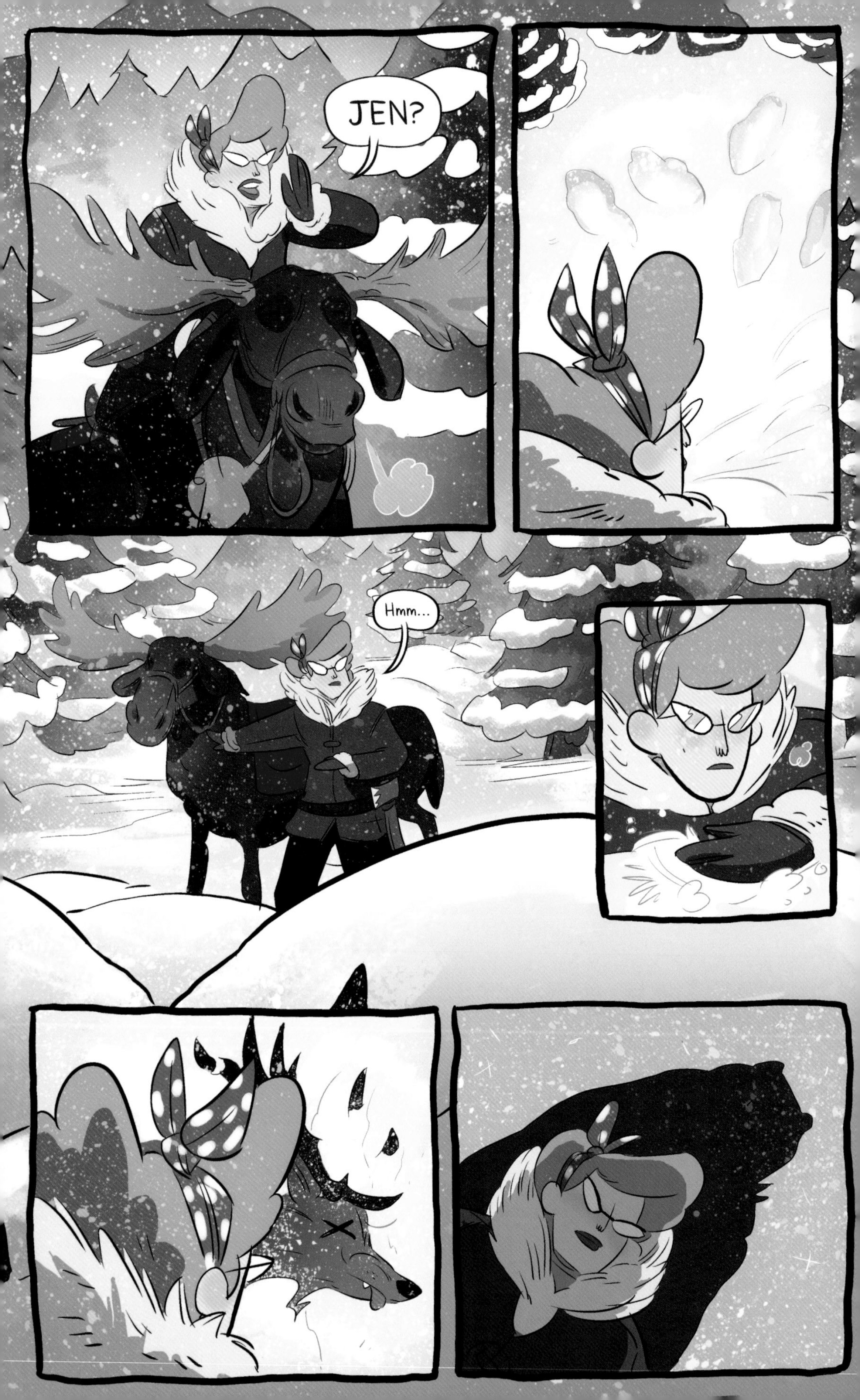
JEN?
Hmm...

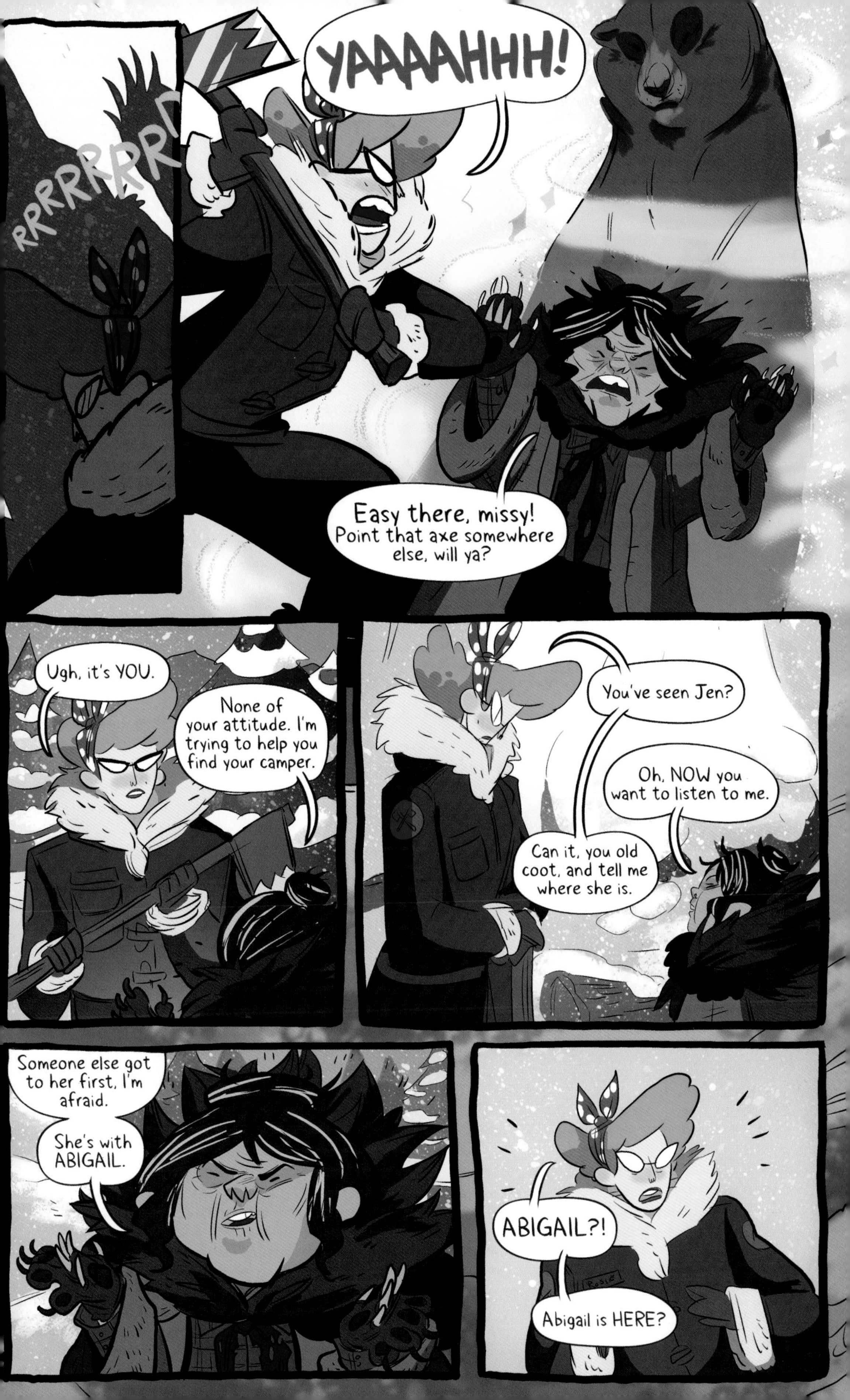
YAAAAHHH!
RRRRRRR
Easy there, missy! Point that axe somewhere else, will ya?
Ugh, it's YOU.
None of your attitude. I'm trying to help you find your camper.
You've seen Jen?
Oh, NOW you want to listen to me.
Can it, you old coot, and tell me where she is.
Someone else got to her first, I'm afraid.
She's with ABIGAIL.
ABIGAIL?!
Abigail is HERE?

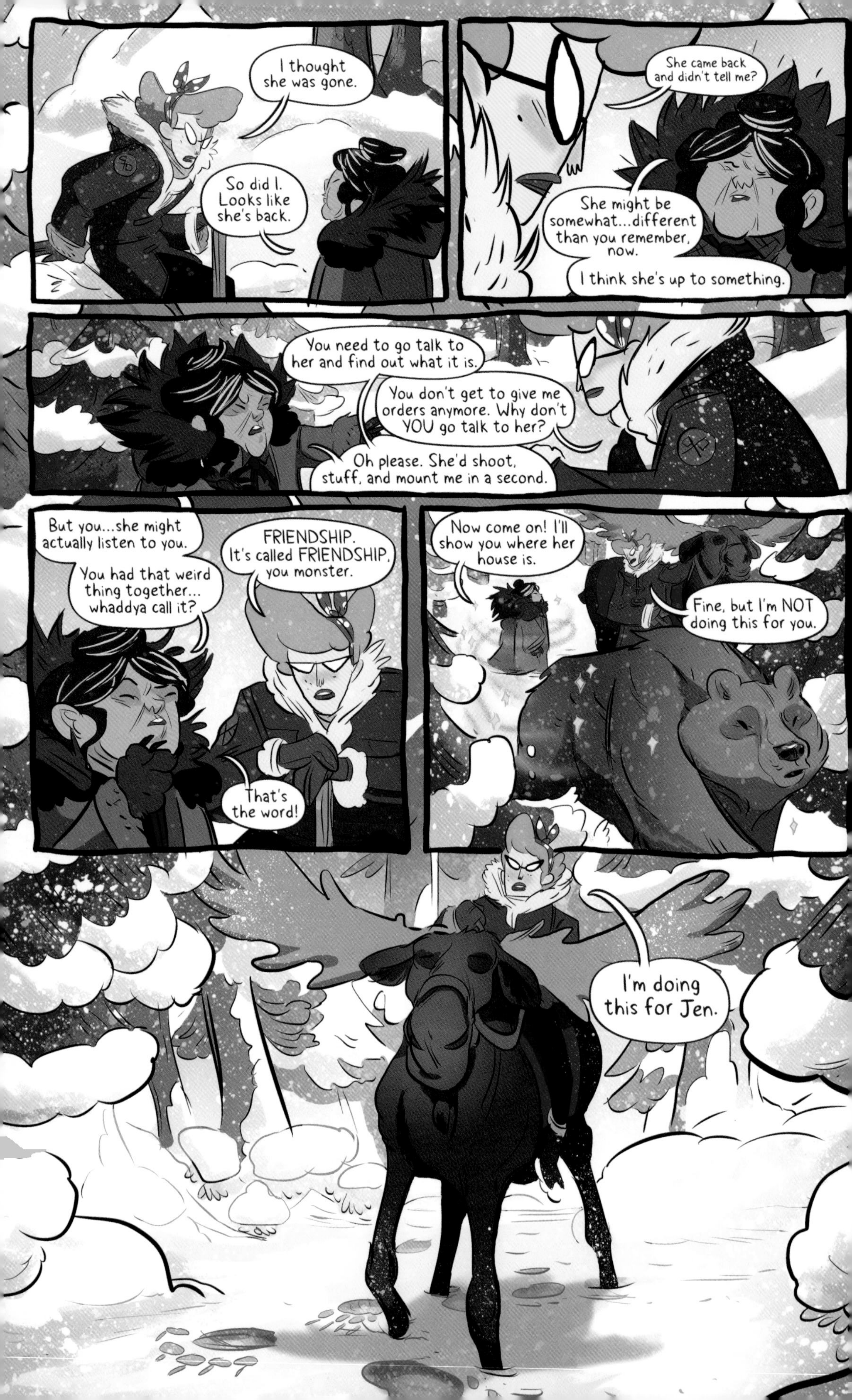
I thought she was gone.
So did I. Looks like she's back.
She came back and didn't tell me?
She might be somewhat...different than you remember, now.
I think she's up to something.
You need to go talk to her and find out what it is.
You don't get to give me orders anymore. Why don't YOU go talk to her?
Oh please. She'd shoot, stuff, and mount me in a second.
But you...she might actually listen to you.
You had that weird thing together... whaddya call it?
FRIENDSHIP. It's called FRIENDSHIP, you monster.
That's the word!
Now come on! I'll show you where her house is.
Fine, but I'm NOT doing this for you.
I'm doing this for Jen.

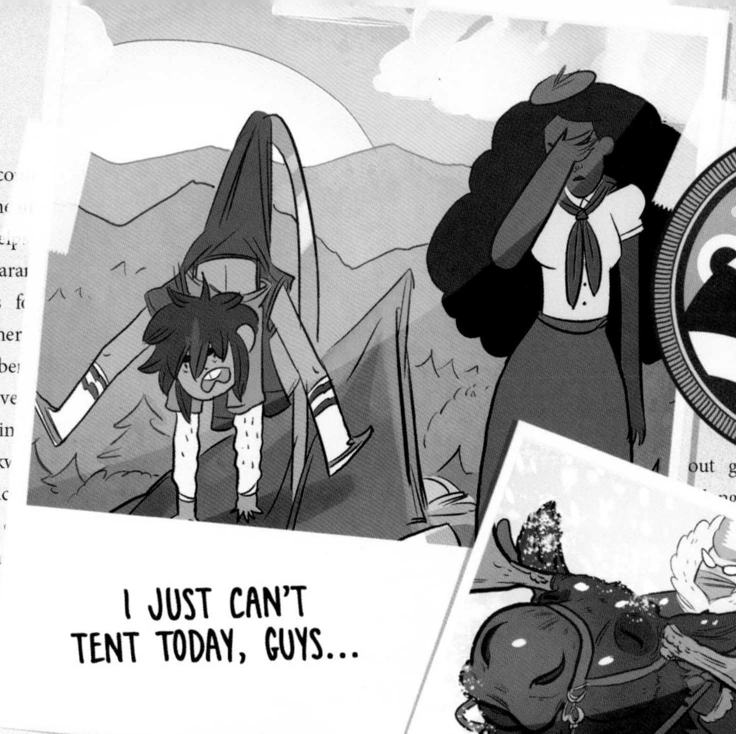
I JUST CAN'T
TENT TODAY, GUYS...

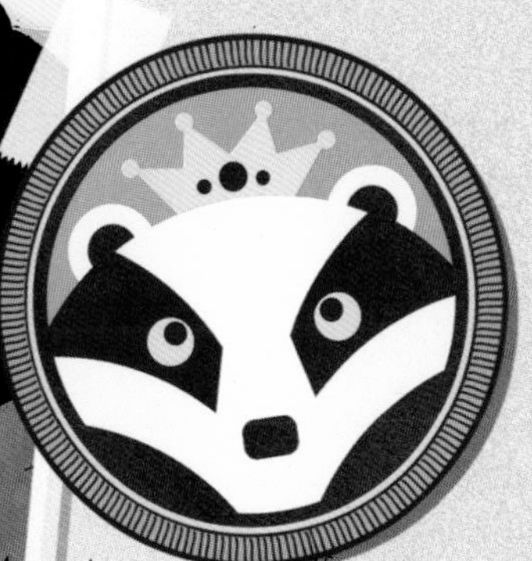

will co…

The… It he… appearan… dress f… Further… Lumbe… to have… part in… Thiskv… Hardc… have… them…

…out grows her uniform or …ng to another Lumberjane. …insignia she has …her …her

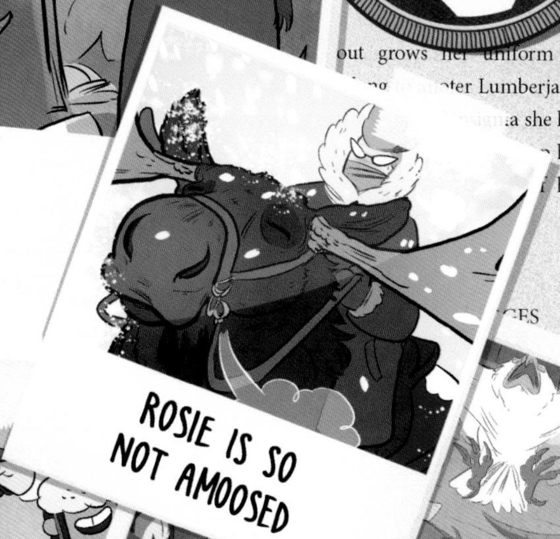
ROSIE IS SO
NOT AMOOSED

The… yellow, short sl… emb… the w… choose… slacks, made o… out-of-d… green bere… the colla… Shoes ma… heels, rou… …ings or socks shou… …with the shoe… the uniform. Ne… bracelets, or… belong with a Lumberjane unifo…

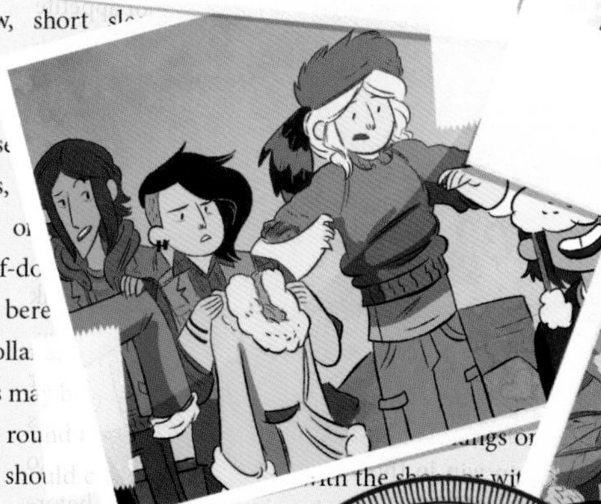

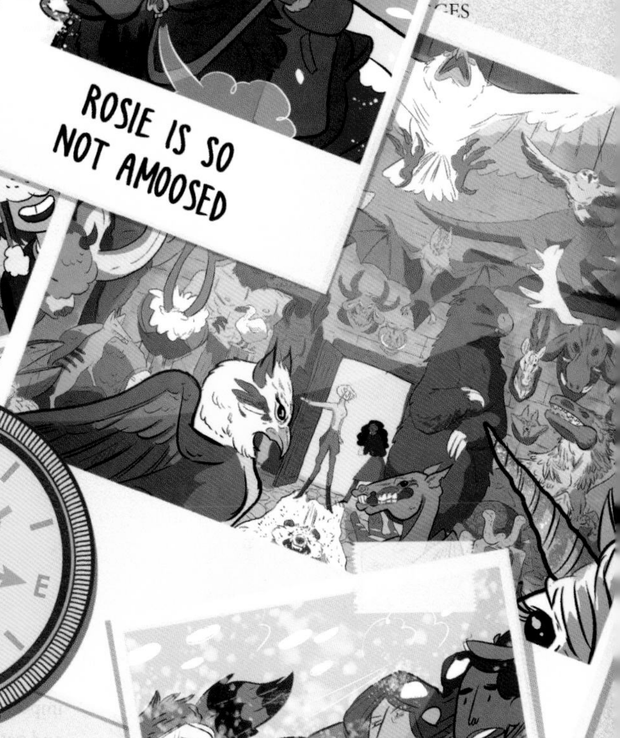

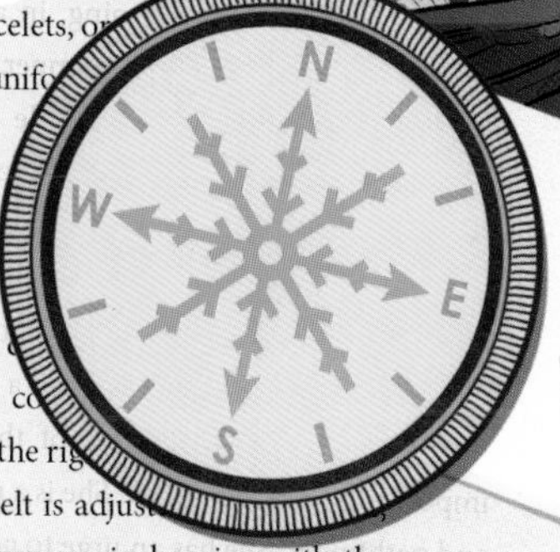
N
E
S
W

HOW TO WEAR…

To look well in a uniform … uniform be kept in good co… pressed. See that the skirt is the ri… height and build, that the belt is adjus… that your shoes and stockings are in keeping with the uniform, that you watch your posture and carry yourself with dignity and grace. If the beret is removed indoors, be sure that your hair is neat and kept in place with an insonspicuous clip or ribbon. When you wear a Lumberjane uniform you are identified as a member of this organization and you should be doubly careful to conduct yourself in a way that will show everyone that courtesy and thoughtfullness are part of being a Lumberjane. People are likely to judge a whole nation by the selfishness of a few individuals, to criticize a whole family because of the misconduct of one member, and to feel unkindly toward and organization because of the

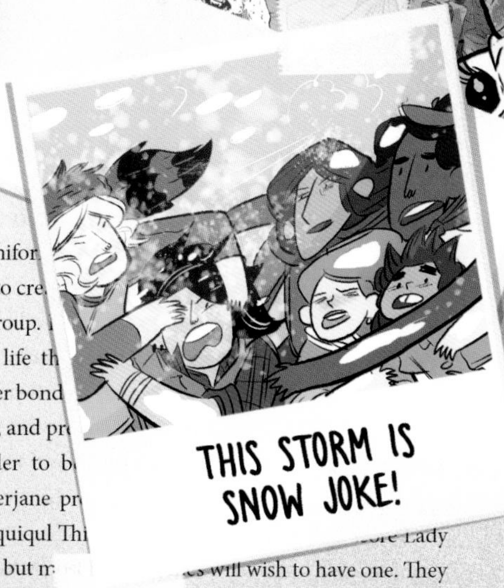
THIS STORM IS
SNOW JOKE!

The unifor… helps to cre… in a group. … active life th… another bond… future, and pr… in order to b… Lumberjane pr… Penniquiqul Thi… …ore Lady Types, but m… …s will wish to have one. They can either bu… …uniform, or make it themselves from materials available at the trading post.

LUMBERJANES FIELD MANUAL

CHAPTER FOURTEEN

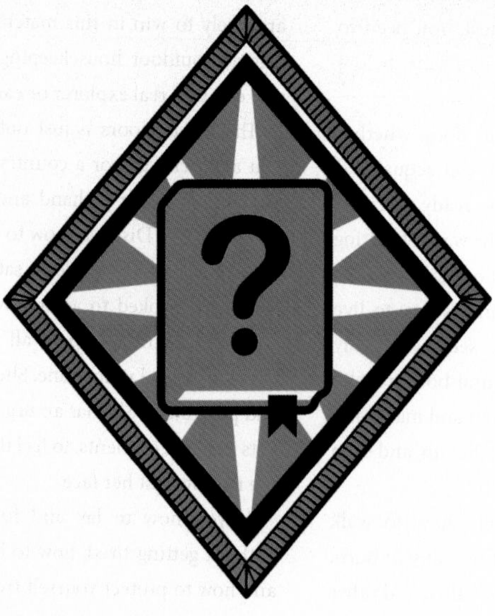

Lumberjanes "Literature" Program Field

THE MYSTERY OF HISTORY BADGE

"It's not about what's remembered, it's about why."

The amazing thing about memory is that it can be tricked. You can go through life knowing one thing as a fact but still be proven wrong at a later date. This is because if someone believes in something strong enough, they can make it feel like a fact for them. They can make something the truth, even though it wasn't. Which is why history is important, but might not always be reliable. As a Lumberjane, it will be important to not only keep an open mind to the occurrences around you but to stay on top of all the changes that happen around you. Everyone has their own unique experience, even if it's all the same event, because we are all unique individuals with our own unique backgrounds. This is what makes us great, what makes us human, what makes us Lumberjanes. All Lumberjanes must have a journal that they keep on themselves and use these journals to keep track of the events that happen to them at this camp, and hopefully the events that happen outside of the camp as well.

The Mystery of History badge is a badge that can only be earned in the library. Every scout will go to the camp's library and pick out a book. It can be any book, from humor to non-fiction, and they will research everything that went into the creation of the book. They will learn about the authors, about their life, about what inspired them to create the book and find all the information that they wouldn't be able to find in the book they chose by itself. One of the many fun opportunities with this badge is the chance to get a better knowledge of how things change from what actually happened to what ends up on paper. Capture the flag will be and will always be the biggest battle of the summer, but the real challenge to the game actually isn't getting the flag. It's breaking out of your enemies prison.

To obtain *The Mystery of History* badge a Lumberjane

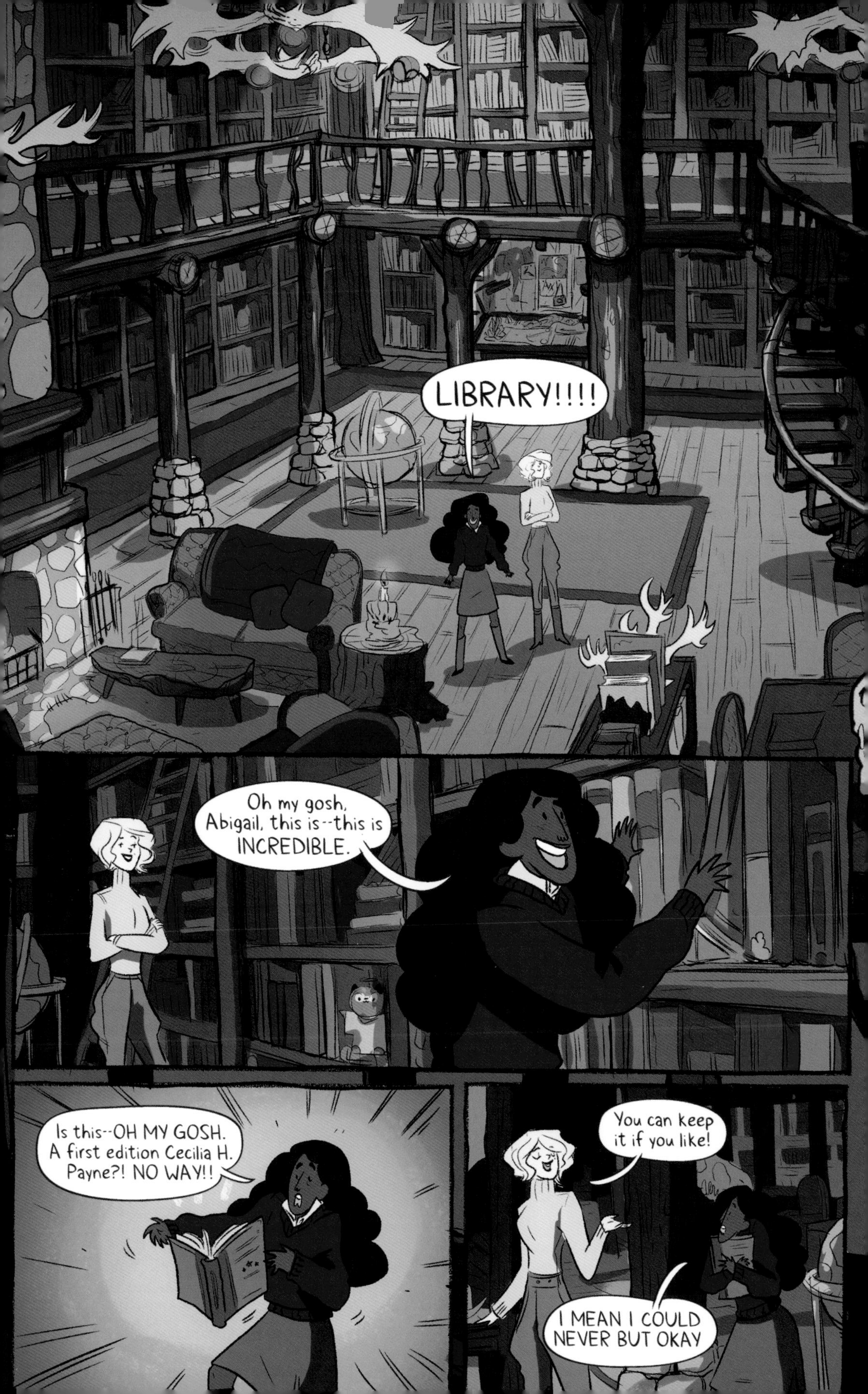
LIBRARY!!!!
Oh my gosh, Abigail, this is--this is INCREDIBLE.
Is this--OH MY GOSH. A first edition Cecilia H. Payne?! NO WAY!!
You can keep it if you like!
I MEAN I COULD NEVER BUT OKAY

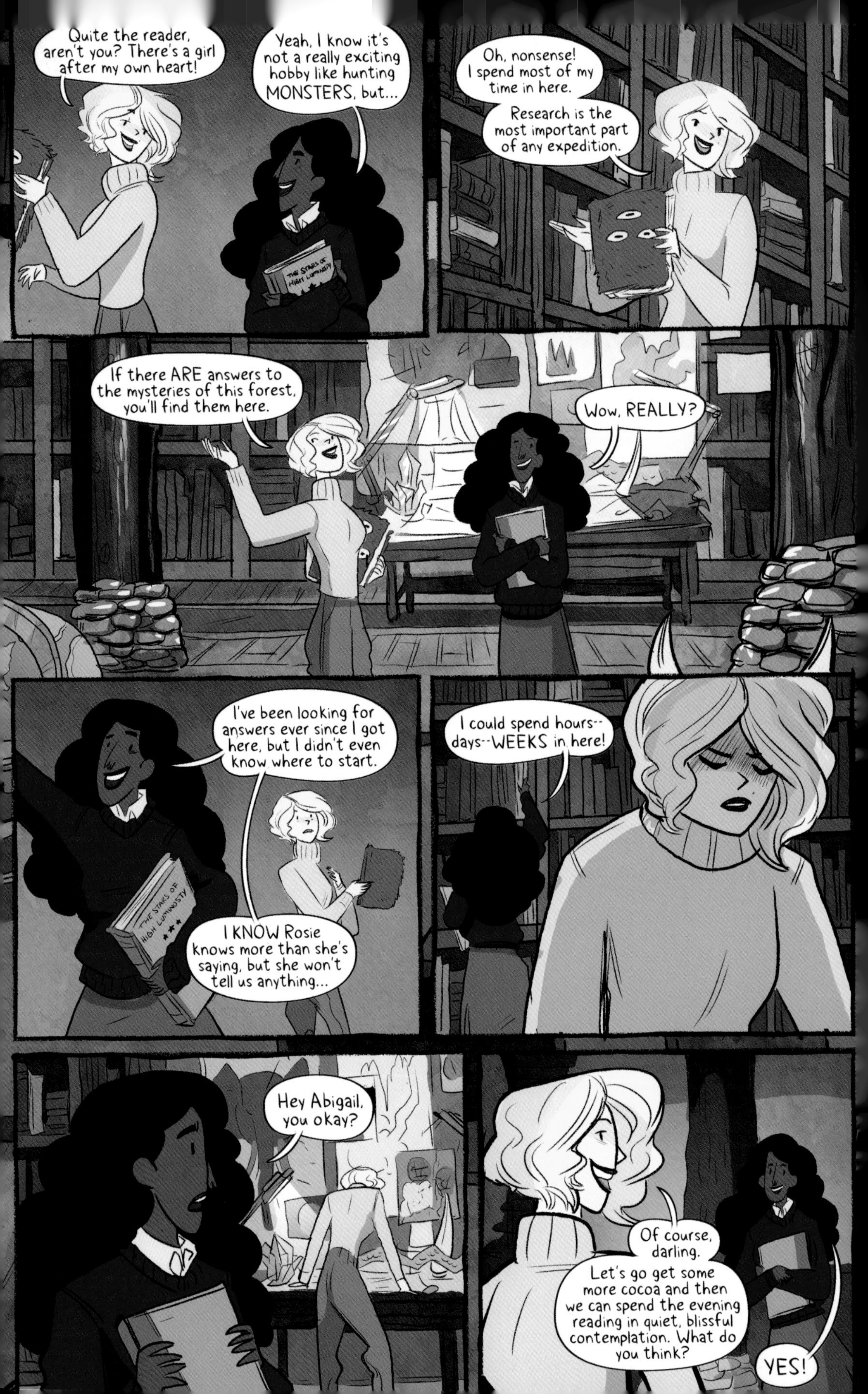
Quite the reader, aren't you? There's a girl after my own heart!
Yeah, I know it's not a really exciting hobby like hunting MONSTERS, but...
THE STARS OF HIGH LUMINOSITY
Oh, nonsense! I spend most of my time in here.
Research is the most important part of any expedition.
If there ARE answers to the mysteries of this forest, you'll find them here.
Wow, REALLY?
I've been looking for answers ever since I got here, but I didn't even know where to start.
I KNOW Rosie knows more than she's saying, but she won't tell us anything...
THE STARS OF HIGH LUMINOSITY
I could spend hours--days--WEEKS in here!
Hey Abigail, you okay?
Of course, darling.
Let's go get some more cocoa and then we can spend the evening reading in quiet, blissful contemplation. What do you think?
YES!

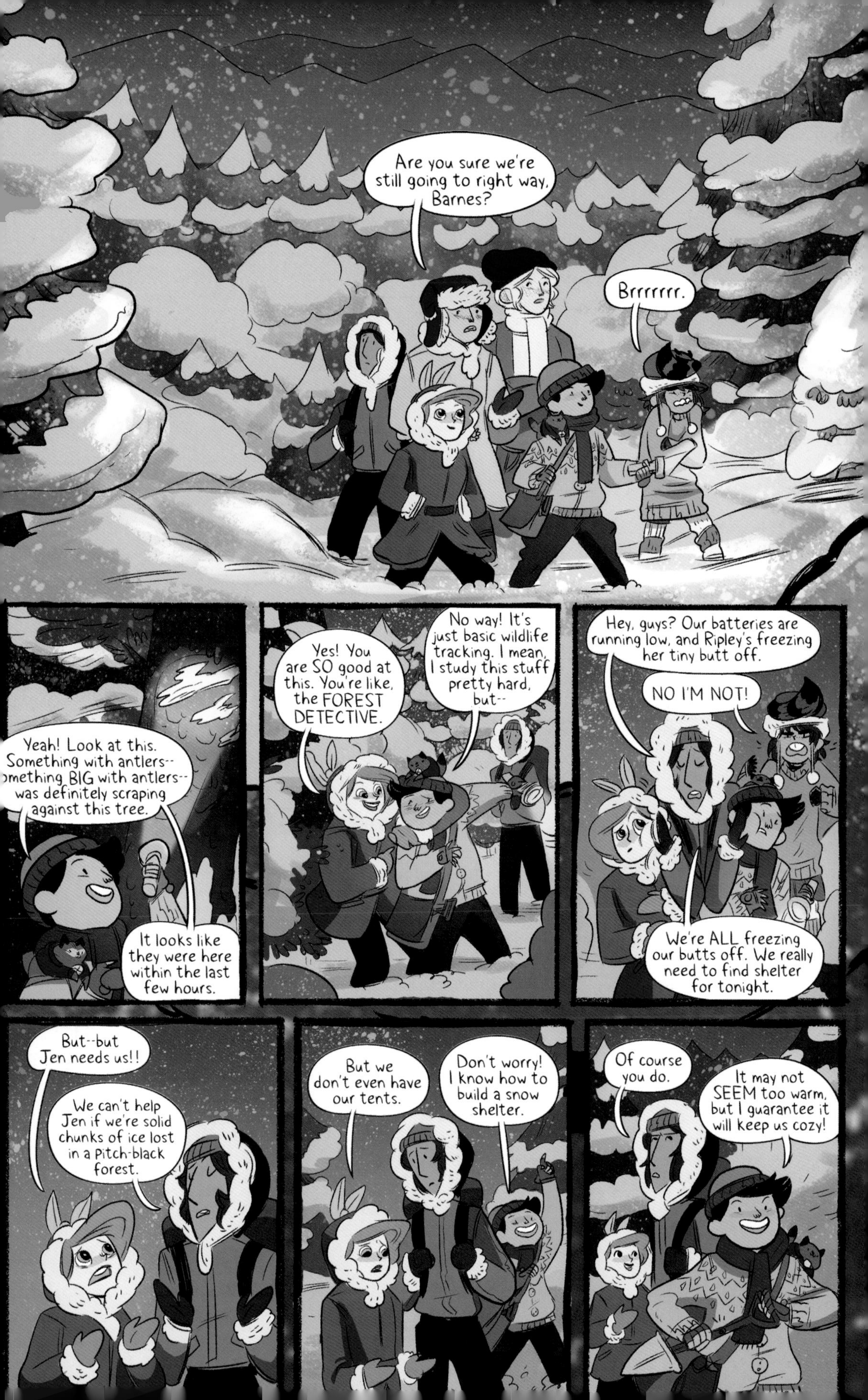
Are you sure we're still going to right way, Barnes?
Brrrrrrr.
Yeah! Look at this. Something with antlers-- omething BIG with antlers-- was definitely scraping against this tree.
It looks like they were here within the last few hours.
Yes! You are SO good at this. You're like, the FOREST DETECTIVE.
No way! It's just basic wildlife tracking. I mean, I study this stuff pretty hard, but--
Hey, guys? Our batteries are running low, and Ripley's freezing her tiny butt off.
NO I'M NOT!
We're ALL freezing our butts off. We really need to find shelter for tonight.
But--but Jen needs us!!
We can't help Jen if we're solid chunks of ice lost in a pitch-black forest.
But we don't even have our tents.
Don't worry! I know how to build a snow shelter.
Of course you do.
It may not SEEM too warm, but I guarantee it will keep us cozy!

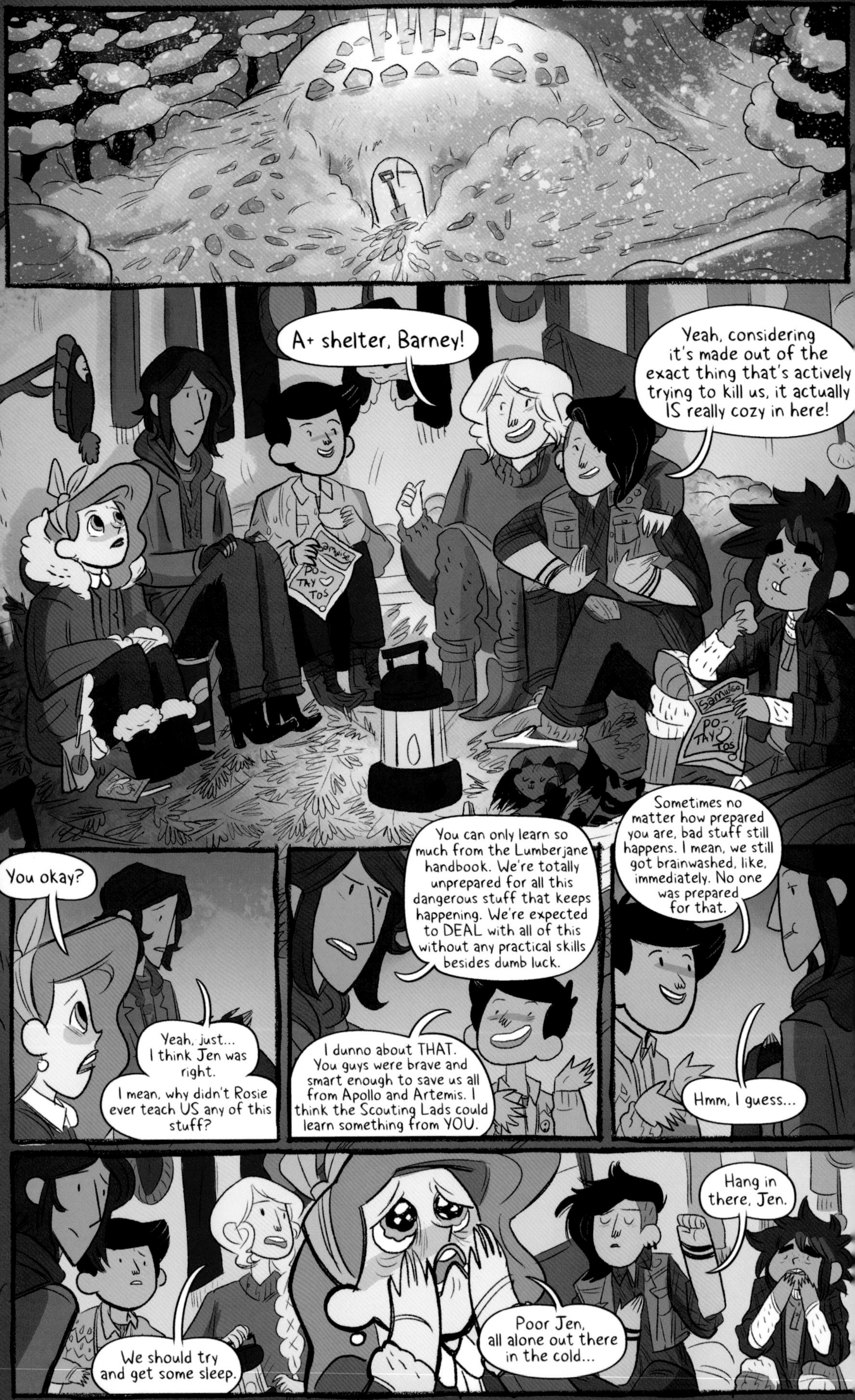

A+ shelter, Barney!
Yeah, considering it's made out of the exact thing that's actively trying to kill us, it actually IS really cozy in here!
Samwise PO-TAY-TOS
You okay?
Yeah, just... I think Jen was right.
I mean, why didn't Rosie ever teach US any of this stuff?
You can only learn so much from the Lumberjane handbook. We're totally unprepared for all this dangerous stuff that keeps happening. We're expected to DEAL with all of this without any practical skills besides dumb luck.
I dunno about THAT. You guys were brave and smart enough to save us all from Apollo and Artemis. I think the Scouting Lads could learn something from YOU.
Sometimes no matter how prepared you are, bad stuff still happens. I mean, we still got brainwashed, like, immediately. No one was prepared for that.
Hmm, I guess...
Hang in there, Jen.
We should try and get some sleep.
Poor Jen, all alone out there in the cold...

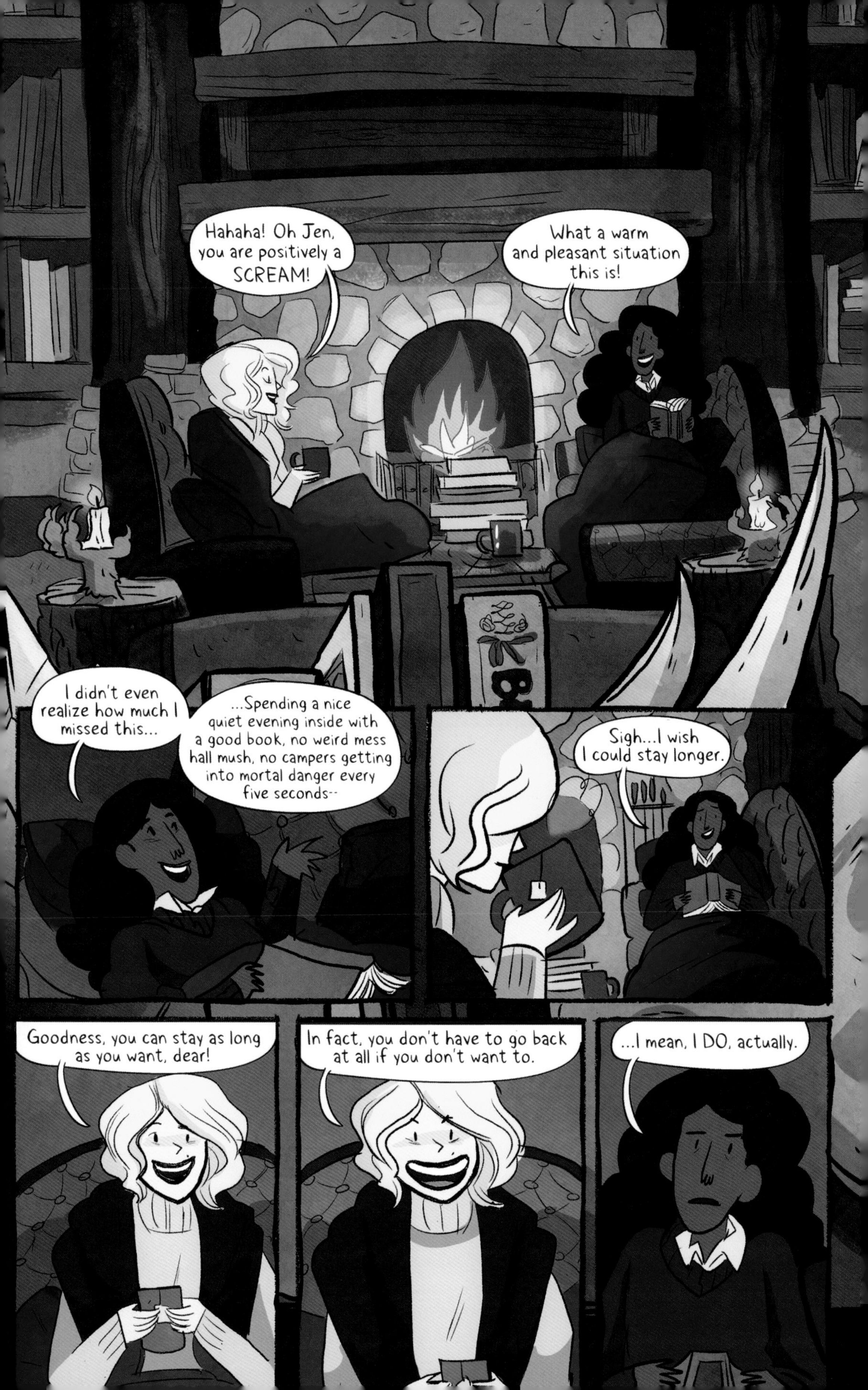

Hahaha! Oh Jen, you are positively a SCREAM!
What a warm and pleasant situation this is!
I didn't even realize how much I missed this...
...Spending a nice quiet evening inside with a good book, no weird mess hall mush, no campers getting into mortal danger every five seconds--
Sigh...I wish I could stay longer.
Goodness, you can stay as long as you want, dear!
In fact, you don't have to go back at all if you don't want to.
...I mean, I DO, actually.

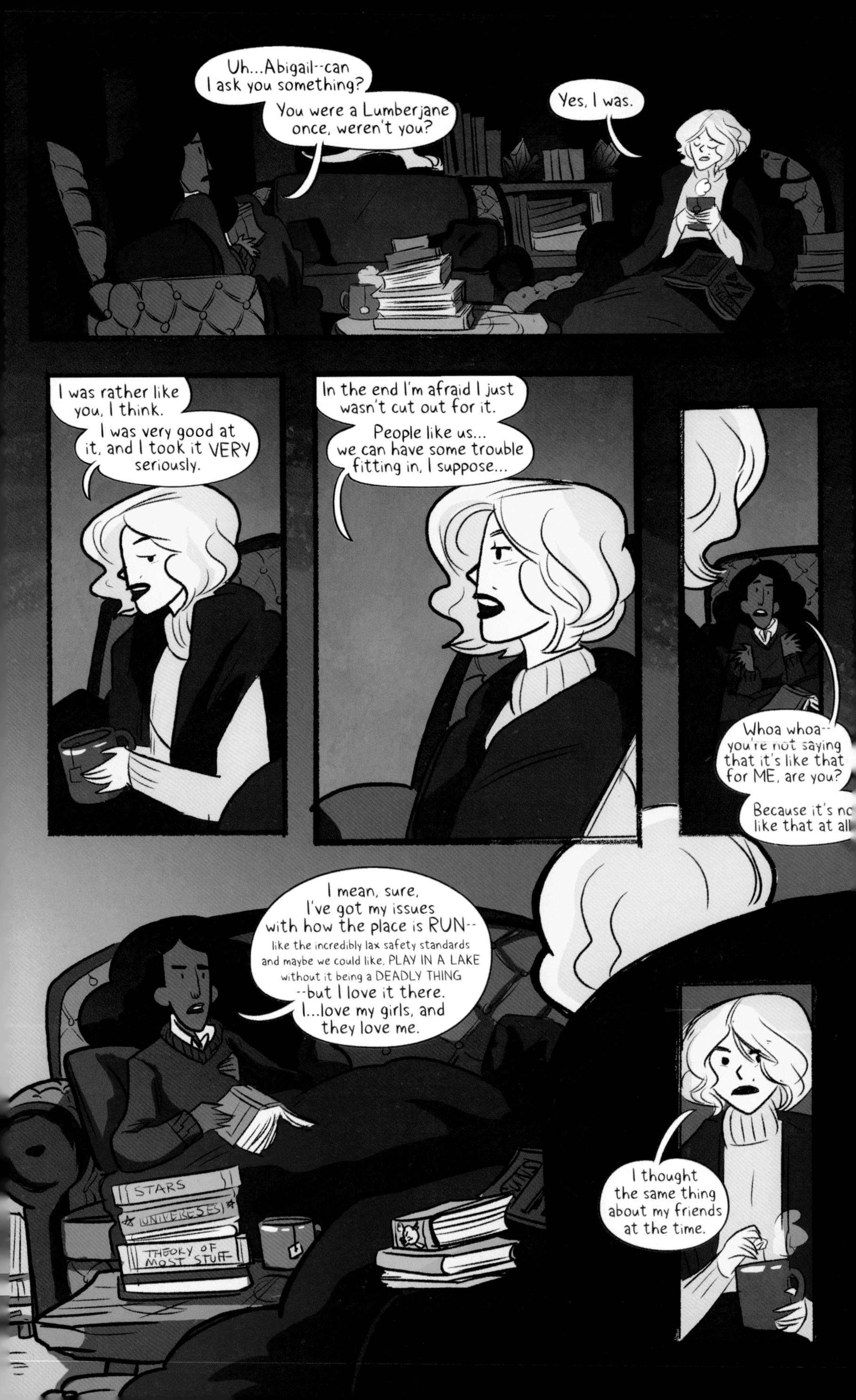
Uh...Abigail--can I ask you something?
You were a Lumberjane once, weren't you?
Yes, I was.
I was rather like you, I think.
I was very good at it, and I took it VERY seriously.
In the end I'm afraid I just wasn't cut out for it.
People like us... we can have some trouble fitting in, I suppose...
Whoa whoa--you're not saying that it's like that for ME, are you?
Because it's no like that at all
I mean, sure, I've got my issues with how the place is RUN--like the incredibly lax safety standards and maybe we could like, PLAY IN A LAKE without it being a DEADLY THING--but I love it there. I...love my girls, and they love me.
STARS
THEORY OF MOST STUFF
I thought the same thing about my friends at the time.

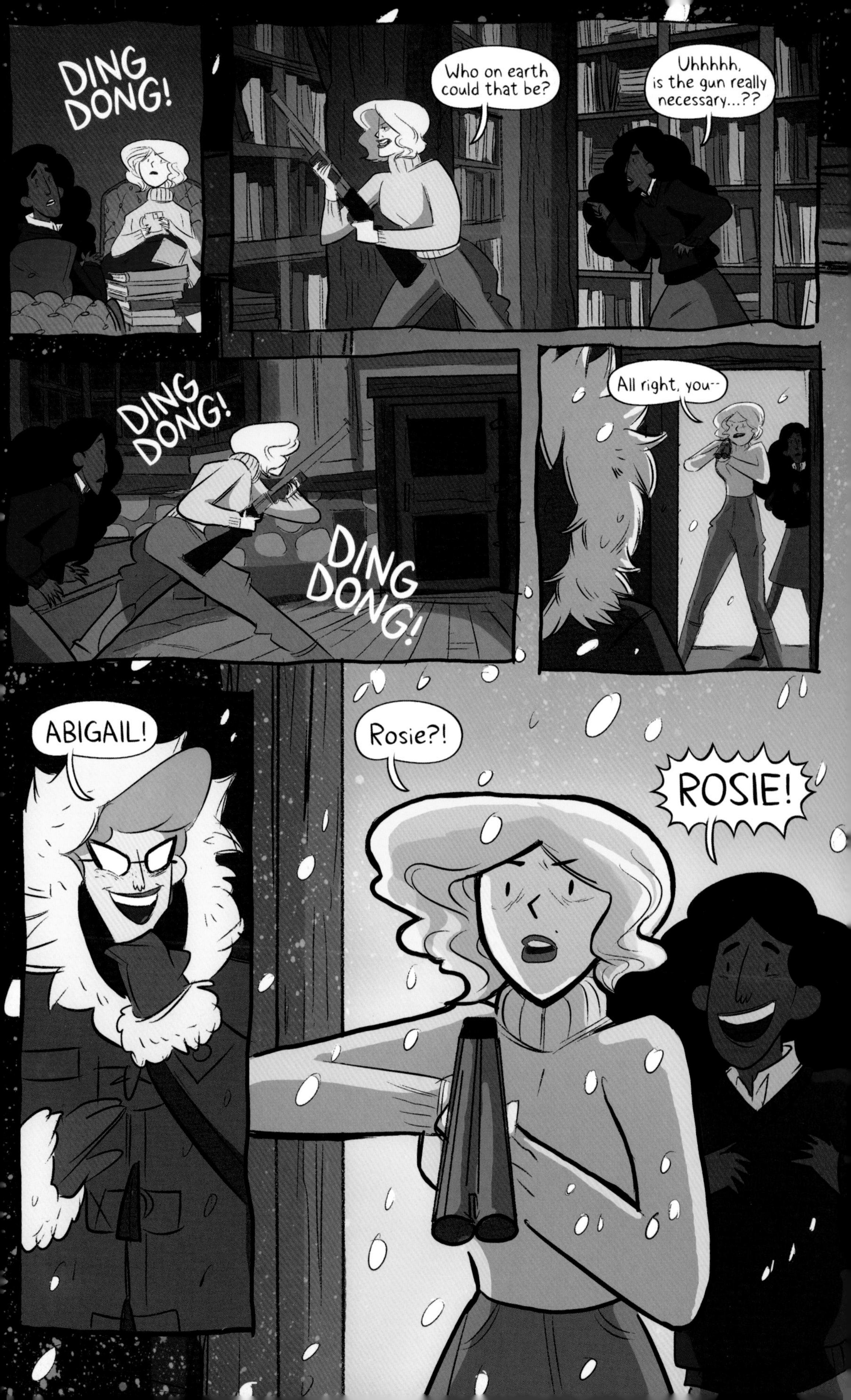
DING DONG!
Who on earth could that be?
Uhhhhh, is the gun really necessary...??
DING DONG!
DING DONG!
All right, you--
ABIGAIL!
Rosie?!
ROSIE!

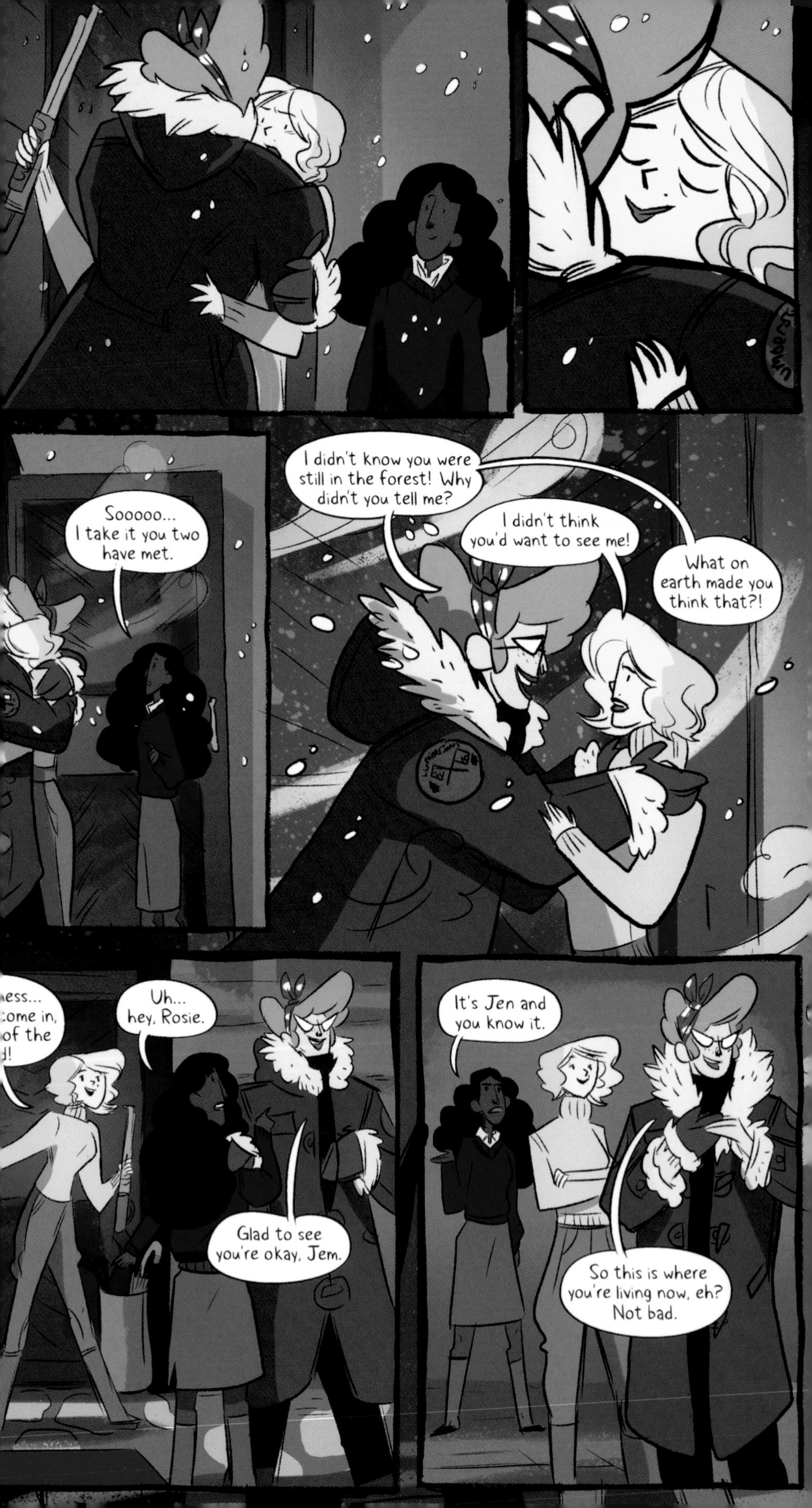
Sooooo... I take it you two have met.
I didn't know you were still in the forest! Why didn't you tell me?
I didn't think you'd want to see me!
What on earth made you think that?!
ess... come in, of the d!
Uh... hey, Rosie.
Glad to see you're okay, Jem.
It's Jen and you know it.
So this is where you're living now, eh? Not bad.

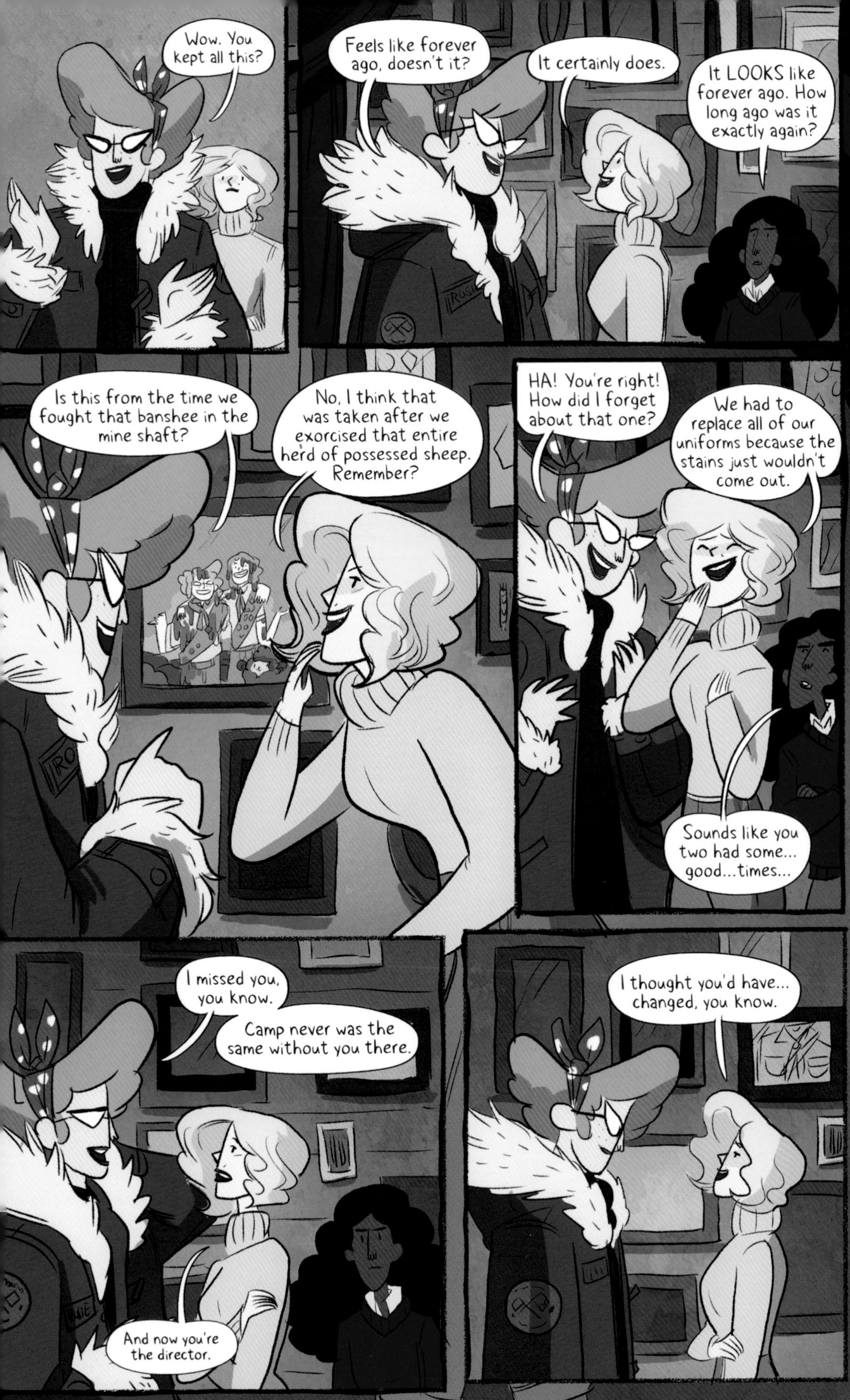
Wow. You kept all this?
Feels like forever ago, doesn't it?
It certainly does.
It LOOKS like forever ago. How long ago was it exactly again?
Is this from the time we fought that banshee in the mine shaft?
No, I think that was taken after we exorcised that entire herd of possessed sheep. Remember?
HA! You're right! How did I forget about that one?
We had to replace all of our uniforms because the stains just wouldn't come out.
Sounds like you two had some... good...times...
I missed you, you know.
Camp never was the same without you there.
And now you're the director.
I thought you'd have... changed, you know.

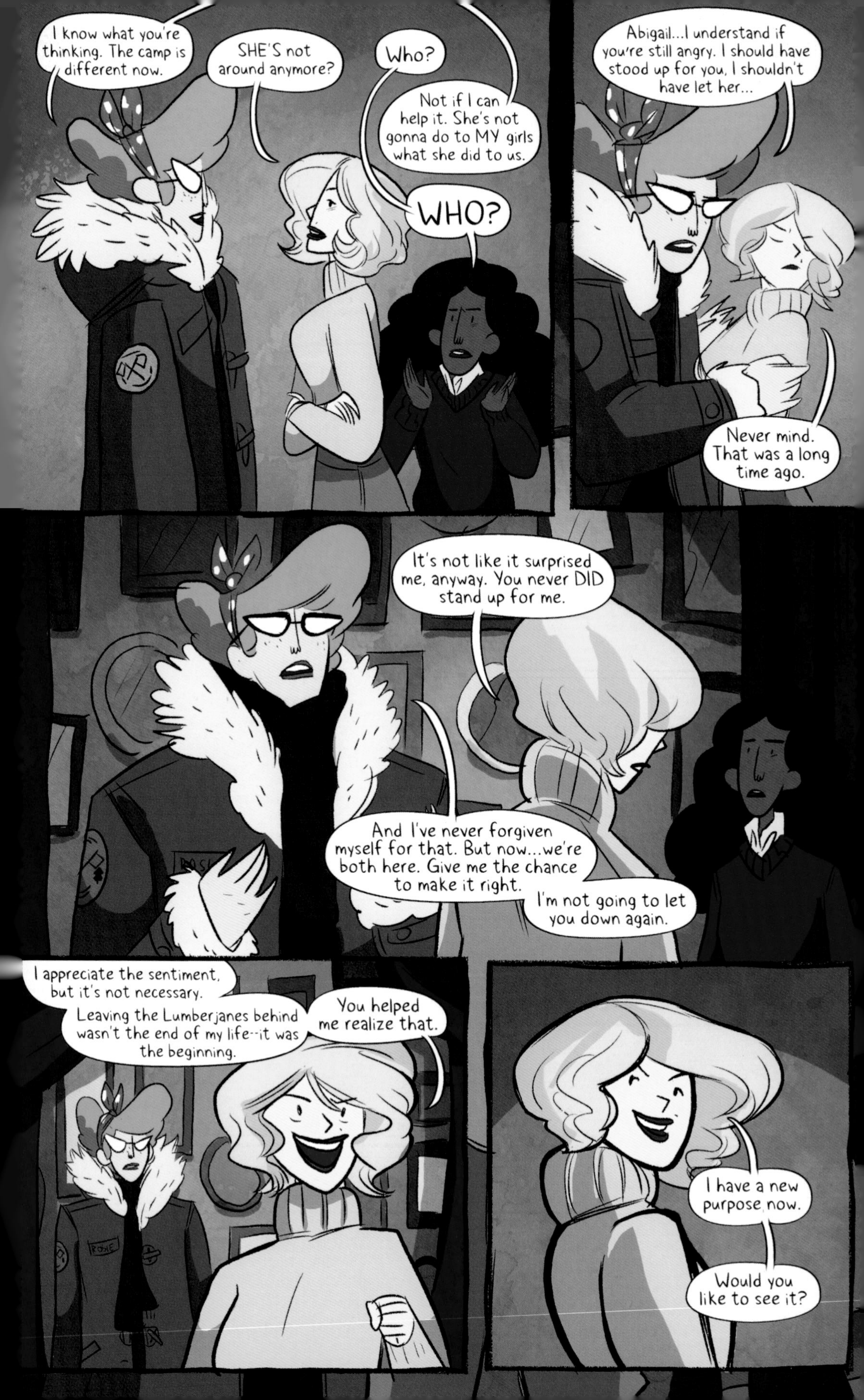
I know what you're thinking. The camp is different now.
SHE'S not around anymore?
Who?
Not if I can help it. She's not gonna do to MY girls what she did to us.
WHO?
Abigail...I understand if you're still angry. I should have stood up for you, I shouldn't have let her...
Never mind. That was a long time ago.
It's not like it surprised me, anyway. You never DID stand up for me.
And I've never forgiven myself for that. But now...we're both here. Give me the chance to make it right.
I'm not going to let you down again.
I appreciate the sentiment, but it's not necessary.
Leaving the Lumberjanes behind wasn't the end of my life--it was the beginning.
You helped me realize that.
I have a new purpose now.
Would you like to see it?

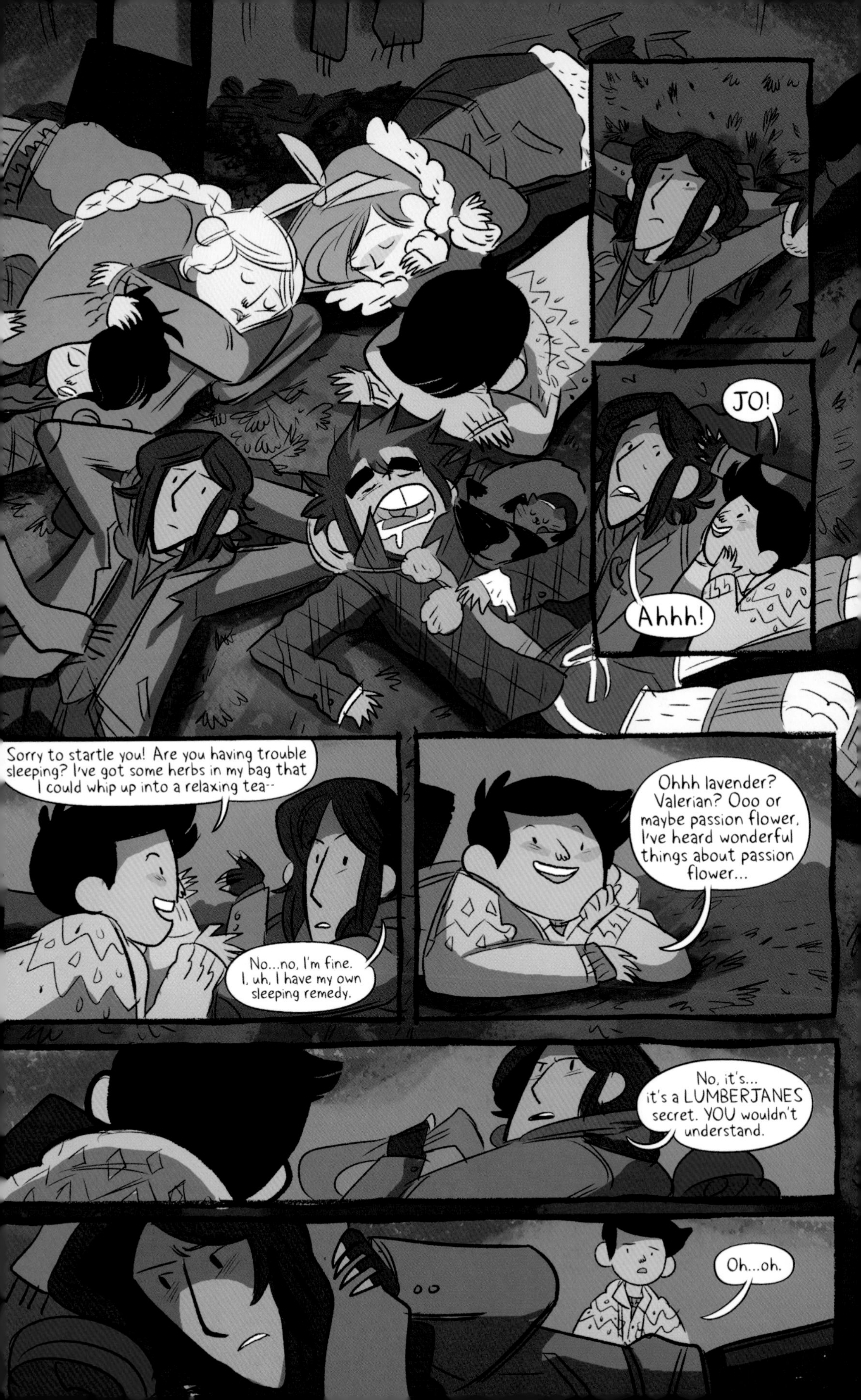
JO!
Ahhh!
Sorry to startle you! Are you having trouble sleeping? I've got some herbs in my bag that I could whip up into a relaxing tea--
No...no, I'm fine. I, uh, I have my own sleeping remedy.
Ohhh lavender? Valerian? Ooo or maybe passion flower. I've heard wonderful things about passion flower...
No, it's... it's a LUMBERJANES secret. YOU wouldn't understand.
Oh...oh.

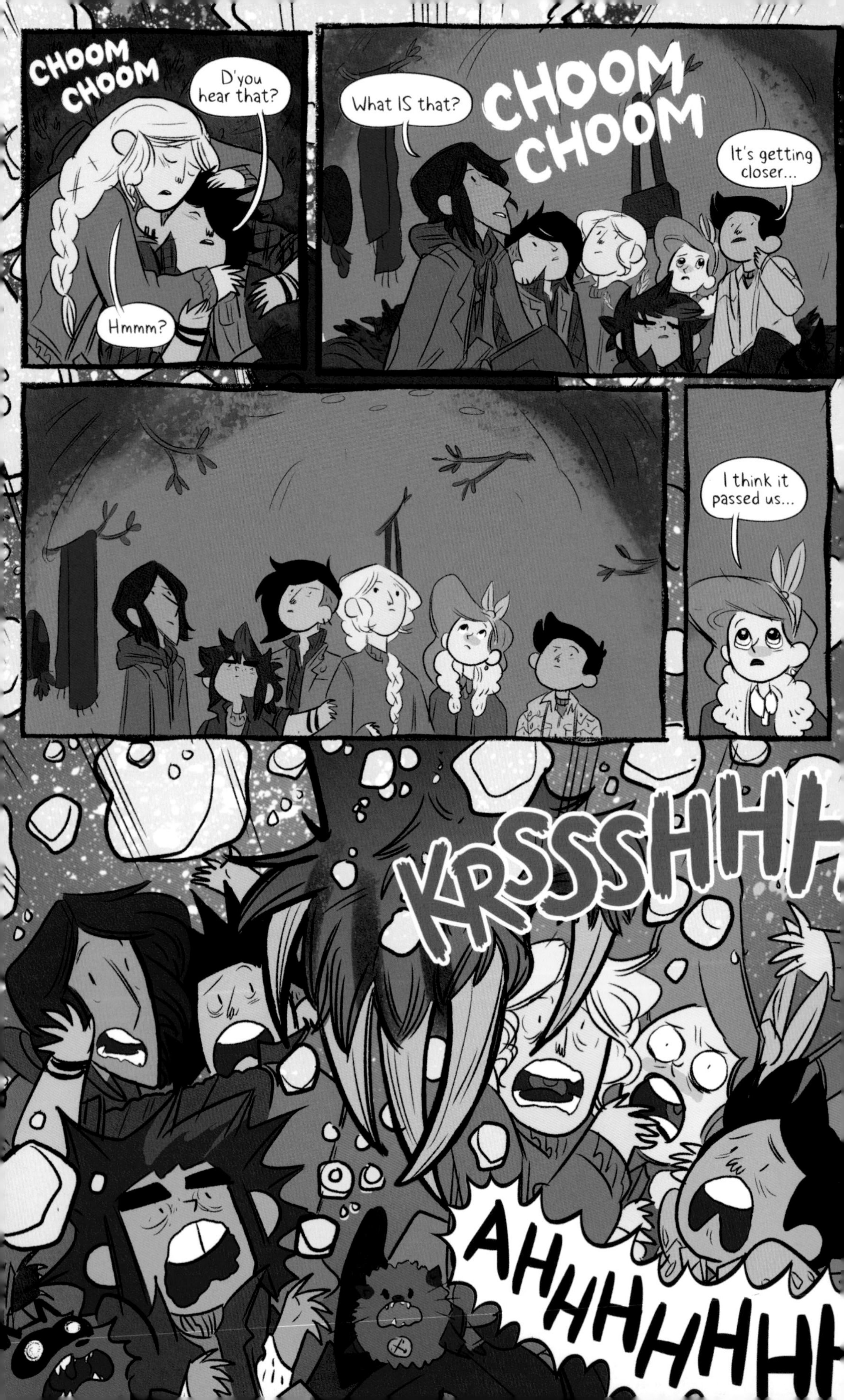
CHOOM CHOOM
D'you hear that?
Hmmm?
What IS that?
CHOOM CHOOM
It's getting closer...
I think it passed us...
KRSSSHHH
AHHHHHHHH

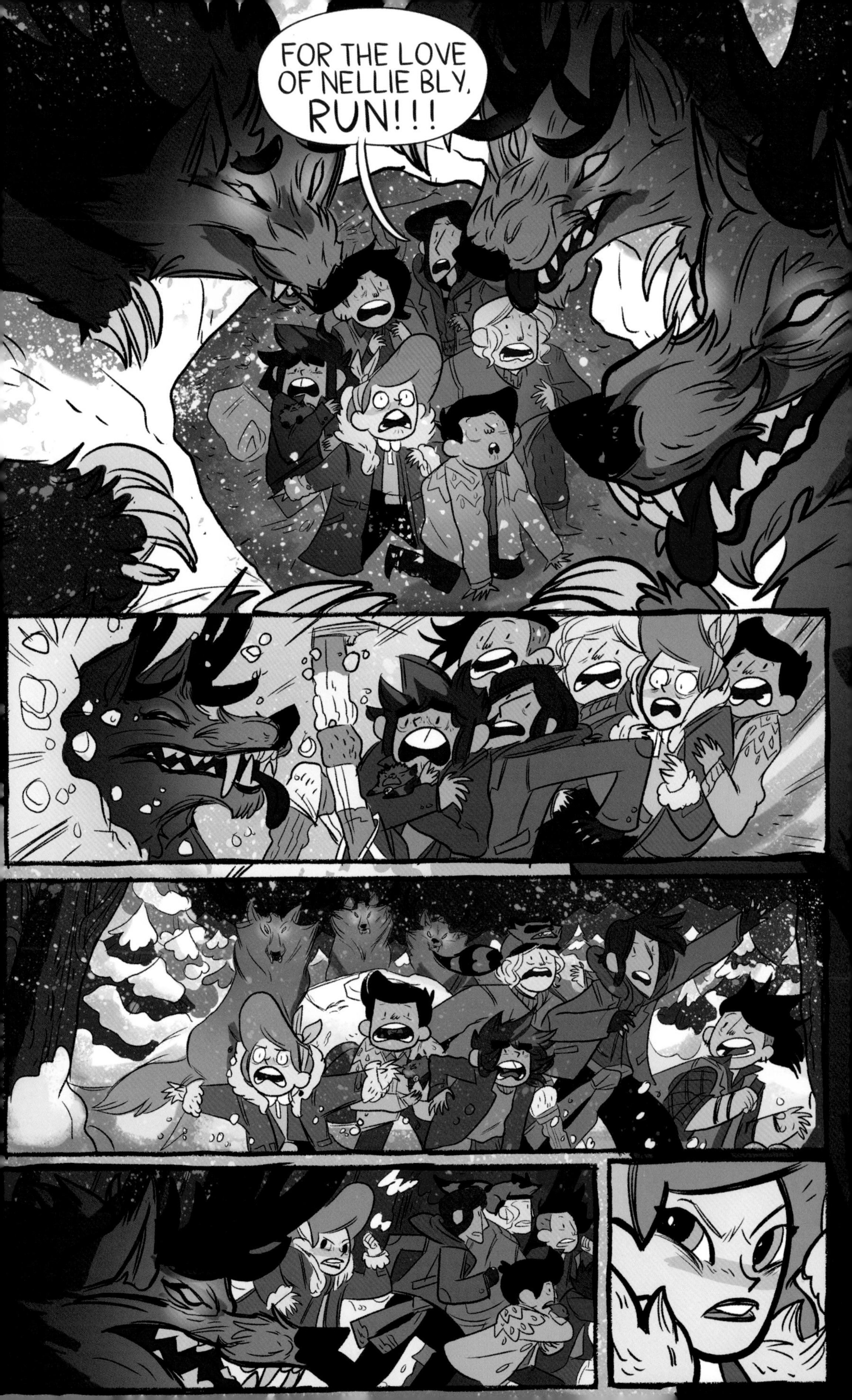
FOR THE LOVE OF NELLIE BLY, RUN!!!

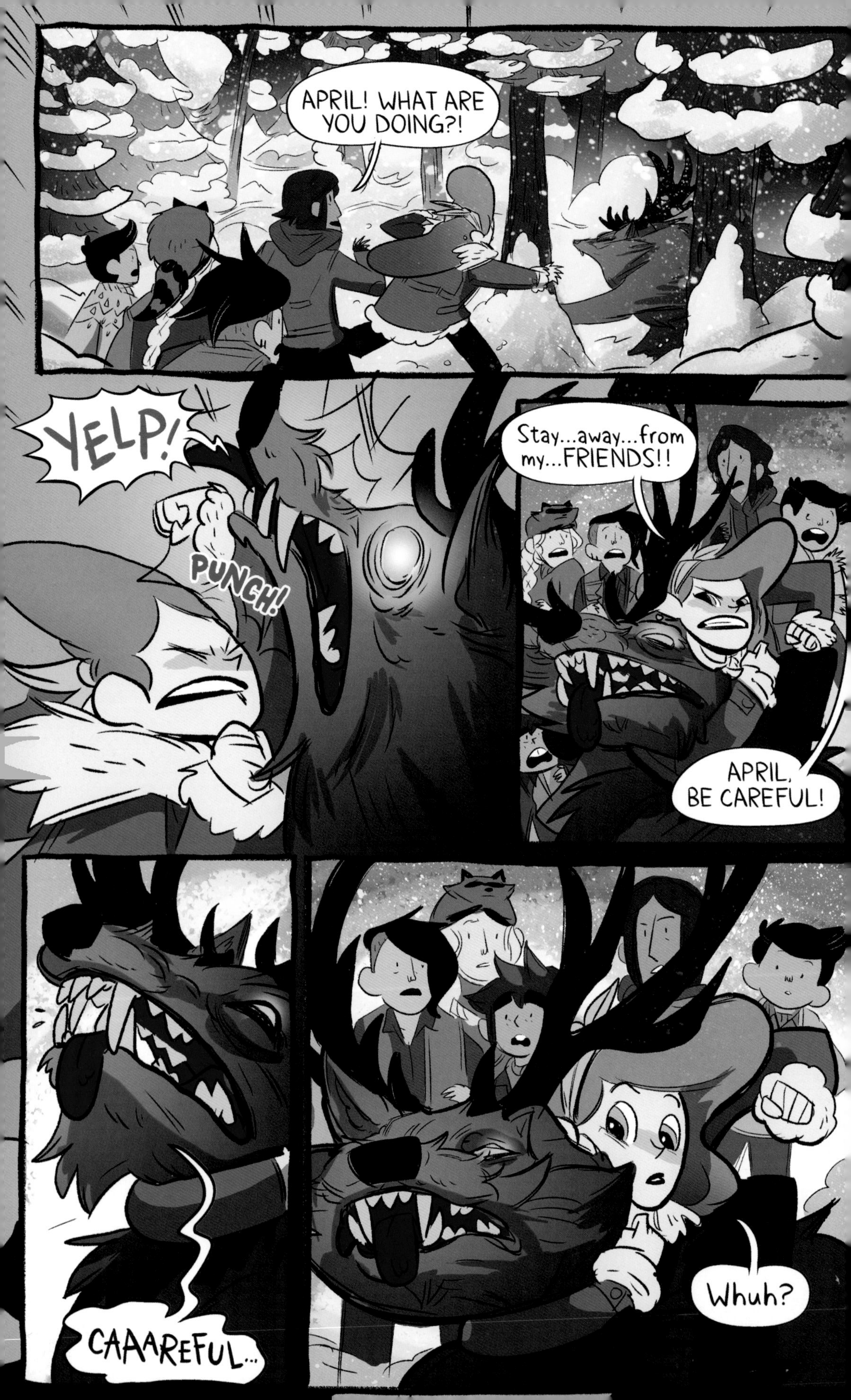
APRIL! WHAT ARE YOU DOING?!
YELP!
PUNCH!
Stay...away...from my...FRIENDS!!
APRIL, BE CAREFUL!
CAAAREFUL...
Whuh?

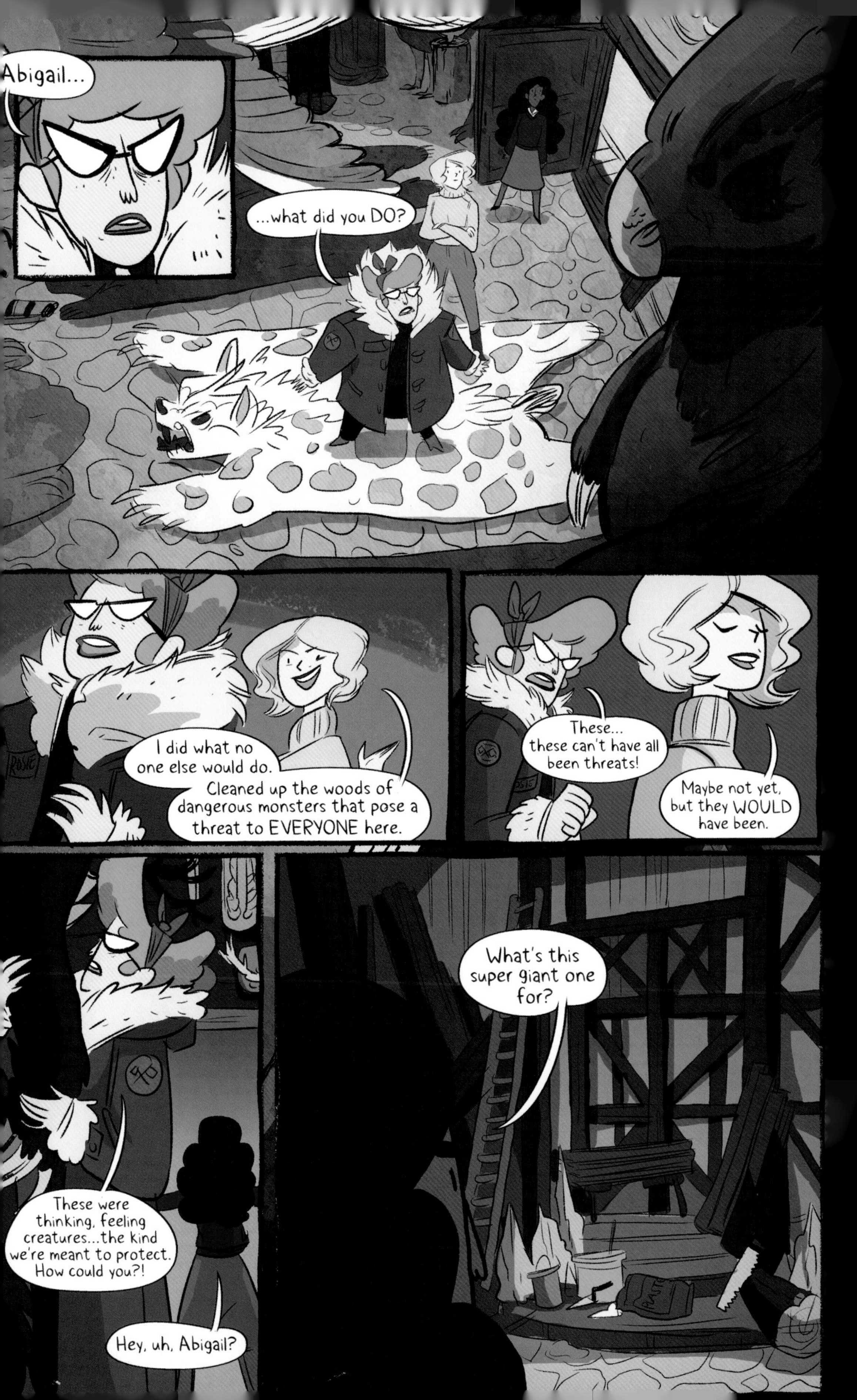
Abigail...
...what did you DO?
I did what no one else would do.
Cleaned up the woods of dangerous monsters that pose a threat to EVERYONE here.
These... these can't have all been threats!
Maybe not yet, but they WOULD have been.
These were thinking, feeling creatures...the kind we're meant to protect. How could you?!
Hey, uh, Abigail?
What's this super giant one for?

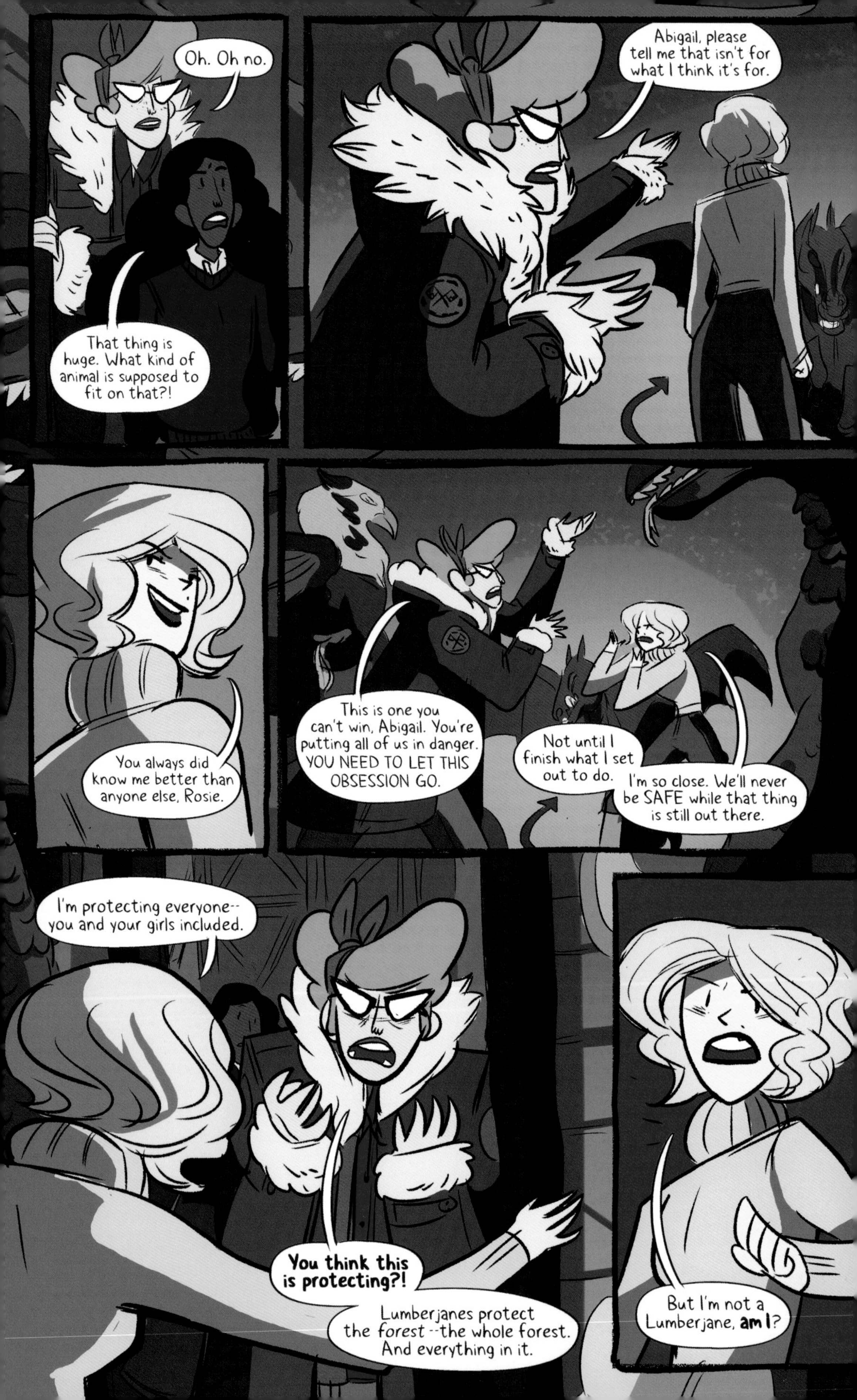
Oh. Oh no.
That thing is huge. What kind of animal is supposed to fit on that?!
Abigail, please tell me that isn't for what I think it's for.
You always did know me better than anyone else, Rosie.
This is one you can't win, Abigail. You're putting all of us in danger. YOU NEED TO LET THIS OBSESSION GO.
Not until I finish what I set out to do.
I'm so close. We'll never be SAFE while that thing is still out there.
I'm protecting everyone-- you and your girls included.
You think this is protecting?!
Lumberjanes protect the forest --the whole forest. And everything in it.
But I'm not a Lumberjane, **am I**?

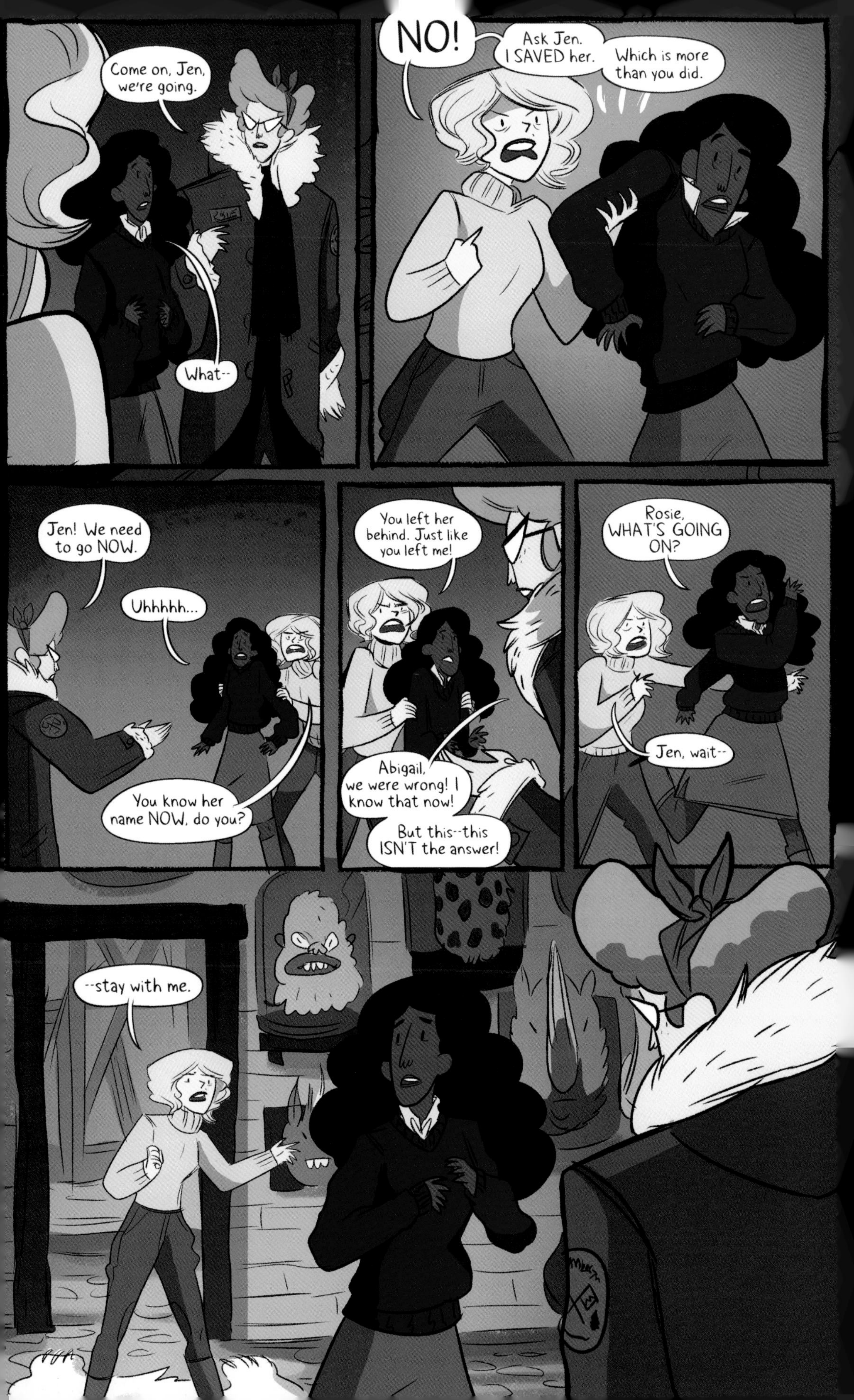
Come on, Jen, we're going.
What--
NO!
Ask Jen. I SAVED her.
Which is more than you did.
Jen! We need to go NOW.
Uhhhhh...
You know her name NOW, do you?
You left her behind. Just like you left me!
Abigail, we were wrong! I know that now!
But this--this ISN'T the answer!
Rosie, WHAT'S GOING ON?
Jen, wait--
--stay with me.

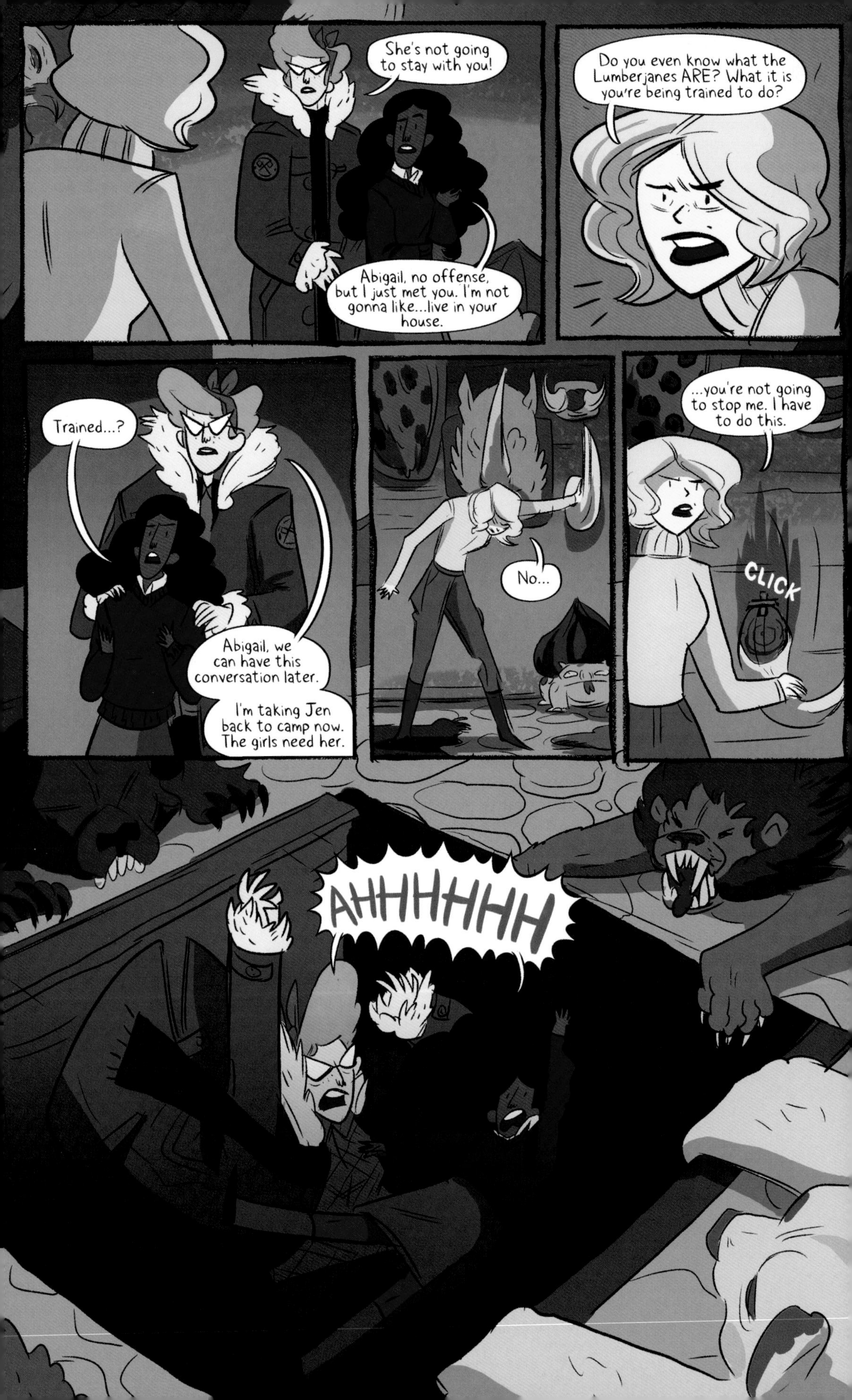
She's not going to stay with you!
Abigail, no offense, but I just met you. I'm not gonna like...live in your house.
Do you even know what the Lumberjanes ARE? What it is you're being trained to do?
Trained...?
Abigail, we can have this conversation later.
I'm taking Jen back to camp now. The girls need her.
No...
...you're not going to stop me. I have to do this.
CLICK
AHHHHHH

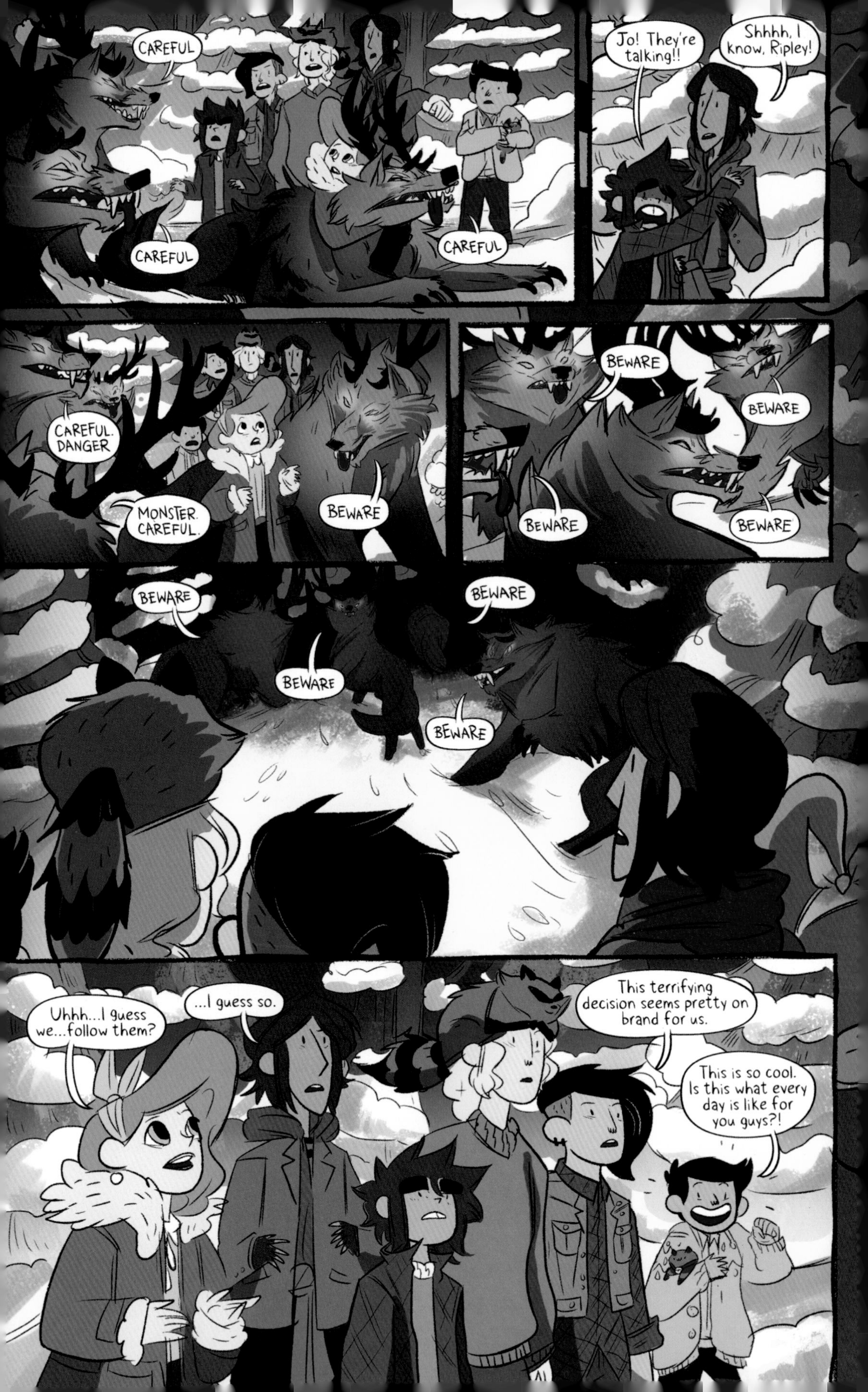
CAREFUL
CAREFUL
CAREFUL
Jo! They're talking!!
Shhhh, I know, Ripley!
CAREFUL. DANGER
MONSTER. CAREFUL.
BEWARE
BEWARE
BEWARE
BEWARE
BEWARE
BEWARE
BEWARE
BEWARE
BEWARE
Uhhh...I guess we...follow them?
...I guess so.
This terrifying decision seems pretty on brand for us.
This is so cool. Is this what every day is like for you guys?!

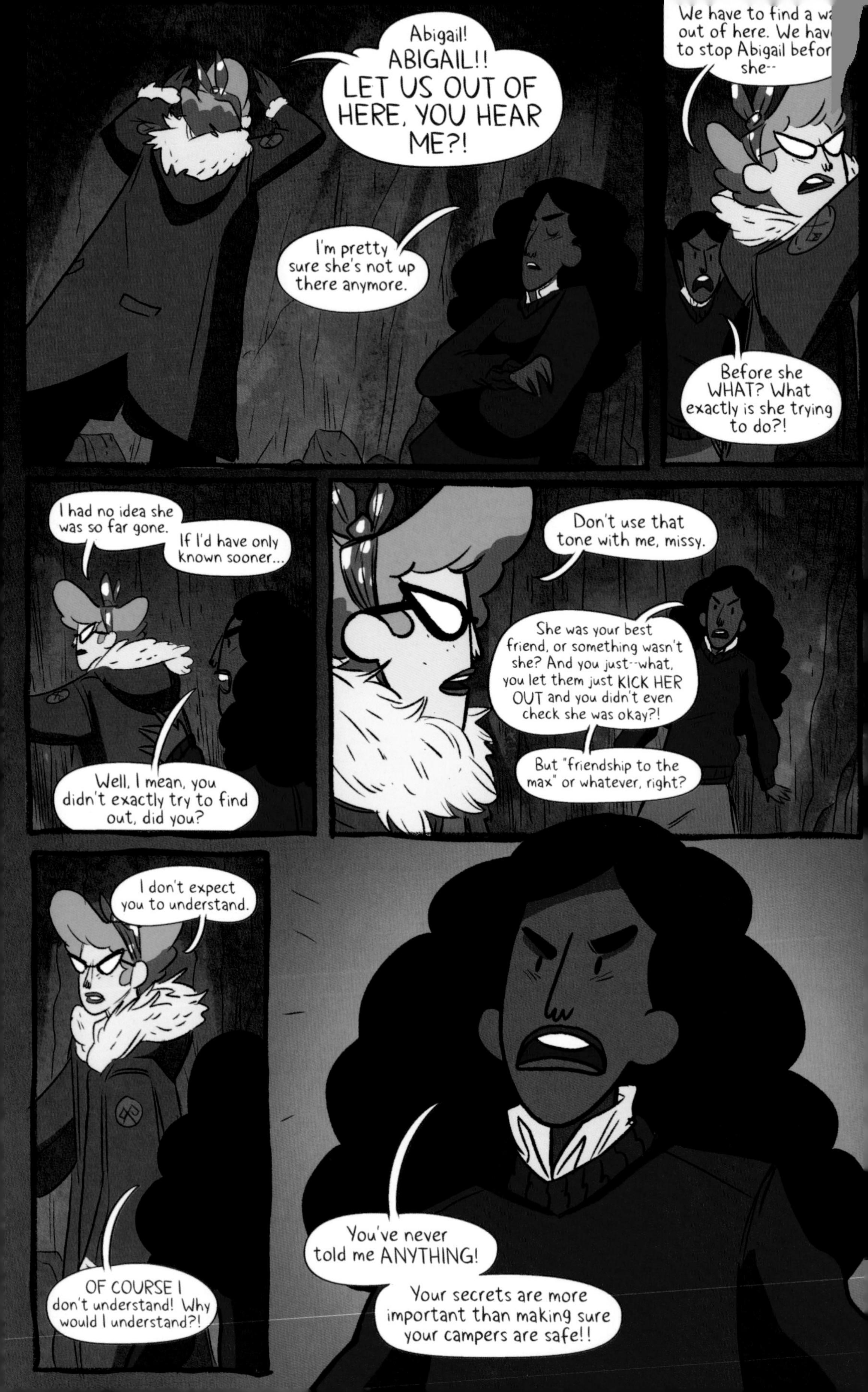
Abigail! ABIGAIL!! LET US OUT OF HERE, YOU HEAR ME?!
I'm pretty sure she's not up there anymore.
We have to find a wa out of here. We hav to stop Abigail befor she--
Before she WHAT? What exactly is she trying to do?!
I had no idea she was so far gone.
If I'd have only known sooner...
Well, I mean, you didn't exactly try to find out, did you?
Don't use that tone with me, missy.
She was your best friend, or something wasn't she? And you just--what, you let them just KICK HER OUT and you didn't even check she was okay?!
But "friendship to the max" or whatever, right?
I don't expect you to understand.
OF COURSE I don't understand! Why would I understand?!
You've never told me ANYTHING!
Your secrets are more important than making sure your campers are safe!!

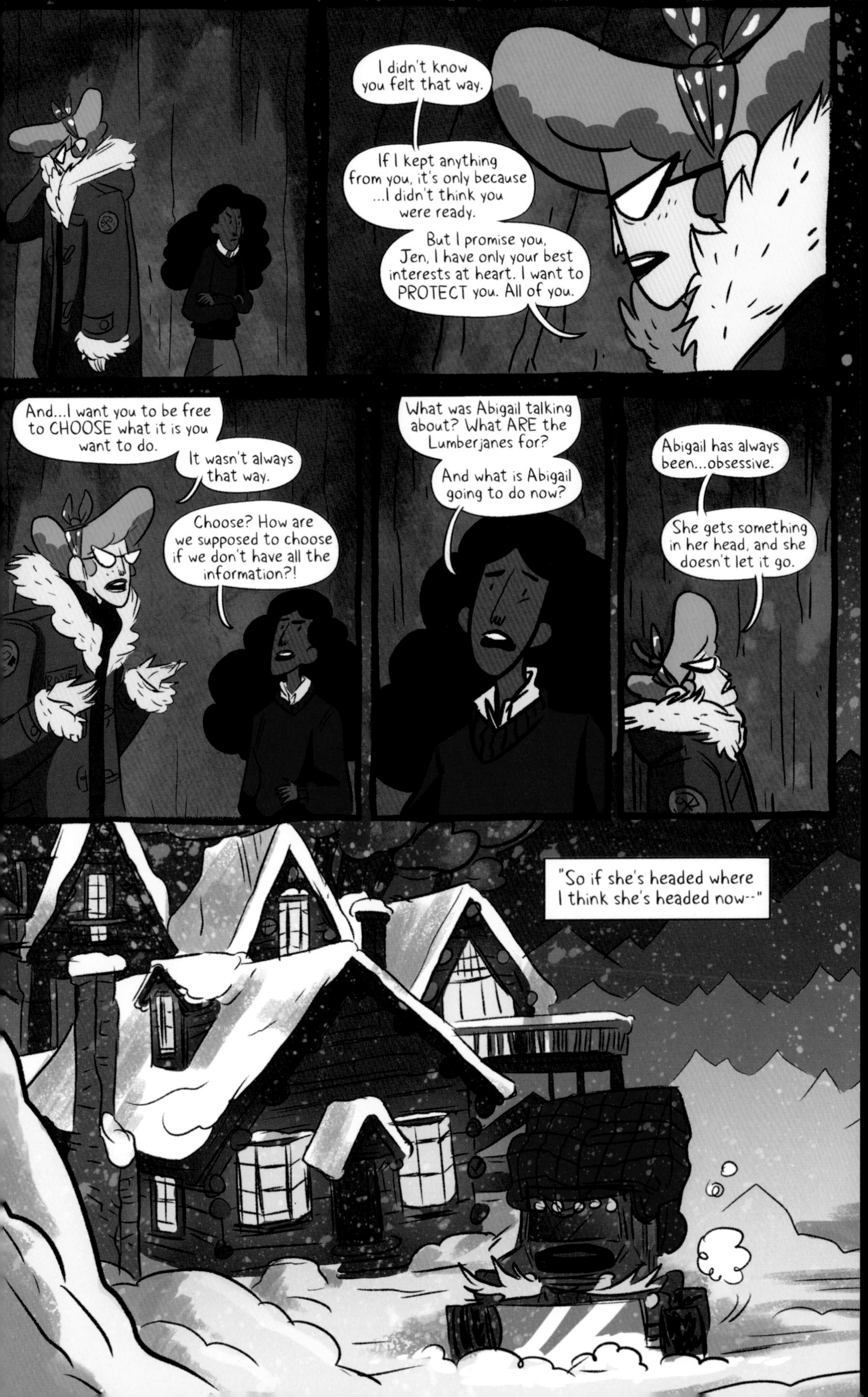
I didn't know you felt that way.
If I kept anything from you, it's only because ...I didn't think you were ready.
But I promise you, Jen, I have only your best interests at heart. I want to PROTECT you. All of you.
And...I want you to be free to CHOOSE what it is you want to do.
It wasn't always that way.
Choose? How are we supposed to choose if we don't have all the information?!
ROSIE
What was Abigail talking about? What ARE the Lumberjanes for?
And what is Abigail going to do now?
Abigail has always been...obsessive.
She gets something in her head, and she doesn't let it go.
"So if she's headed where I think she's headed now--"

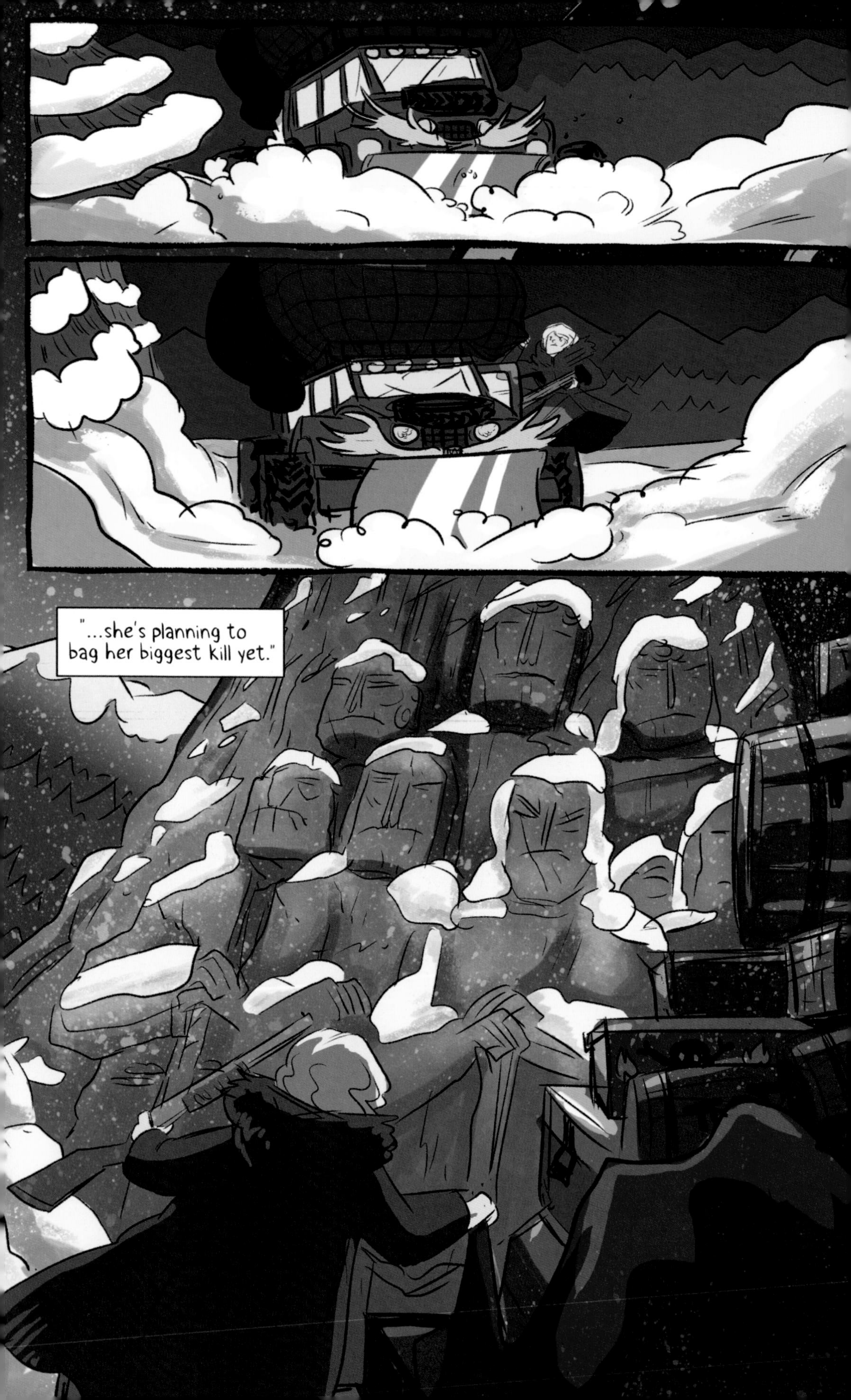
"...she's planning to
bag her biggest kill yet."

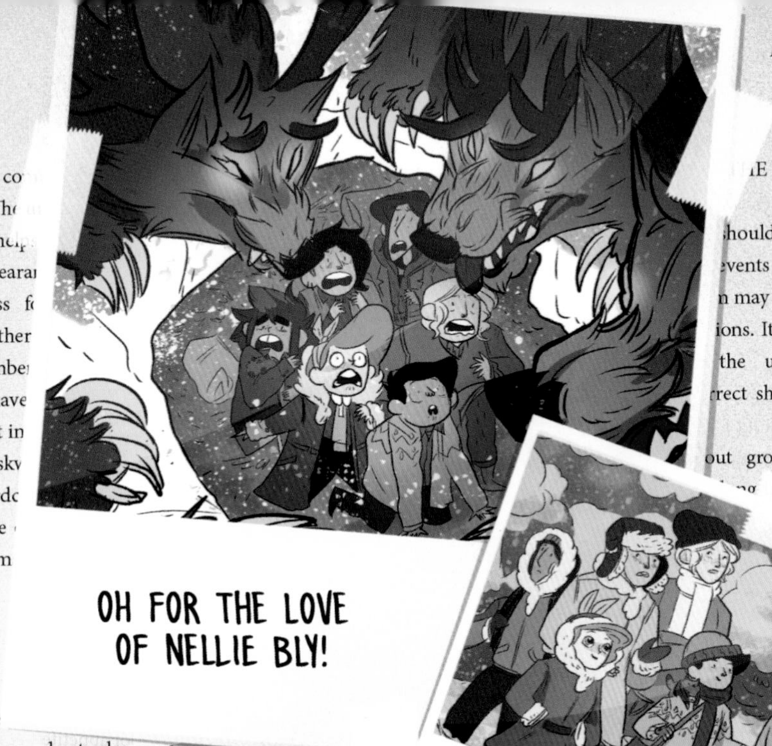
OH FOR THE LOVE
OF NELLIE BLY!

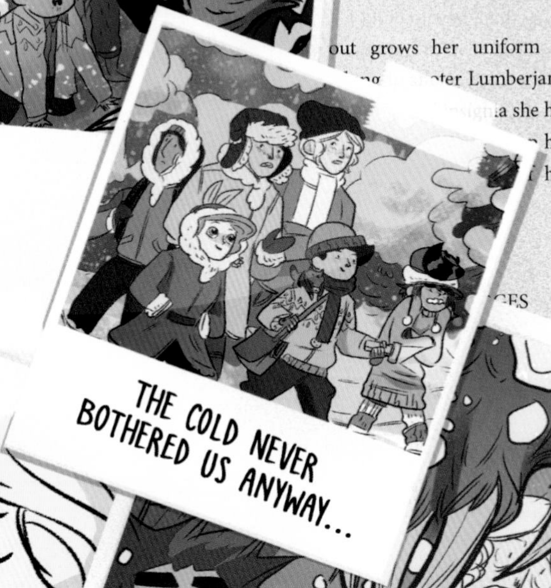
THE COLD NEVER
BOTHERED US ANYWAY...

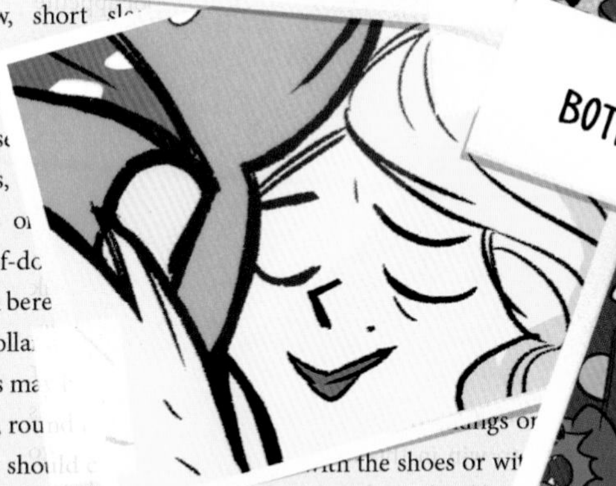

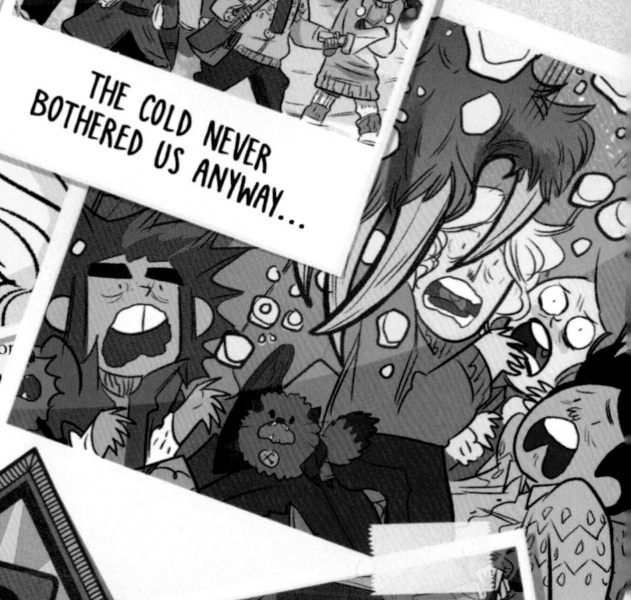

will co
The
It he
appeara
dress f
Further
Lumbe
to have
part in
Thiskv
Hardc
have
them

HE UNIFORM

should be worn at camp
events when Lumberjanes
n may also be worn at other
ions. It should be worn as a
the uniform dress with
rrect shoes, and stocking or

out grows her uniform or
ter Lumberjane.
a she has
her
her

GES

The
yellow, short sl
emb
the w
choos
slacks,
made o
out-of-do
green bere
the colla
Shoes ma
heels, rou ... kings or
socks shou ... with the shoes or wi
the uniform. Ne... es, bracelets, or other jewelry do
belong with a Lumberjane uniform.

HOW TO WEAR THE UNIFO

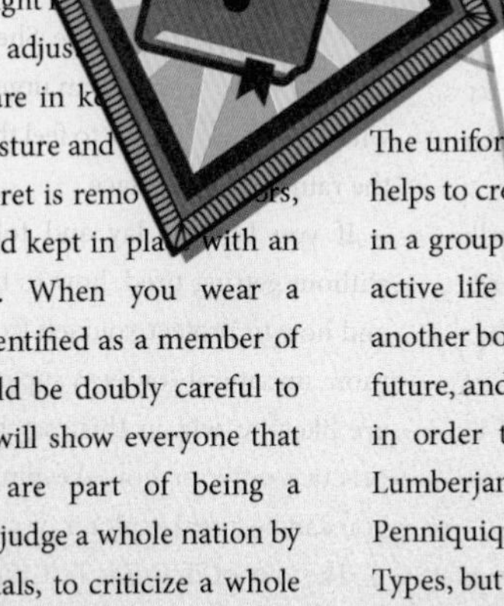

To look well in a uniform dema
uniform be kept in good condit
pressed. See that the skirt is the right
height and build, that the belt is adjus
that your shoes and stockings are in k
uniform, that you watch your posture and
with dignity and grace. If the beret is remo ... rs,
be sure that your hair is neat and kept in pla ... with an
insonspicuous clip or ribbon. When you wear a Lumberjane uniform you are identified as a member of this organization and you should be doubly careful to conduct yourself in a way that will show everyone that courtesy and thoughtfullness are part of being a Lumberjane. People are likely to judge a whole nation by the selfishness of a few individuals, to criticize a whole family because of the misconduct of one member, and to feel unkindly toward and organization because of the

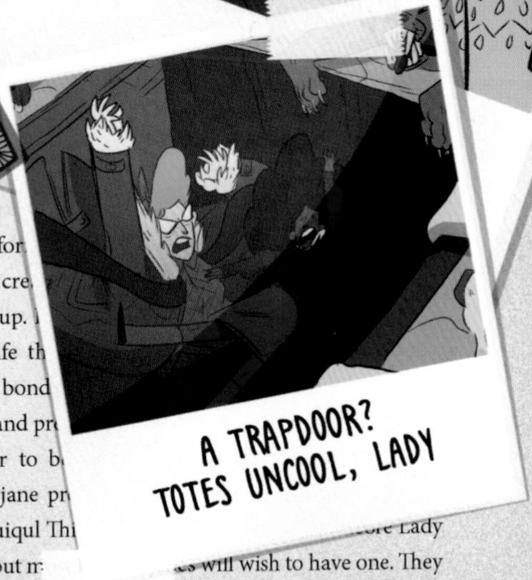
A TRAPDOOR?
TOTES UNCOOL, LADY

The unifor
helps to cre
in a group.
active life th
another bond
future, and pr
in order to b
Lumberjane pr
Penniquiqul Thi ... ore Lady
Types, but m ... will wish to have one. They
can either bu ... uniform, or make it themselves from
materials available at the trading post.

LUMBERJANES FIELD MANUAL

CHAPTER FIFTEEN

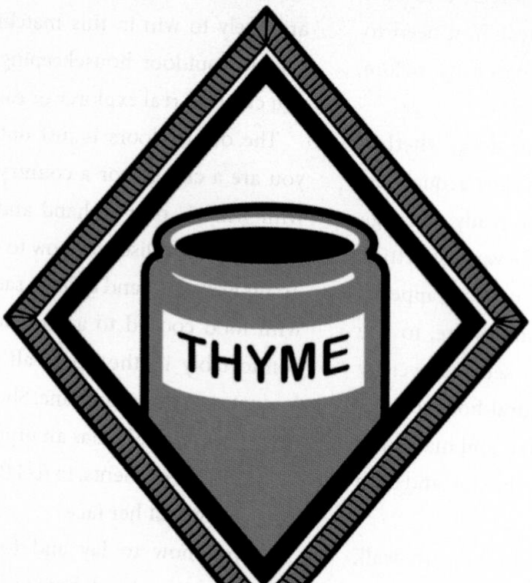
THYME

Lumberjanes "Cooking" Program Field

OUT OF THYME BADGE

"Sometimes expediency is necessary."

Timeliness is next to godliness, or so the saying goes. For a Lumberjane, timeliness is an essential part of everyday life. There are many things that a Lumberjane will learn while at camp, she will learn how to care for the wildlife around her and how to use it to better her life and those around her. She will learn the importance of social customs and manners while at the same time enjoying the chance to break the boundaries that society might place upon her. And above all else, a Lumberjane will learn the importance of being on time.

The *Out of Thyme* badge is not just another badge that helps a Lumberjane understand the importance of seasoning, but it is a badge that helps teach the importance of knowing what time it is and constantly using that to her advantage. Need to slow cook a beef brisket, carve additional chairs for your guests and feed the bees that your neighbor left in your care while they went on their annual Everest hike? Understanding how to use time is the key solution to ensuring that a Lumberjane is not only able to get all of that done, but is able to do it with enough time to spare that they'll be able to handle anything else life might throw her way.

To obtain the *Out of Thyme* badge, a Lumberjanes must show her understanding of spices in the kitchen. On top of that, a Lumberjane must also prove her time management skills through various timed courses. On top of that, she will have to complete several balanced meals in which she will have to feed her cabin. If the cabin decides to earn this badge as a team, which is encouraged, then the cabin will be asked to serve a meal for the entire class. They will have to gather the ingredients themselves, and with the help of their counselor, they will use the kitchens. It is also important that the Lumberjane cleans up after themselves as they

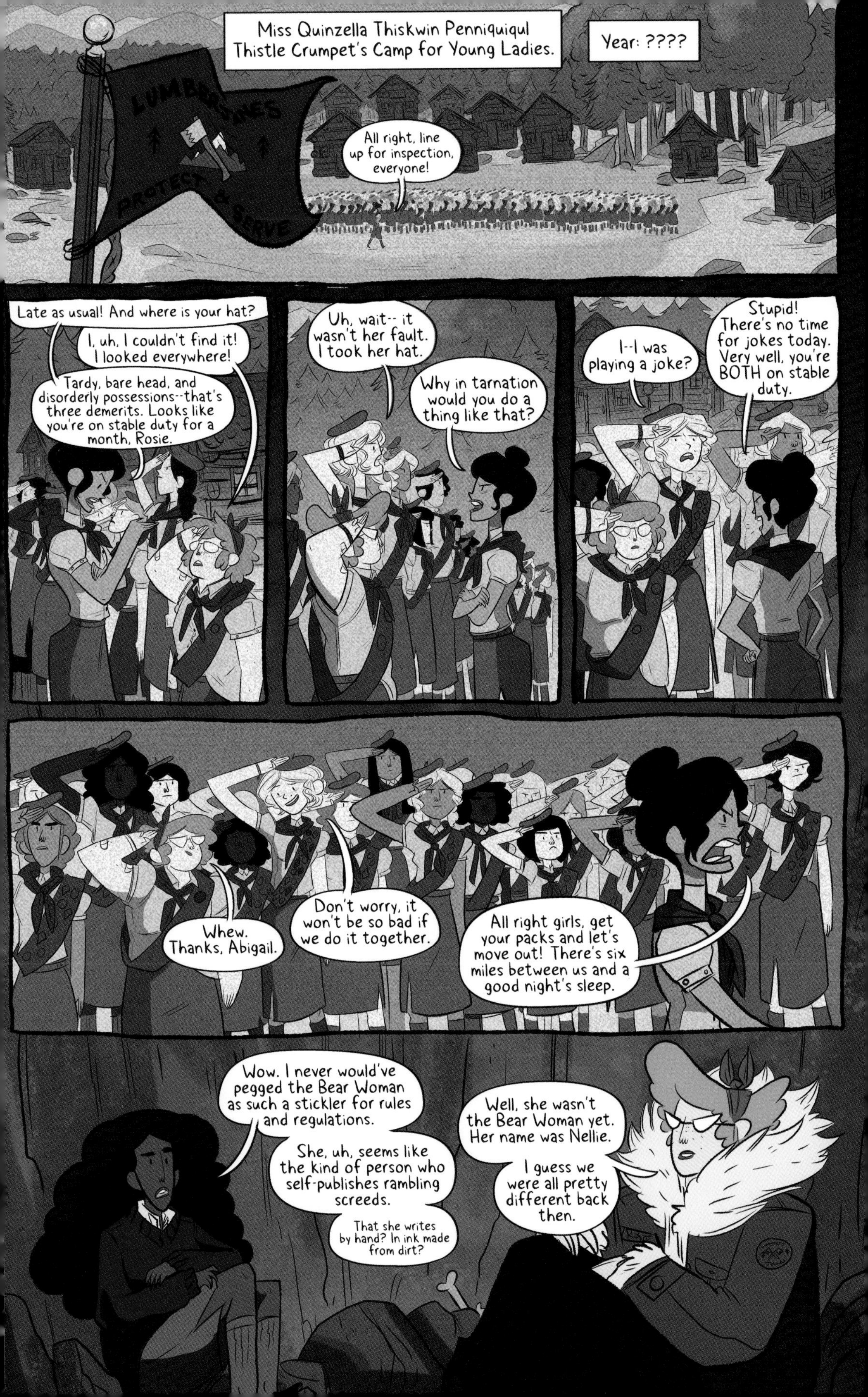
Miss Quinzella Thiskwin Penniquiqul Thistle Crumpet's Camp for Young Ladies.
Year: ????
LUMBERJANES
PROTECT & SERVE
All right, line up for inspection, everyone!
Late as usual! And where is your hat?
I, uh, I couldn't find it! I looked everywhere!
Tardy, bare head, and disorderly possessions--that's three demerits. Looks like you're on stable duty for a month, Rosie.
Uh, wait-- it wasn't her fault. I took her hat.
Why in tarnation would you do a thing like that?
I--I was playing a joke?
Stupid! There's no time for jokes today. Very well, you're BOTH on stable duty.
Whew. Thanks, Abigail.
Don't worry, it won't be so bad if we do it together.
All right girls, get your packs and let's move out! There's six miles between us and a good night's sleep.
Wow. I never would've pegged the Bear Woman as such a stickler for rules and regulations.
She, uh, seems like the kind of person who self-publishes rambling screeds.
That she writes by hand? In ink made from dirt?
Well, she wasn't the Bear Woman yet. Her name was Nellie.
I guess we were all pretty different back then.

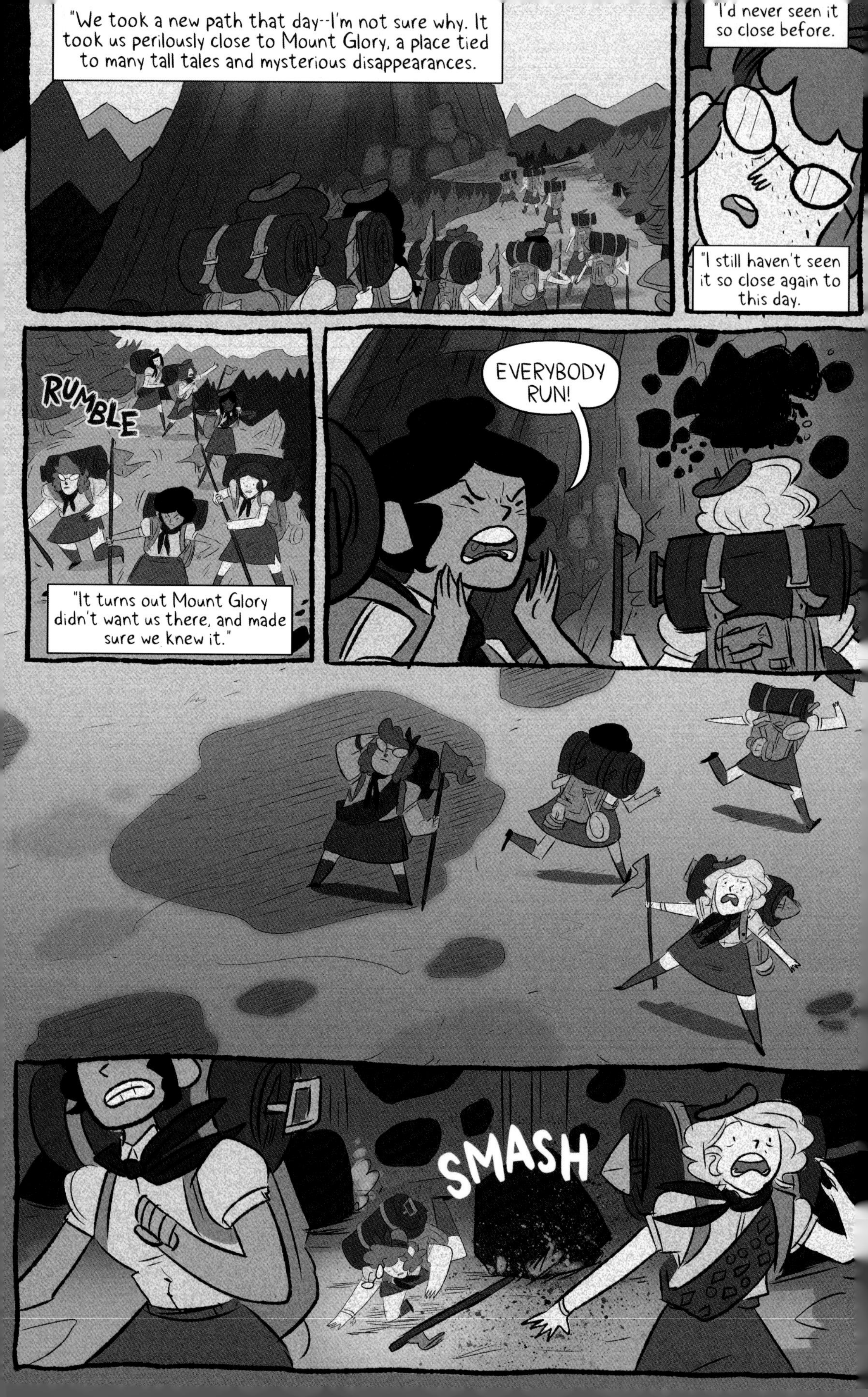
"We took a new path that day--I'm not sure why. It took us perilously close to Mount Glory, a place tied to many tall tales and mysterious disappearances.
"I'd never seen it so close before.
"I still haven't seen it so close again to this day.
RUMBLE
"It turns out Mount Glory didn't want us there, and made sure we knew it."
EVERYBODY RUN!
SMASH

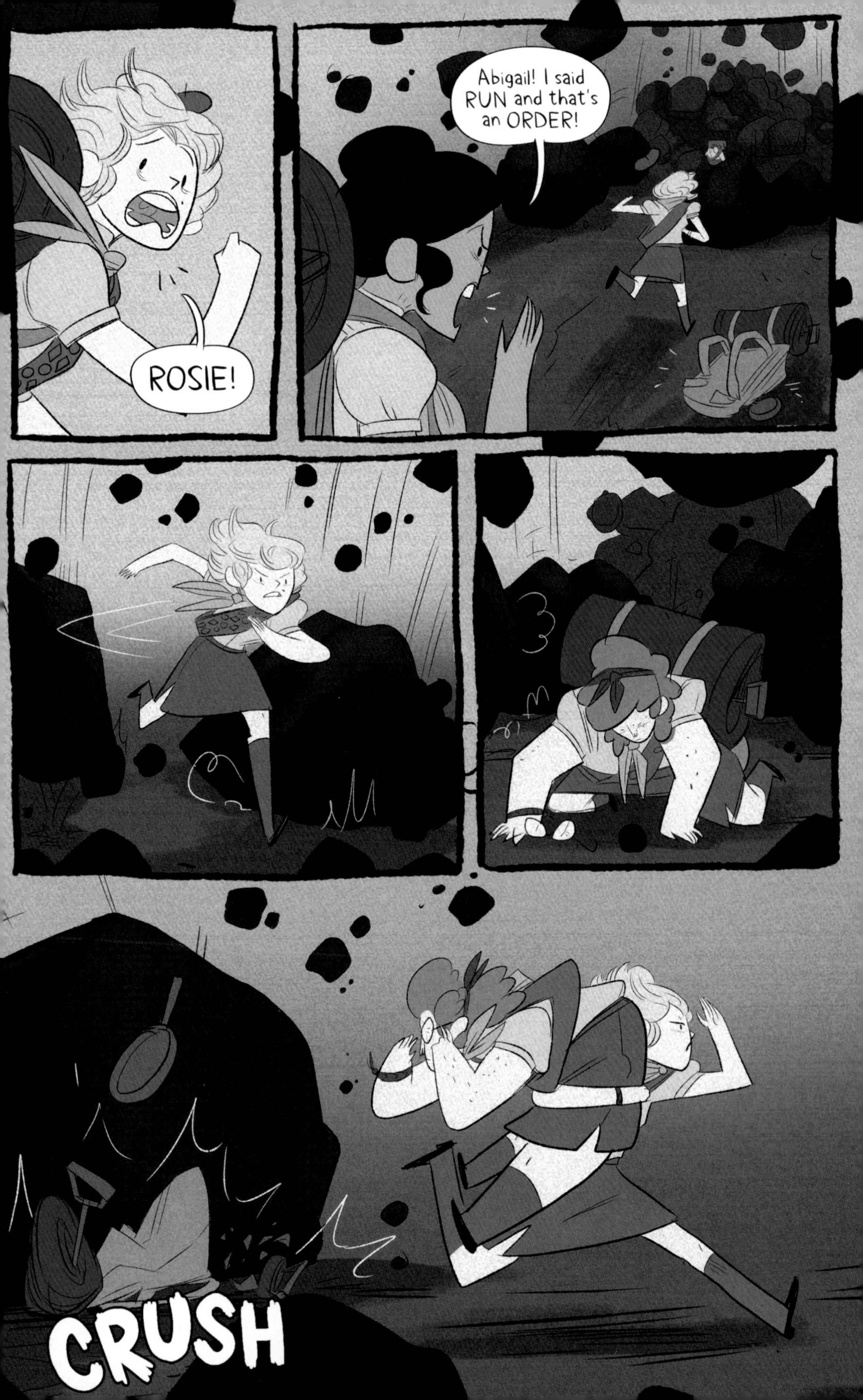
ROSIE!
Abigail! I said RUN and that's an ORDER!
CRUSH

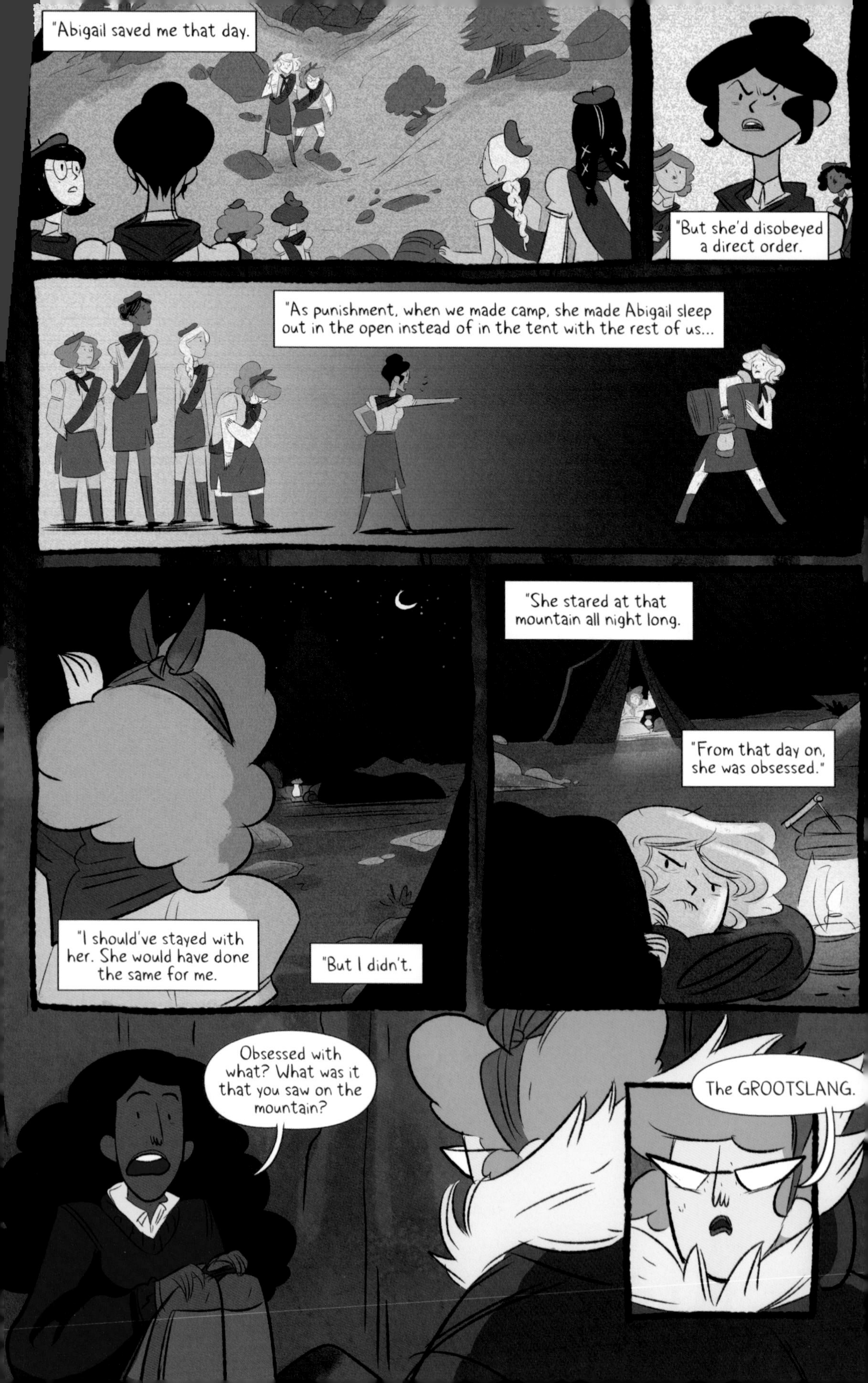
"Abigail saved me that day.
"But she'd disobeyed a direct order.
"As punishment, when we made camp, she made Abigail sleep out in the open instead of in the tent with the rest of us...
"I should've stayed with her. She would have done the same for me.
"But I didn't.
"She stared at that mountain all night long.
"From that day on, she was obsessed."
Obsessed with what? What was it that you saw on the mountain?
The GROOTSLANG.

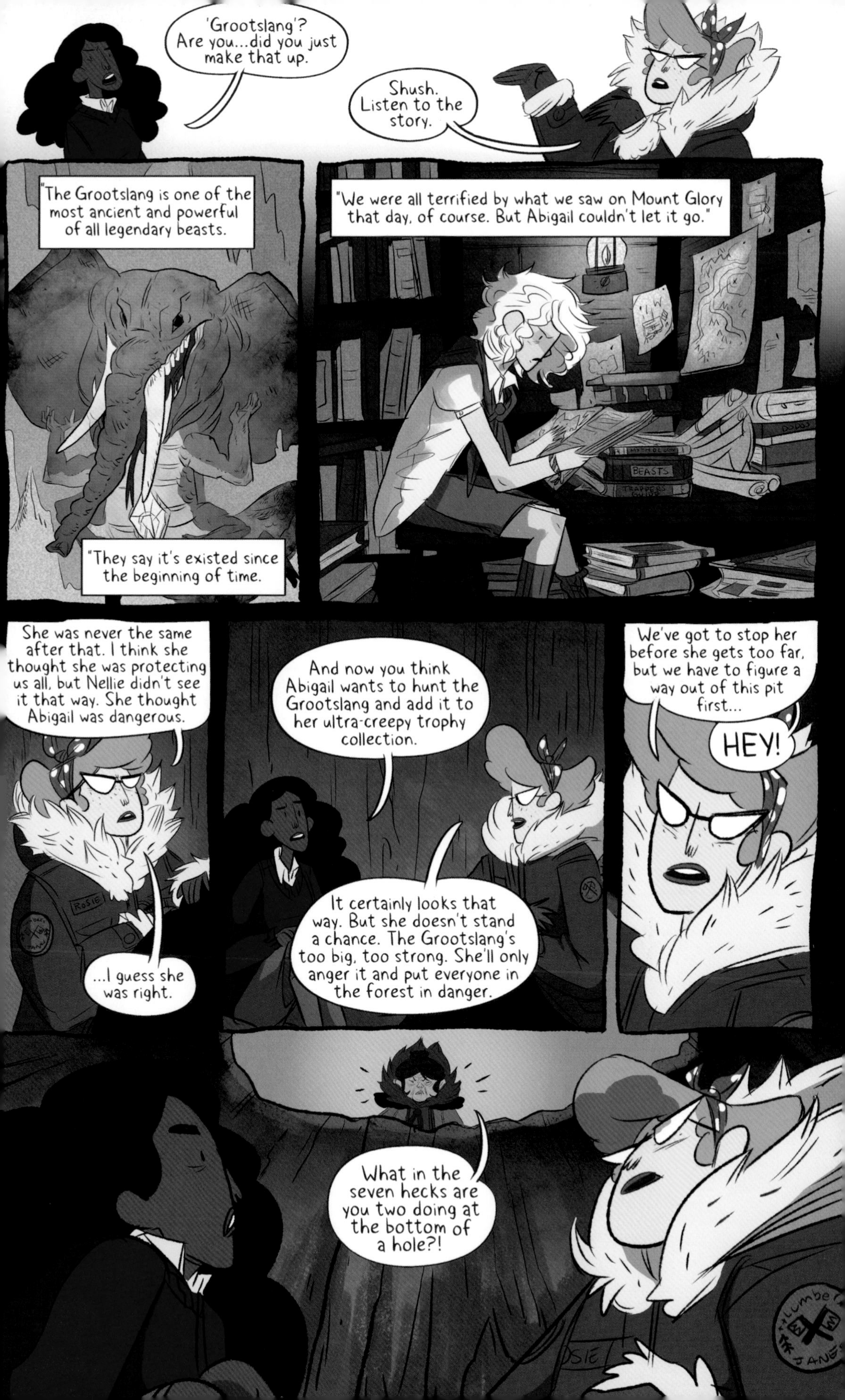
'Grootslang'? Are you...did you just make that up.
Shush. Listen to the story.
"The Grootslang is one of the most ancient and powerful of all legendary beasts.
"They say it's existed since the beginning of time.
"We were all terrified by what we saw on Mount Glory that day, of course. But Abigail couldn't let it go."
MYTHOLOGY
BEASTS
TRAPPERS GUIDE
She was never the same after that. I think she thought she was protecting us all, but Nellie didn't see it that way. She thought Abigail was dangerous.
...I guess she was right.
ROSIE
And now you think Abigail wants to hunt the Grootslang and add it to her ultra-creepy trophy collection.
It certainly looks that way. But she doesn't stand a chance. The Grootslang's too big, too strong. She'll only anger it and put everyone in the forest in danger.
We've got to stop her before she gets too far, but we have to figure a way out of this pit first...
HEY!
What in the seven hecks are you two doing at the bottom of a hole?!

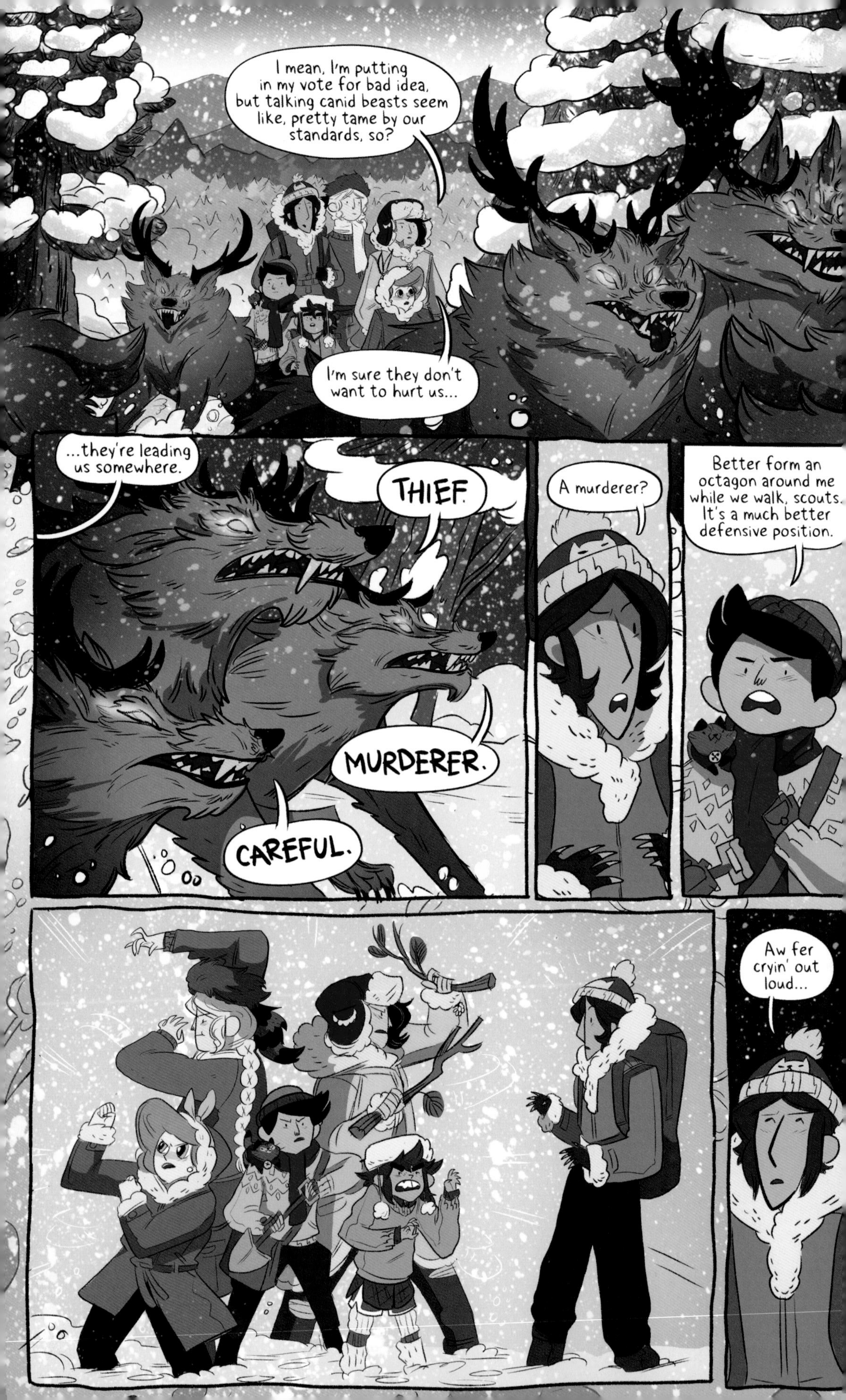
I mean, I'm putting in my vote for bad idea, but talking canid beasts seem like, pretty tame by our standards, so?
I'm sure they don't want to hurt us...
...they're leading us somewhere.
THIEF.
MURDERER.
CAREFUL.
A murderer?
Better form an octagon around me while we walk, scouts. It's a much better defensive position.
Aw fer cryin' out loud...

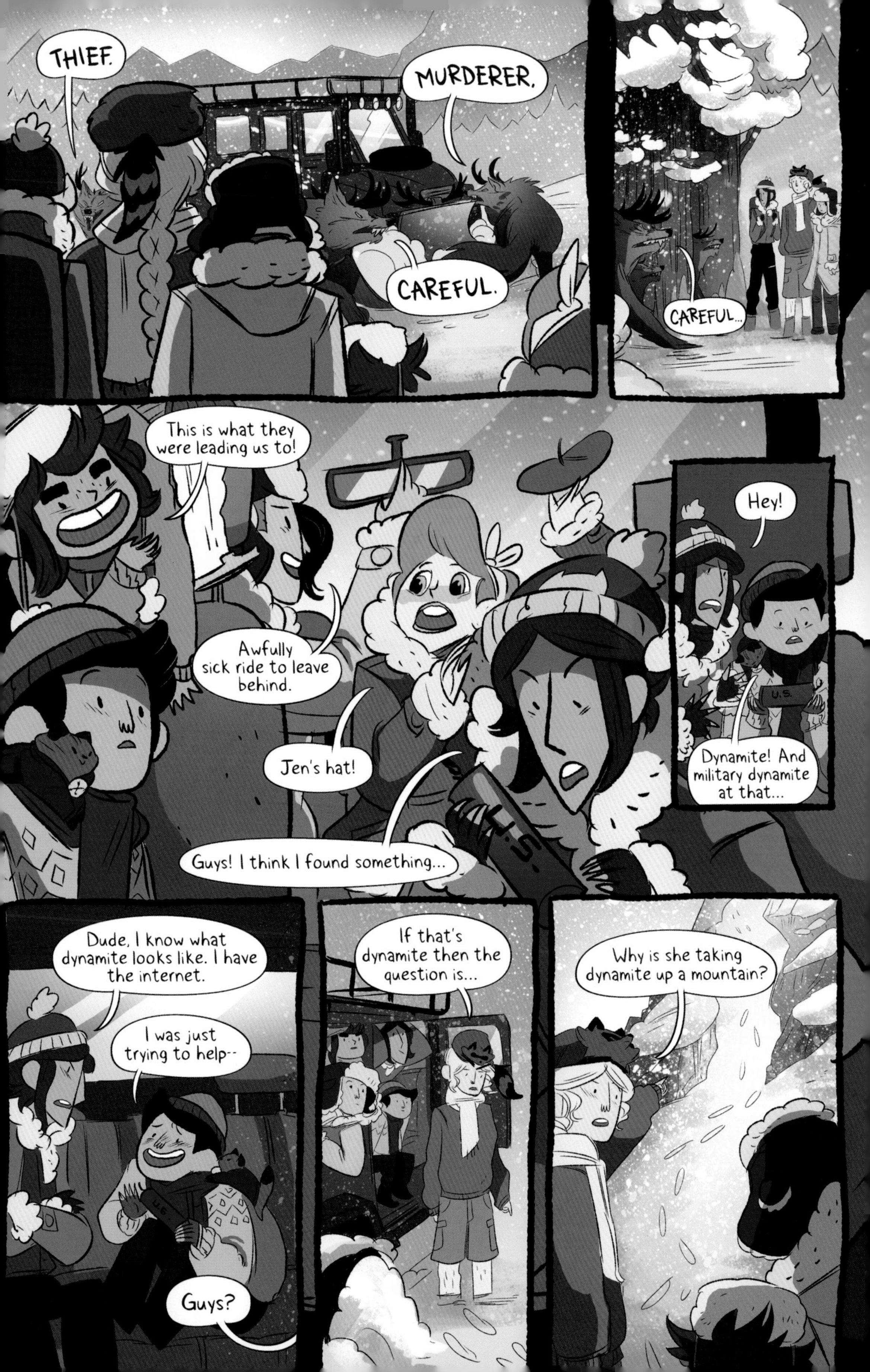
THIEF.
MURDERER.
CAREFUL.
CAREFUL...
This is what they were leading us to!
Awfully sick ride to leave behind.
Jen's hat!
Guys! I think I found something...
Hey!
U.S.
Dynamite! And military dynamite at that...
Dude, I know what dynamite looks like. I have the internet.
I was just trying to help--
Guys?
If that's dynamite then the question is...
Why is she taking dynamite up a mountain?

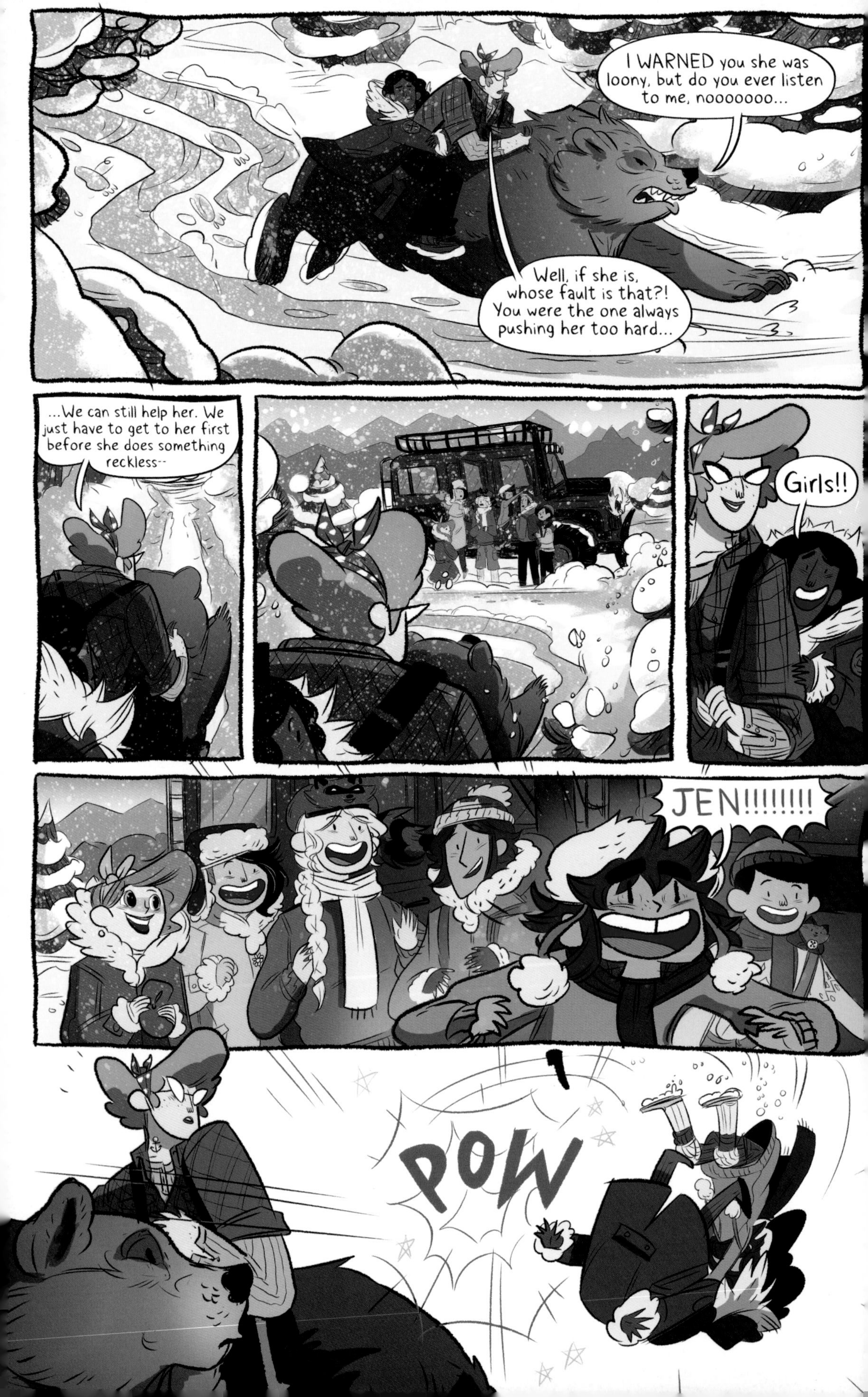
I WARNED you she was loony, but do you ever listen to me, nooooooo...
Well, if she is, whose fault is that?! You were the one always pushing her too hard...
...We can still help her. We just have to get to her first before she does something reckless--
Girls!!
JEN!!!!!!!!!
POW

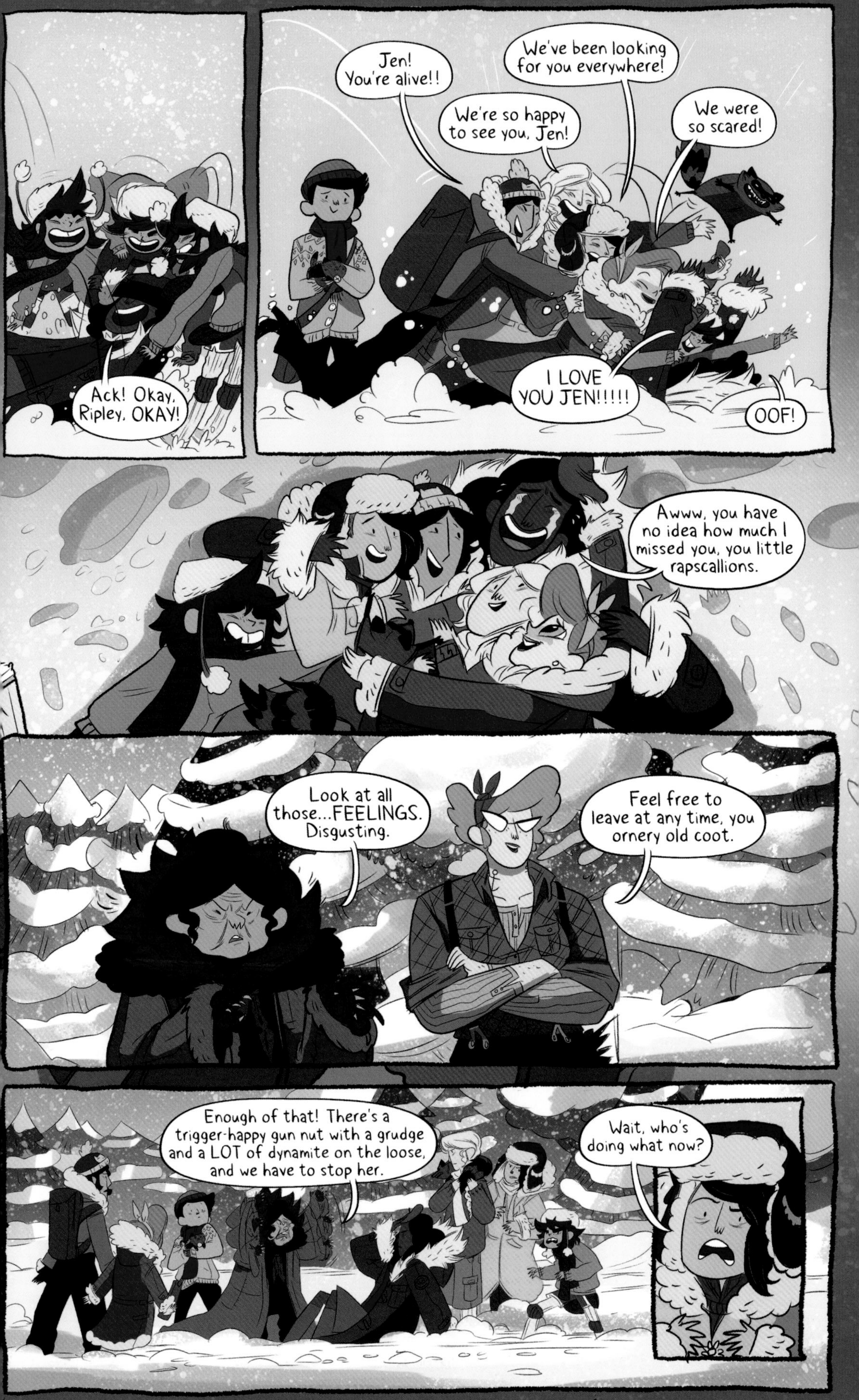
Ack! Okay, Ripley, OKAY!
Jen! You're alive!!
We're so happy to see you, Jen!
We've been looking for you everywhere!
We were so scared!
I LOVE YOU JEN!!!!!
OOF!
Awww, you have no idea how much I missed you, you little rapscallions.
Look at all those...FEELINGS. Disgusting.
Feel free to leave at any time, you ornery old coot.
Enough of that! There's a trigger-happy gun nut with a grudge and a LOT of dynamite on the loose, and we have to stop her.
Wait, who's doing what now?

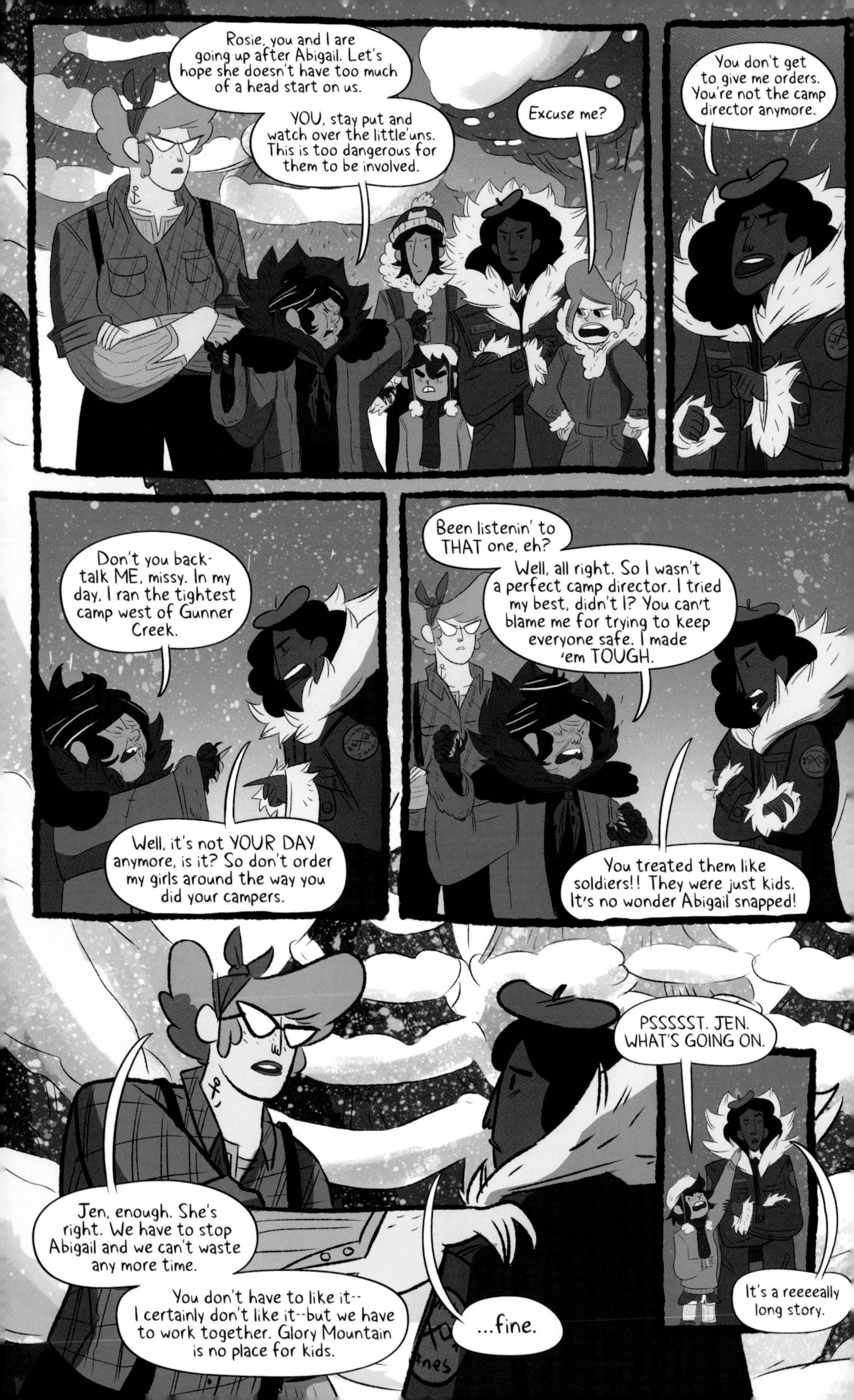

Rosie, you and I are going up after Abigail. Let's hope she doesn't have too much of a head start on us.
YOU, stay put and watch over the little'uns. This is too dangerous for them to be involved.
Excuse me?
You don't get to give me orders. You're not the camp director anymore.
Don't you back-talk ME, missy. In my day, I ran the tightest camp west of Gunner Creek.
Well, it's not YOUR DAY anymore, is it? So don't order my girls around the way you did your campers.
Been listenin' to THAT one, eh?
Well, all right. So I wasn't a perfect camp director. I tried my best, didn't I? You can't blame me for trying to keep everyone safe. I made 'em TOUGH.
You treated them like soldiers!! They were just kids. It's no wonder Abigail snapped!
Jen, enough. She's right. We have to stop Abigail and we can't waste any more time.
You don't have to like it-- I certainly don't like it--but we have to work together. Glory Mountain is no place for kids.
...fine.
PSSSSST. JEN. WHAT'S GOING ON.
It's a reeeeally long story.

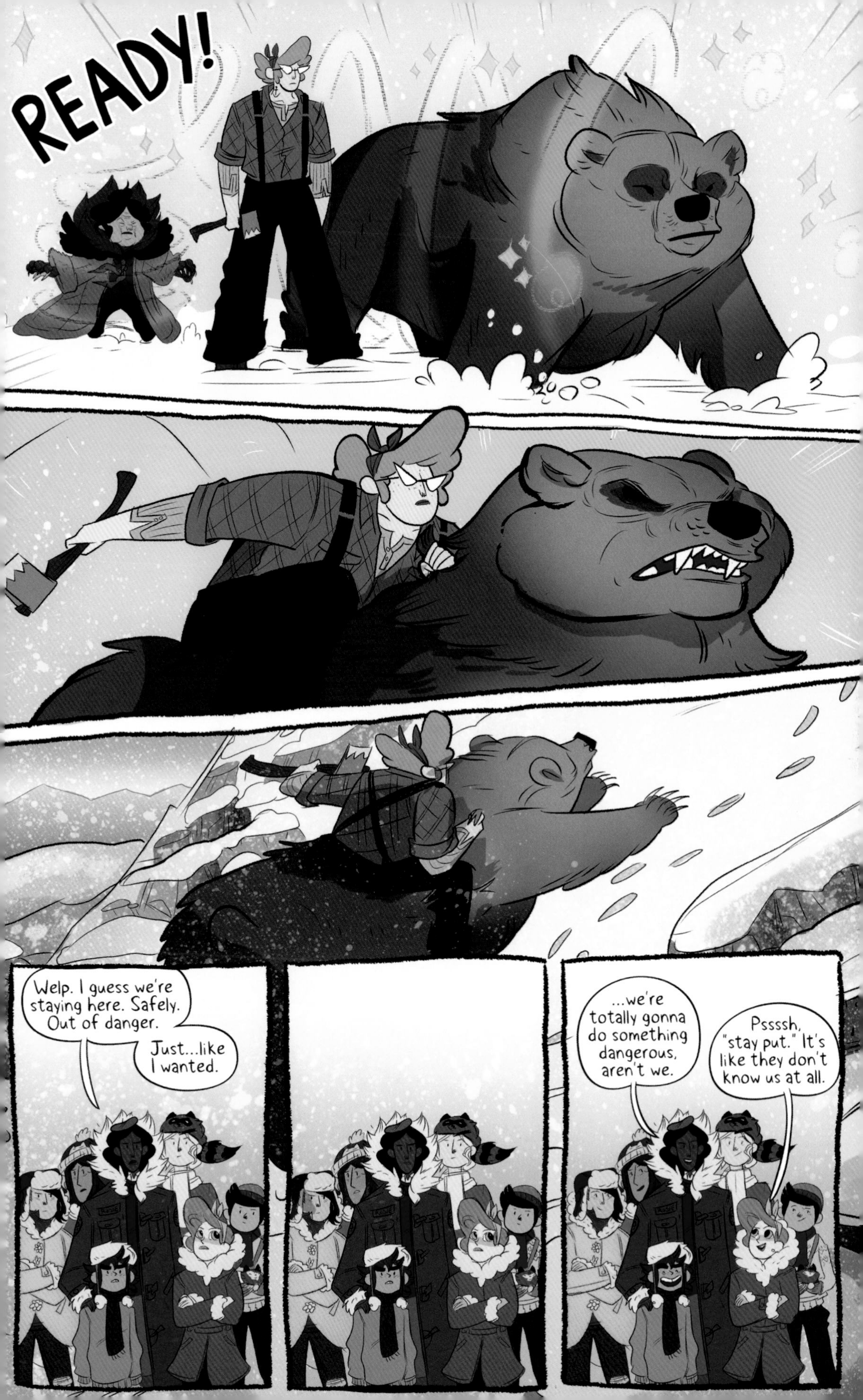
READY!
Welp. I guess we're staying here. Safely. Out of danger.
Just...like I wanted.
...we're totally gonna do something dangerous, aren't we.
Pssssh, "stay put." It's like they don't know us at all.

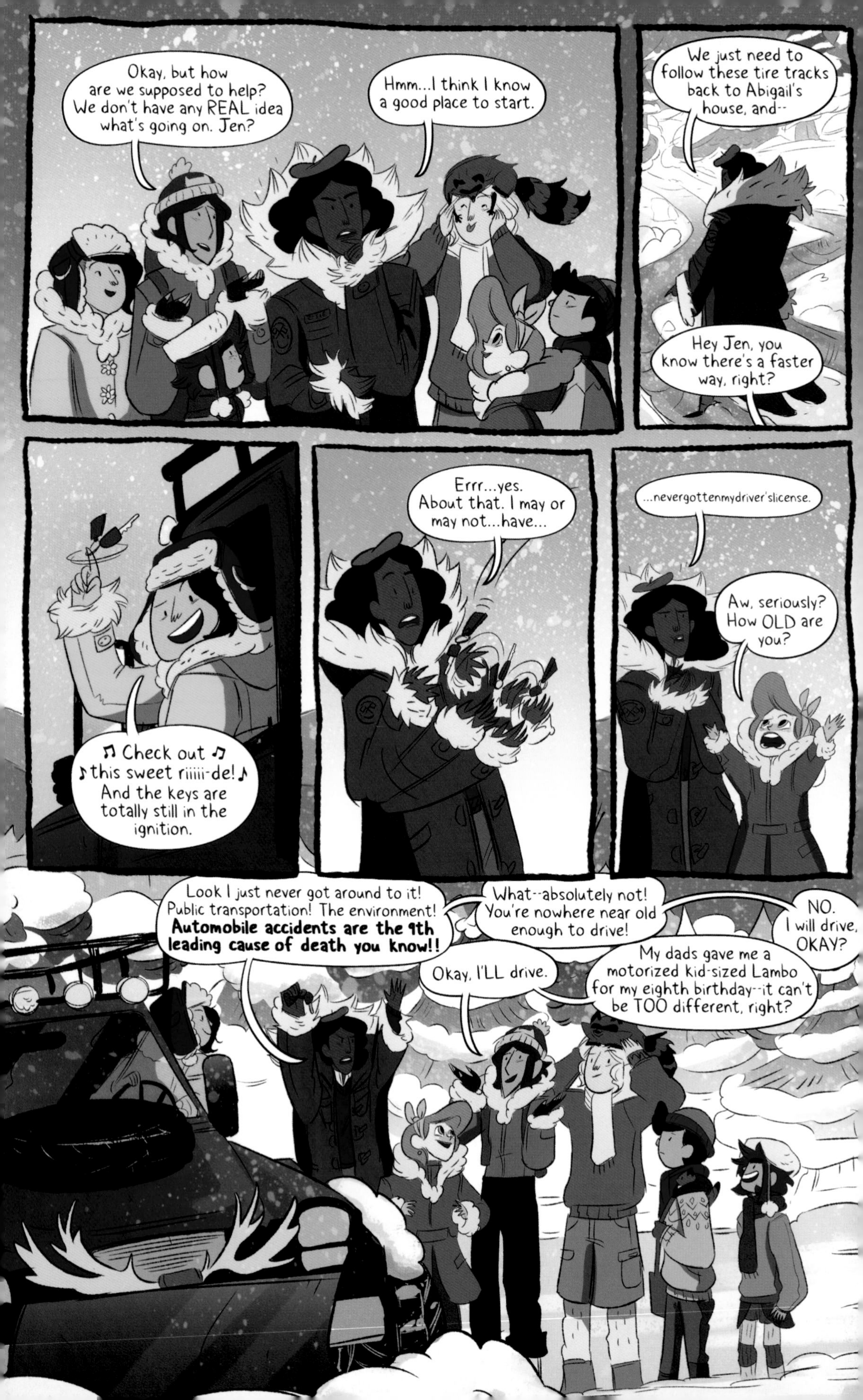
Okay, but how are we supposed to help? We don't have any REAL idea what's going on. Jen?
Hmm...I think I know a good place to start.
We just need to follow these tire tracks back to Abigail's house, and--
Hey Jen, you know there's a faster way, right?
♫ Check out ♫ ♪ this sweet riiiii-de! ♪ And the keys are totally still in the ignition.
Errr...yes. About that. I may or may not...have...
...nevergottenmydriver'slicense.
Aw, seriously? How OLD are you?
Look I just never got around to it! Public transportation! The environment! **Automobile accidents are the 9th leading cause of death you know!!**
What--absolutely not! You're nowhere near old enough to drive!
NO. I will drive, OKAY?
Okay, I'LL drive.
My dads gave me a motorized kid-sized Lambo for my eighth birthday--it can't be TOO different, right?

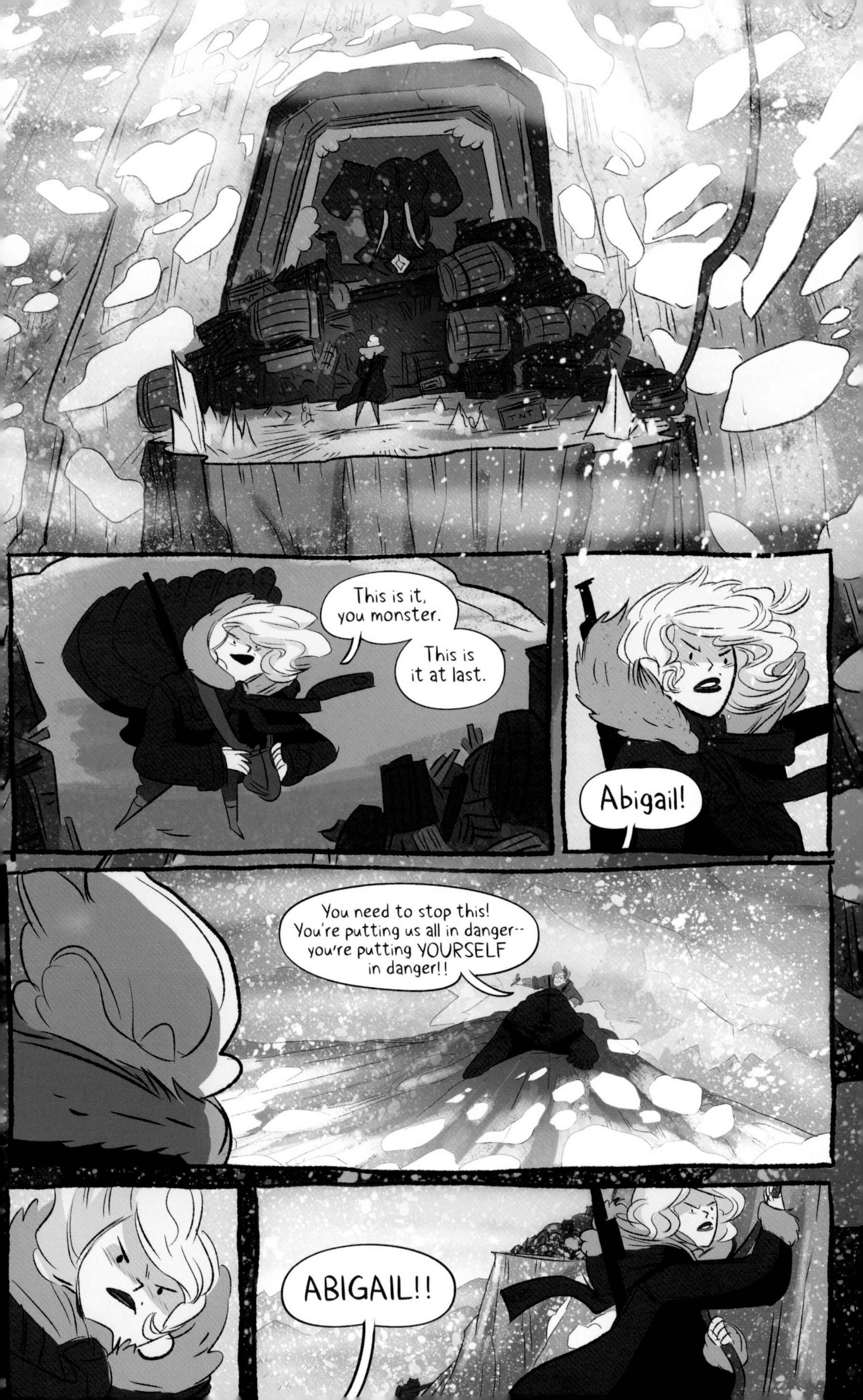
This is it, you monster.
This is it at last.
Abigail!
You need to stop this! You're putting us all in danger-- you're putting YOURSELF in danger!!
ABIGAIL!!

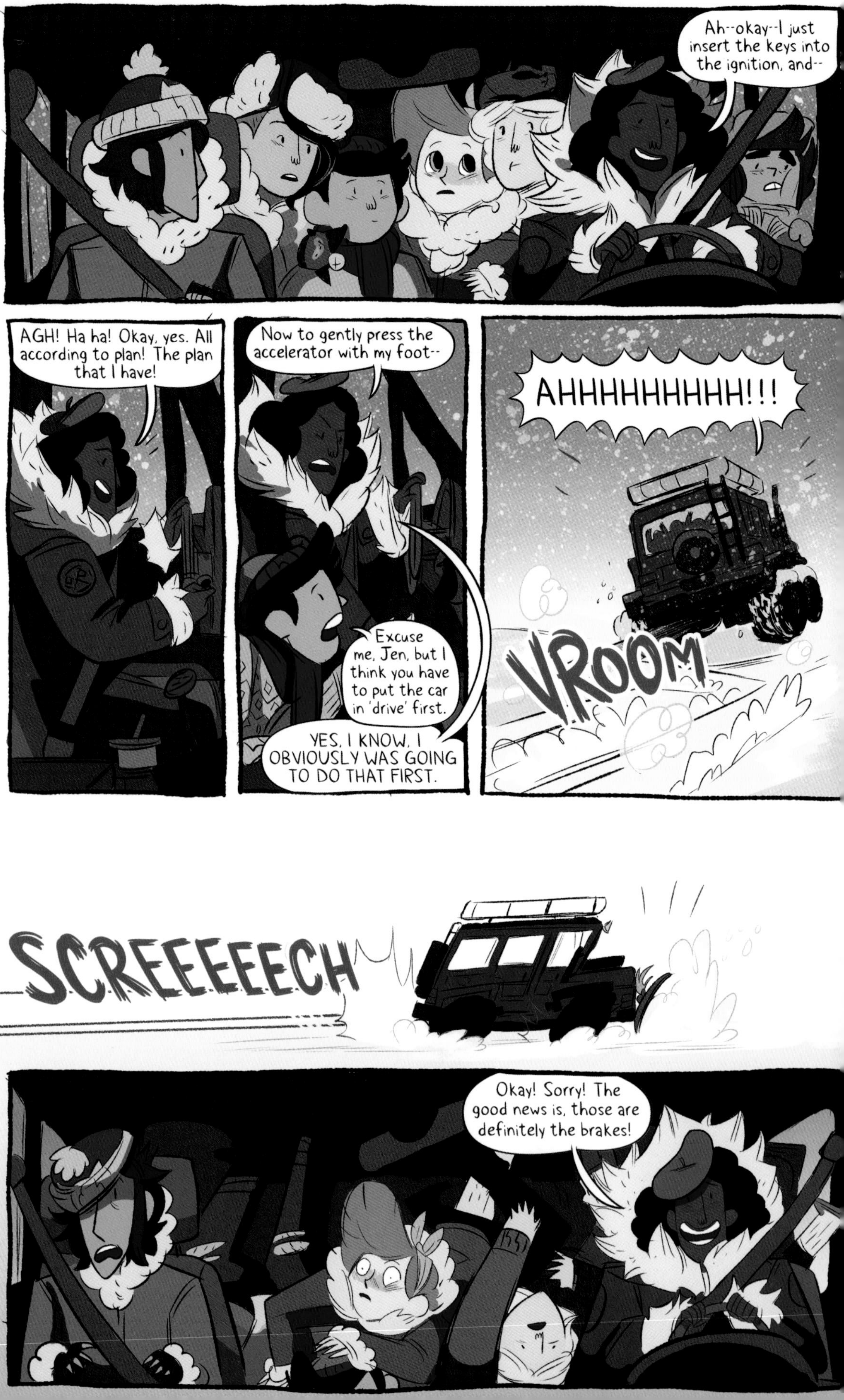

Ah--okay--I just insert the keys into the ignition, and--
AGH! Ha ha! Okay, yes. All according to plan! The plan that I have!
Now to gently press the accelerator with my foot--
Excuse me, Jen, but I think you have to put the car in 'drive' first.
YES, I KNOW, I OBVIOUSLY WAS GOING TO DO THAT FIRST.
AHHHHHHHHH!!!
VROOM
SCREEEEEECH
Okay! Sorry! The good news is, those are definitely the brakes!

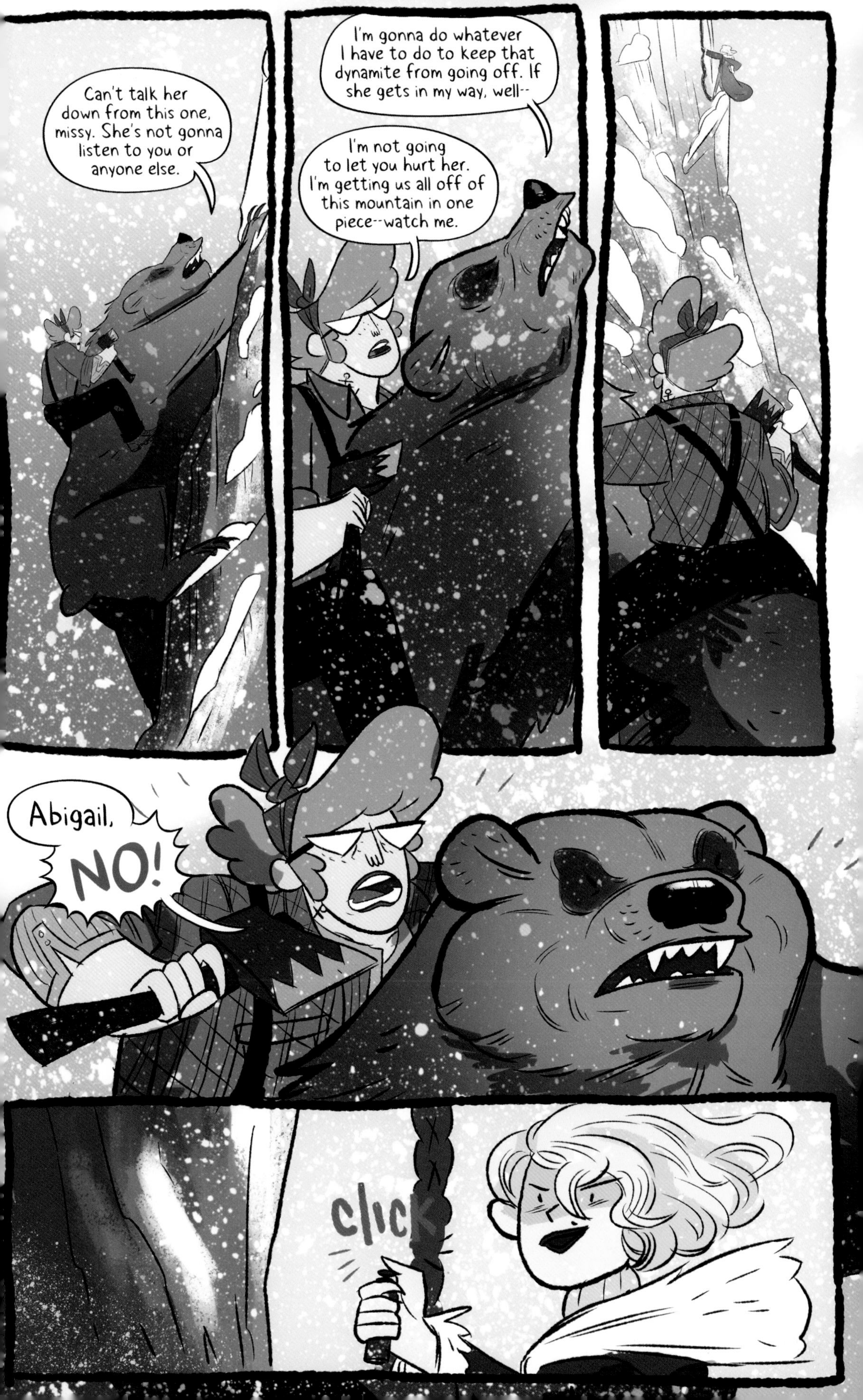
Can't talk her down from this one, missy. She's not gonna listen to you or anyone else.
I'm gonna do whatever I have to do to keep that dynamite from going off. If she gets in my way, well--
I'm not going to let you hurt her. I'm getting us all off of this mountain in one piece--watch me.
Abigail, NO!
CLICK

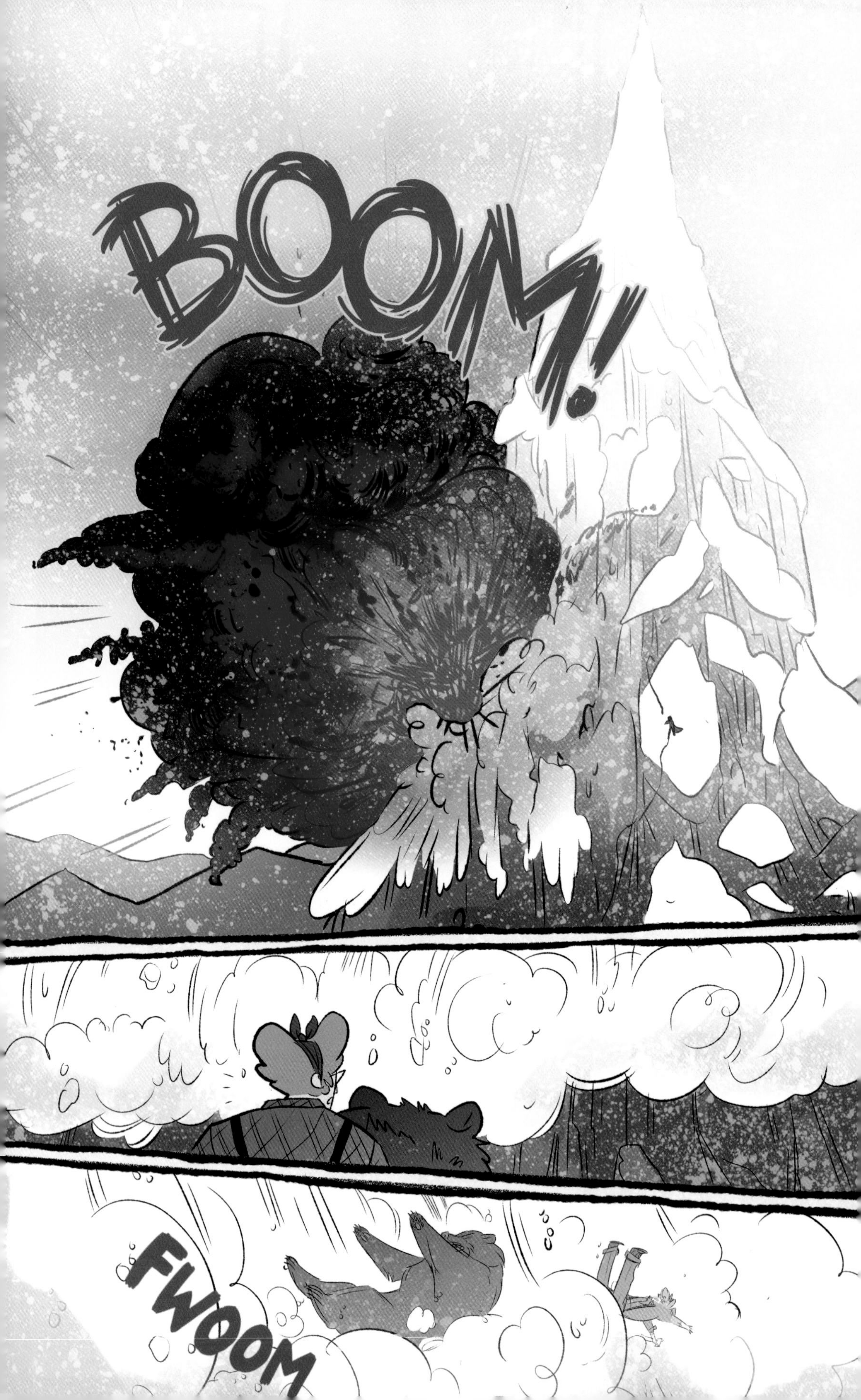
BOOM!
FWOOM

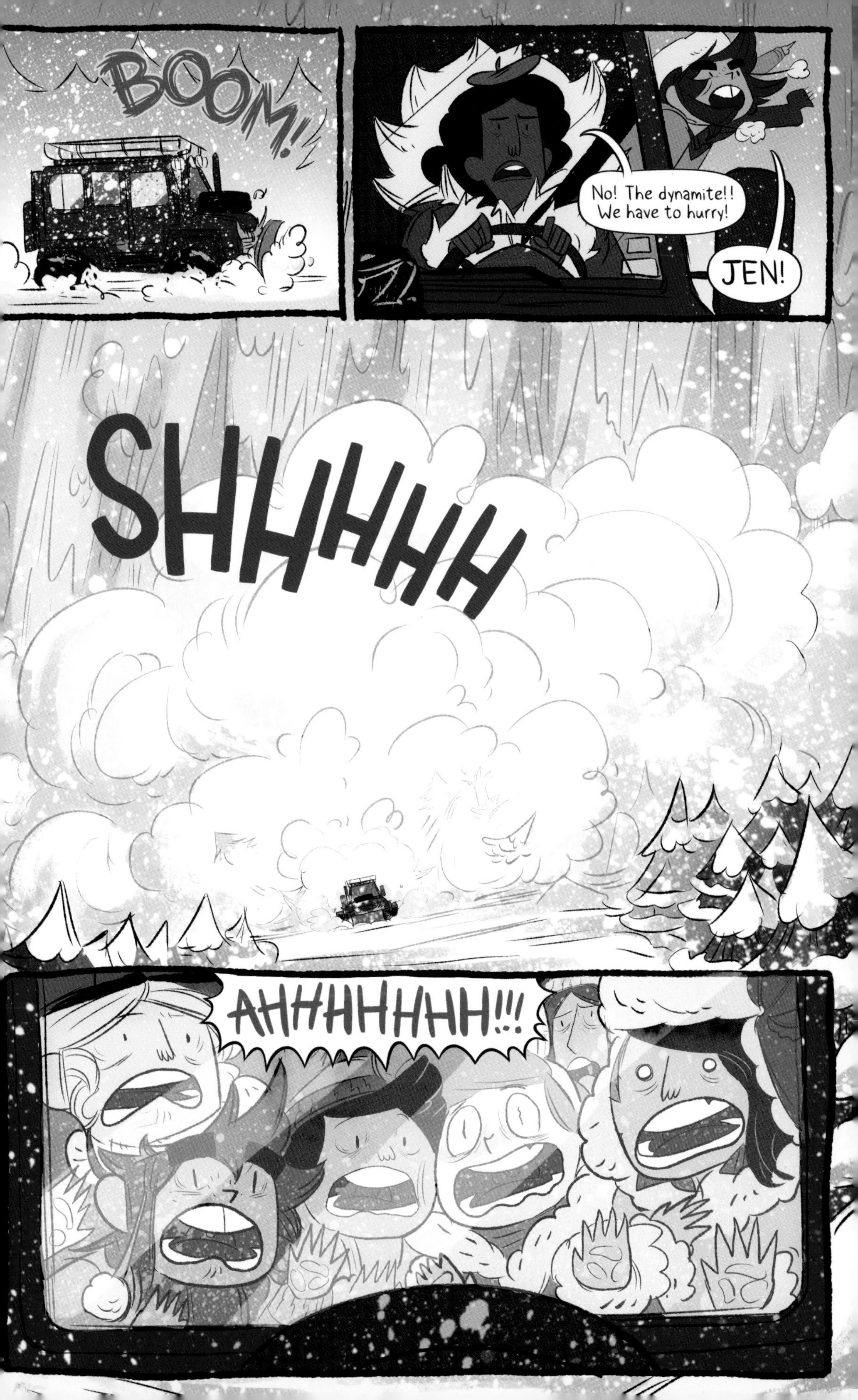
BOOM!!
No! The dynamite!!
We have to hurry!
JEN!
SHHHHHH
AHHHHHHHH!!!

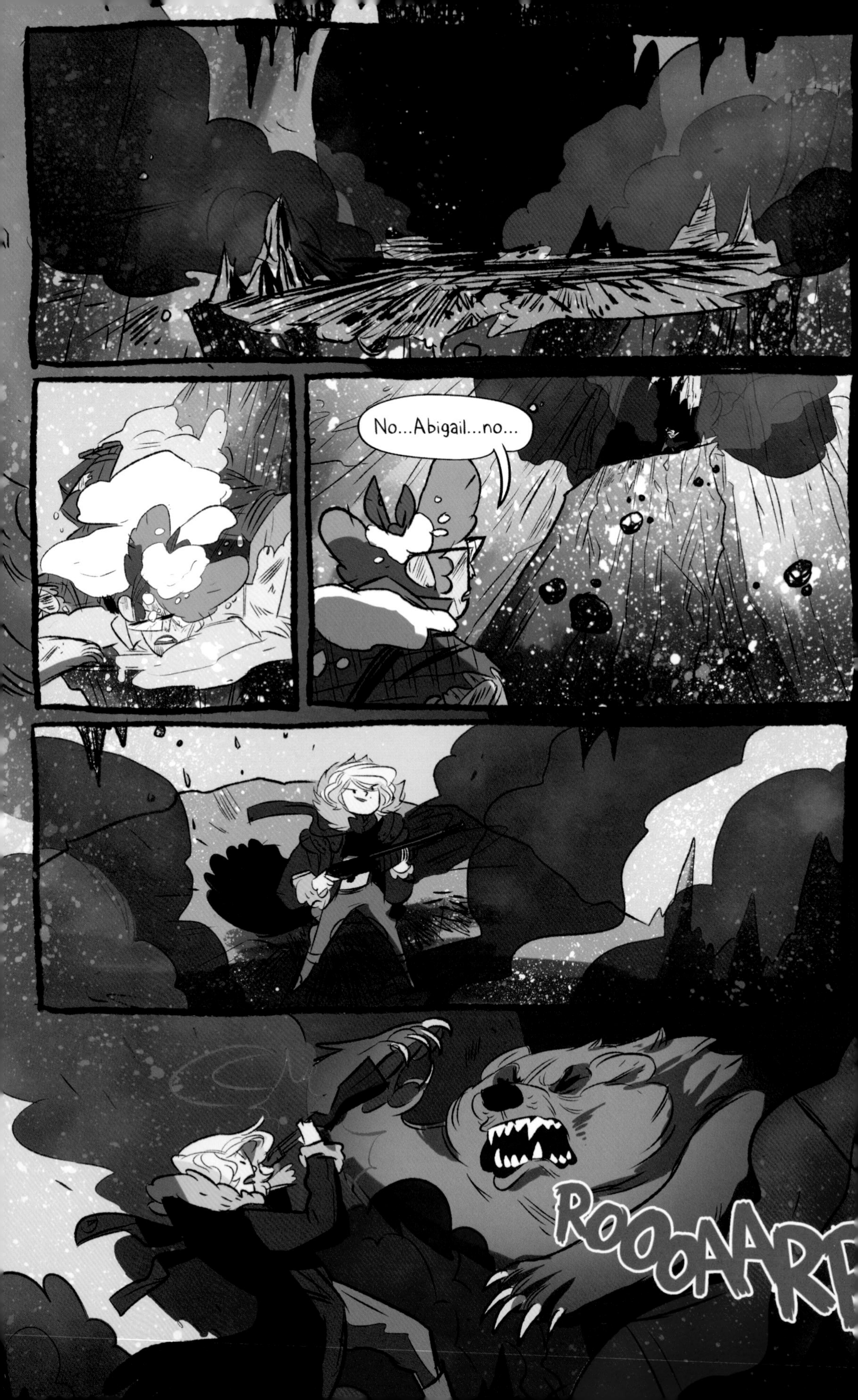
No...Abigail...no...
ROOOAARR

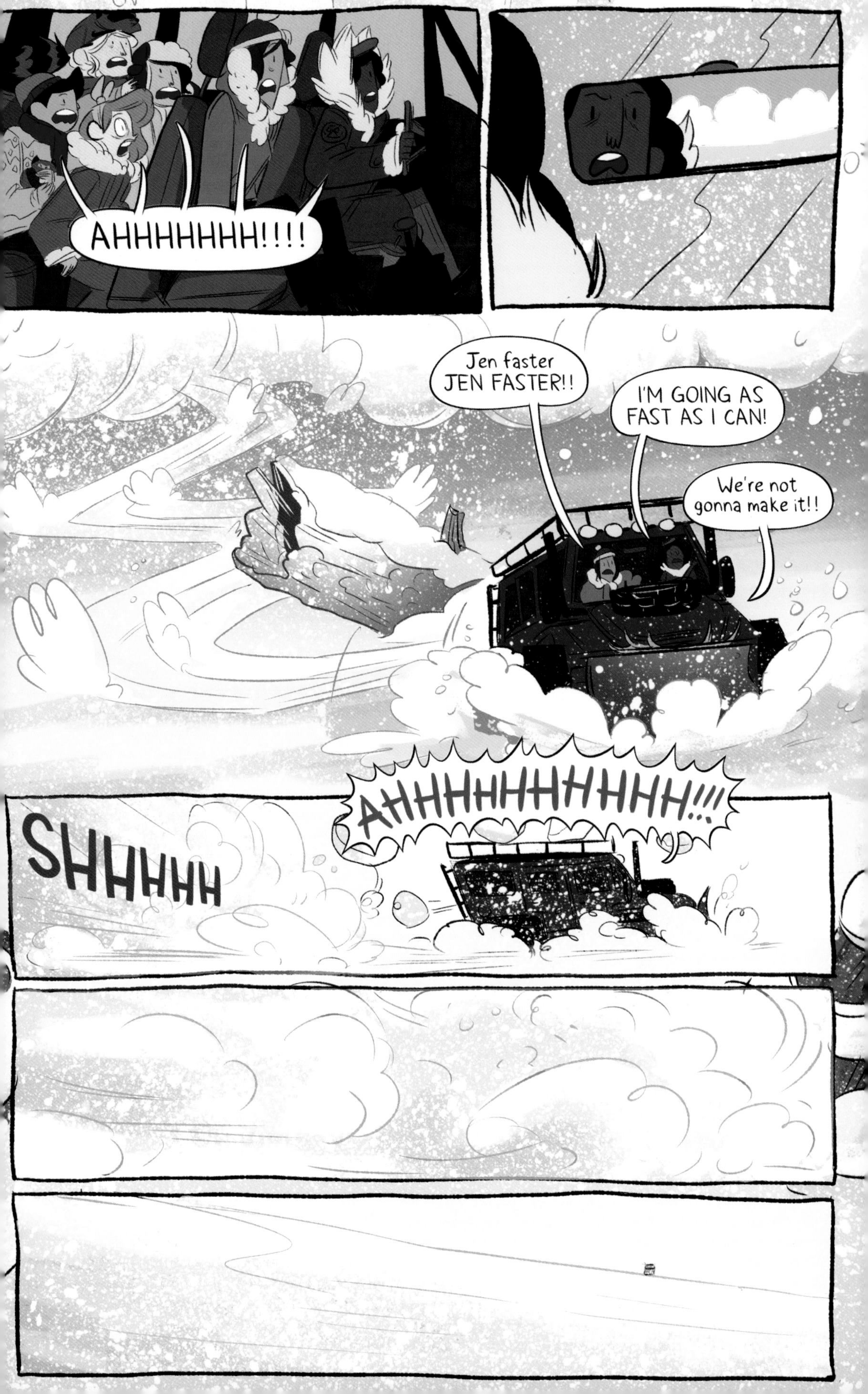
AHHHHHHH!!!!
Jen faster JEN FASTER!!
I'M GOING AS FAST AS I CAN!
We're not gonna make it!!
AHHHHHHHHHHH!!!
SHHHHH

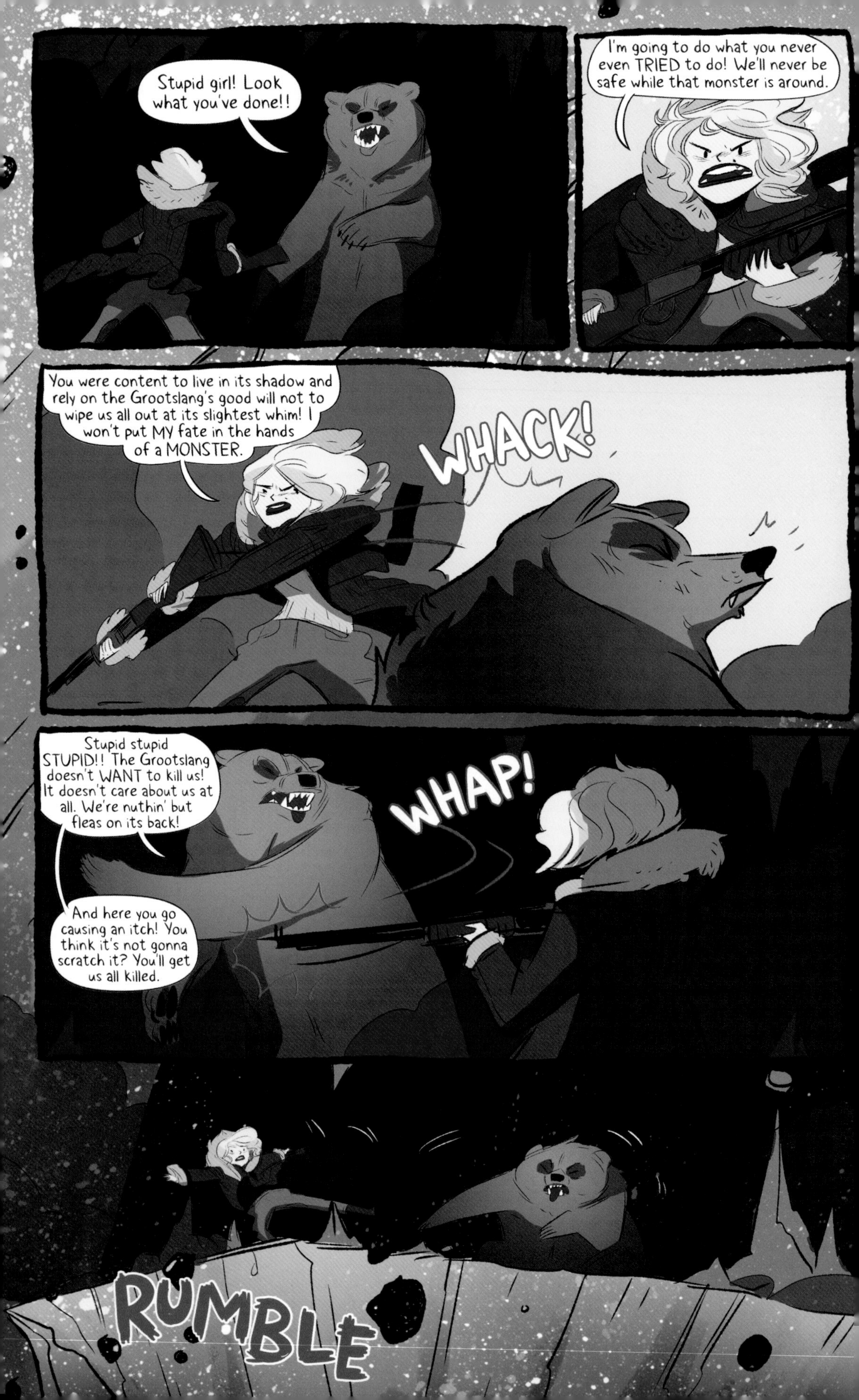
Stupid girl! Look what you've done!!
I'm going to do what you never even TRIED to do! We'll never be safe while that monster is around.
You were content to live in its shadow and rely on the Grootslang's good will not to wipe us all out at its slightest whim! I won't put MY fate in the hands of a MONSTER.
WHACK!
Stupid stupid STUPID!! The Grootslang doesn't WANT to kill us! It doesn't care about us at all. We're nuthin' but fleas on its back!
WHAP!
And here you go causing an itch! You think it's not gonna scratch it? You'll get us all killed.
RUMBLE

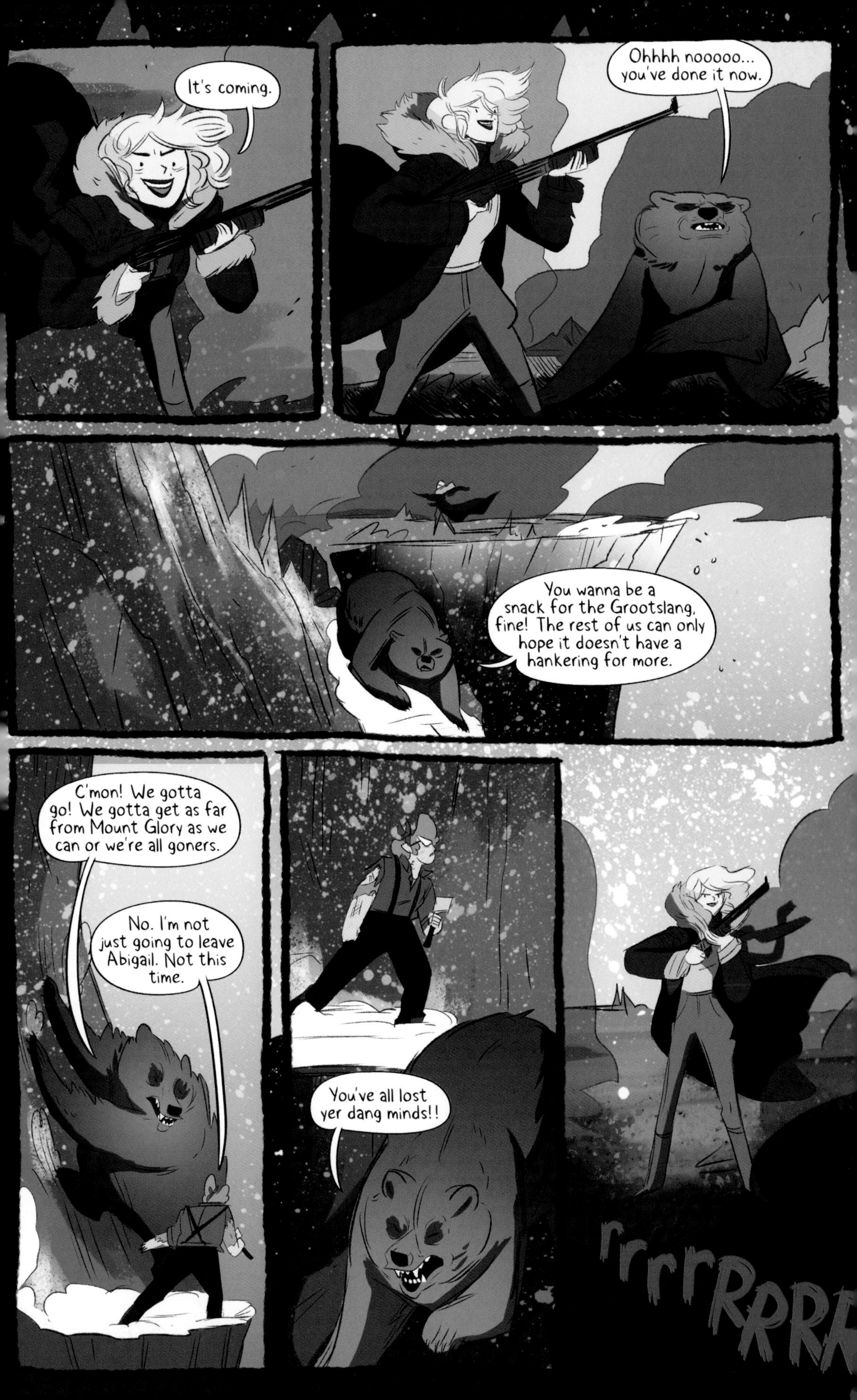
It's coming.
Ohhhh nooooo... you've done it now.
You wanna be a snack for the Grootslang, fine! The rest of us can only hope it doesn't have a hankering for more.
C'mon! We gotta go! We gotta get as far from Mount Glory as we can or we're all goners.
No. I'm not just going to leave Abigail. Not this time.
You've all lost yer dang minds!!
rrrrRRRR

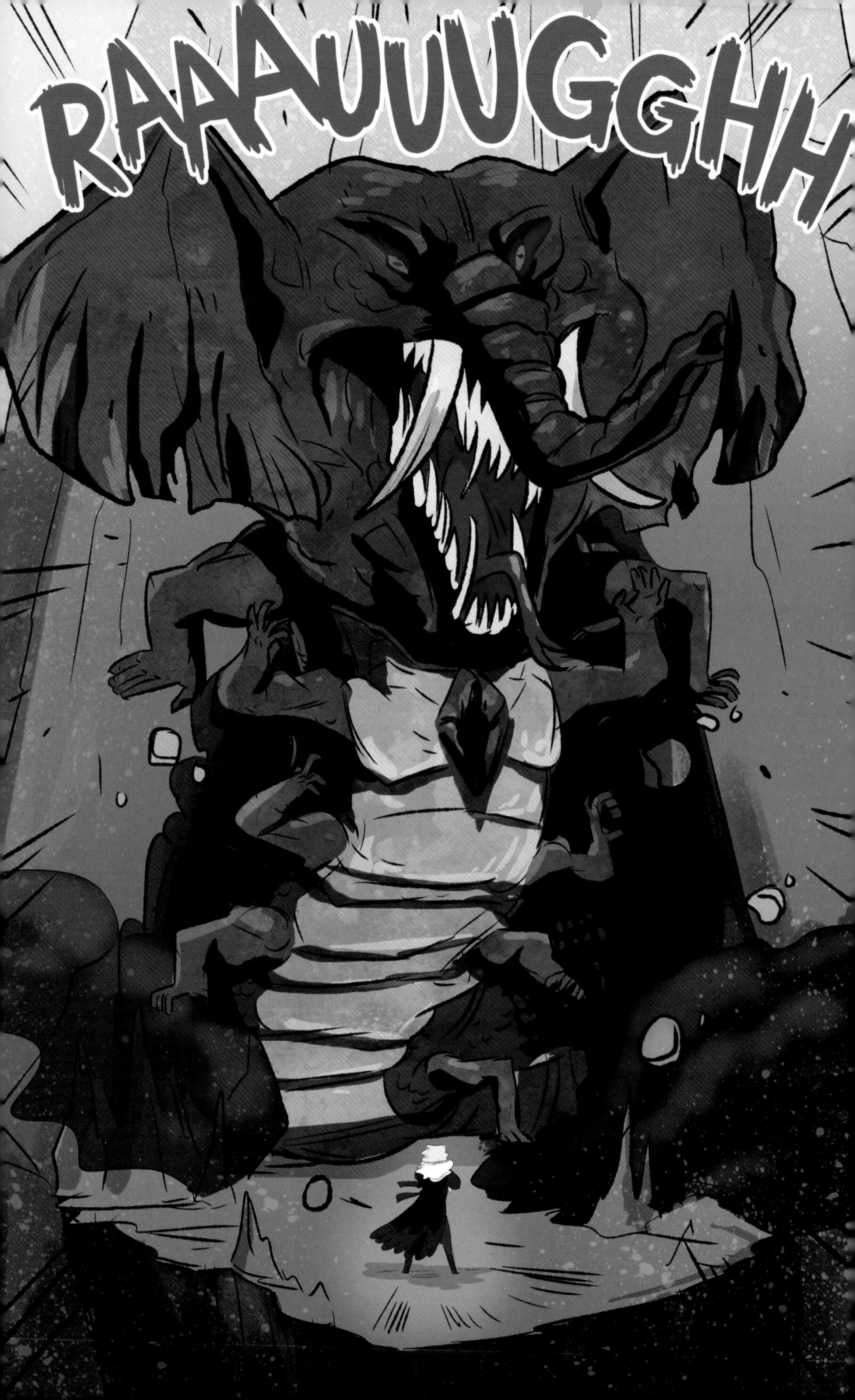
RAAAUUUGGHH

will co...

The...
It he... should be worn at camp
appearan... ...vents when Lumberjanes
dress f... ...may also be worn at other
Further... ...ions. It should be worn as a
Lumber... the uniform dress with
to have... ...rect shoes, and stocking or
part in...
Thiskv... ...out grows her uniform or
Hardc... ...ter Lumberjane.
have... ...ia she has
them... her
...her

THE UNIFORM

The... ...ES
yellow, short sl...
emb...
the w...
choose...
slacks,...
made o...
out-of-do...
green bere...
the colla...
Shoes ma...
heels, roun... ...ngs or
socks shou... ...th the shoes or wi...
the uniform. Ne... ...es, bracelets, or other jewelry do...
belong with a Lumberjane uniform.

WE WERE READY TO KICK SNOW MUCH BUTT!

WE FOUND JEN!

THYME

HOW TO WEAR THE UNIFOR...

To look well in a uniform demans fi...
uniform be kept in good condition...
pressed. See that the skirt is the right...
height and build, that the belt is adjusted...
that your shoes and stockings are in keeping...
uniform, that you watch your posture and carry you... ...e unifor...
with dignity and grace. If the beret is removed indoors, ...elps to cre...
be sure that your hair is neat and kept in place with an in a group. ...
insconspicuous clip or ribbon. When you wear a active life th...
Lumberjane uniform you are identified as a member of another bond...
this organization and you should be doubly careful to future, and pr...
conduct yourself in a way that will show everyone that in order to b...
courtesy and thoughtfullness are part of being a Lumberjane pr...
Lumberjane. People are likely to judge a whole nation by Penniquiqul Thi... ...ore Lady
the selfishness of a few individuals, to criticize a whole Types, but m... ...es will wish to have one. They
family because of the misconduct of one member, and to can either b... ...uniform, or make it themselves from
feel unkindly toward and organization because of the materials available at the trading post.

ABIGAIL HAS AN EXPLOSIVE PERSONALITY

LUMBERJANES FIELD MANUAL

CHAPTER SIXTEEN

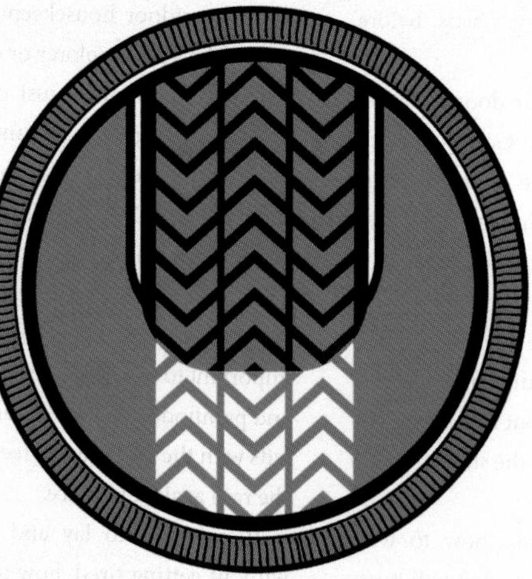

Lumberjanes "Automotive" Program Field

SPARE ME BADGE

"Automobile safety saves."

Like any well rounded young woman, a Lumberjane will understand the importance of automobile safety. The key to this knowledge is understanding the vehicle inside and out. The Lumberjanes will be responsible for the care and upkeep of the camp vehicle in the summer that they are at the camp. The counselor in charge of the auto shop will educate each Lumberjane on how to identify parts of the engine, understand the common problems that are faced on the road, as well as the way to solve those problems with the tools available to them.

Life on the open road will be an experience that most will go through as they transition through their life, and even if it's an experience that not everyone will enjoy, it's definitely something a Lumberjane should be prepared for. From safety features like seat belts to how to change a tire, the *Spare Me* badge is about understanding practical knowledge of automobiles. As a Lumberjane, our campers will understand the importance of keeping their property in tip top shape. They will have experience in taking care of their own belongings as well as helping others with their own, and they will be able see the benefit of taking the time to ensure their property is in great quality so that it will last for a long time.

To obtain the *Spare Me* badge a Lumberjane must choose the camp vehicle they will want to work on. They will learn all practical knowledge there is about the vehicle and will learn safety guidelines and laws from their home state. They will change the oil in the car, and they will learn how to change a flat tire. If they are of age, they will learn how to drive the vehicle without supervision and will be used to help transport campers or run other errands that might be needed. They will meet with the park ranger to talk about the dangers of driving in the mountains, what to look out for if off

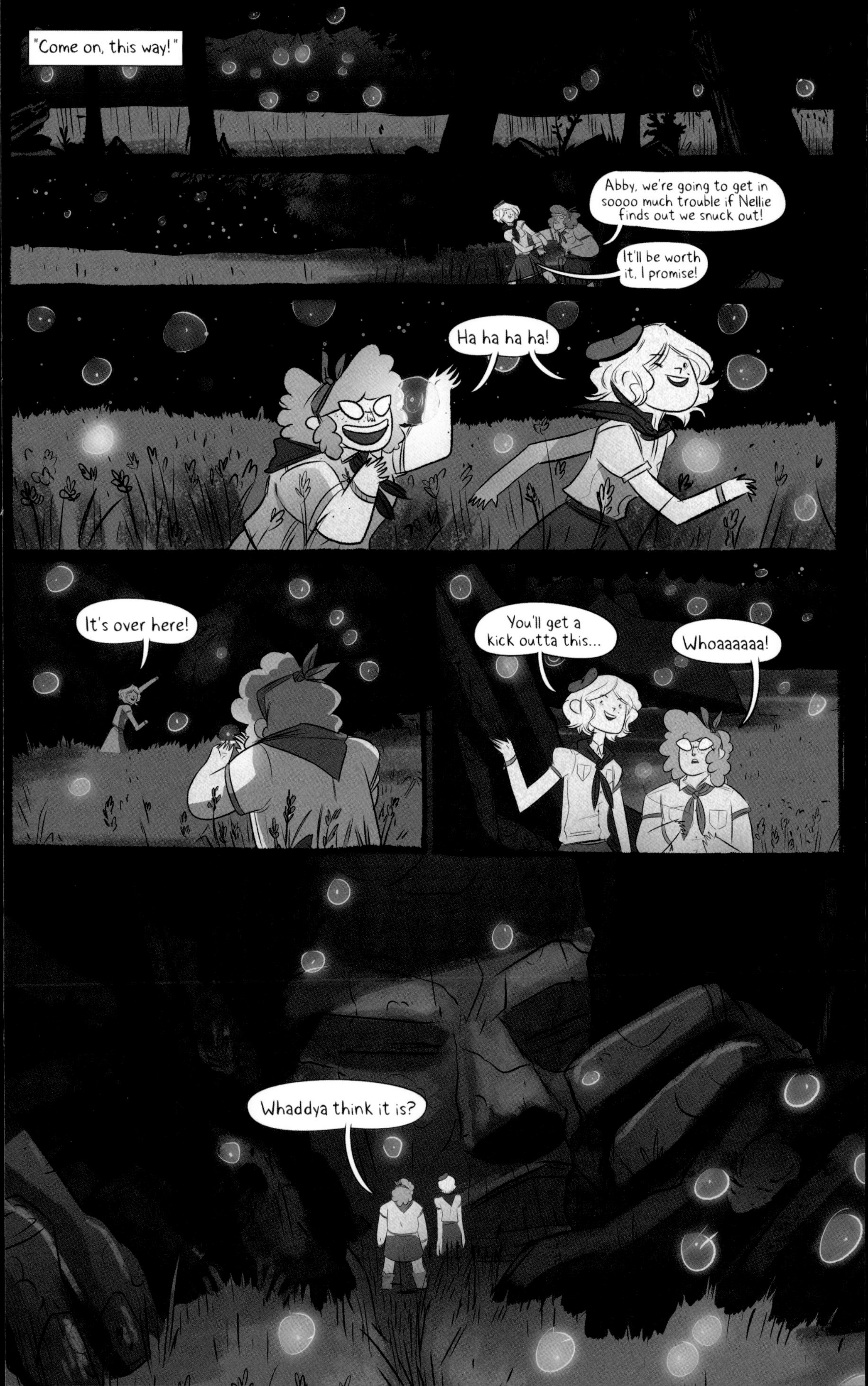
"Come on, this way!"
Abby, we're going to get in soooo much trouble if Nellie finds out we snuck out!
It'll be worth it, I promise!
Ha ha ha ha!
It's over here!
You'll get a kick outta this...
Whoaaaaaa!
Whaddya think it is?

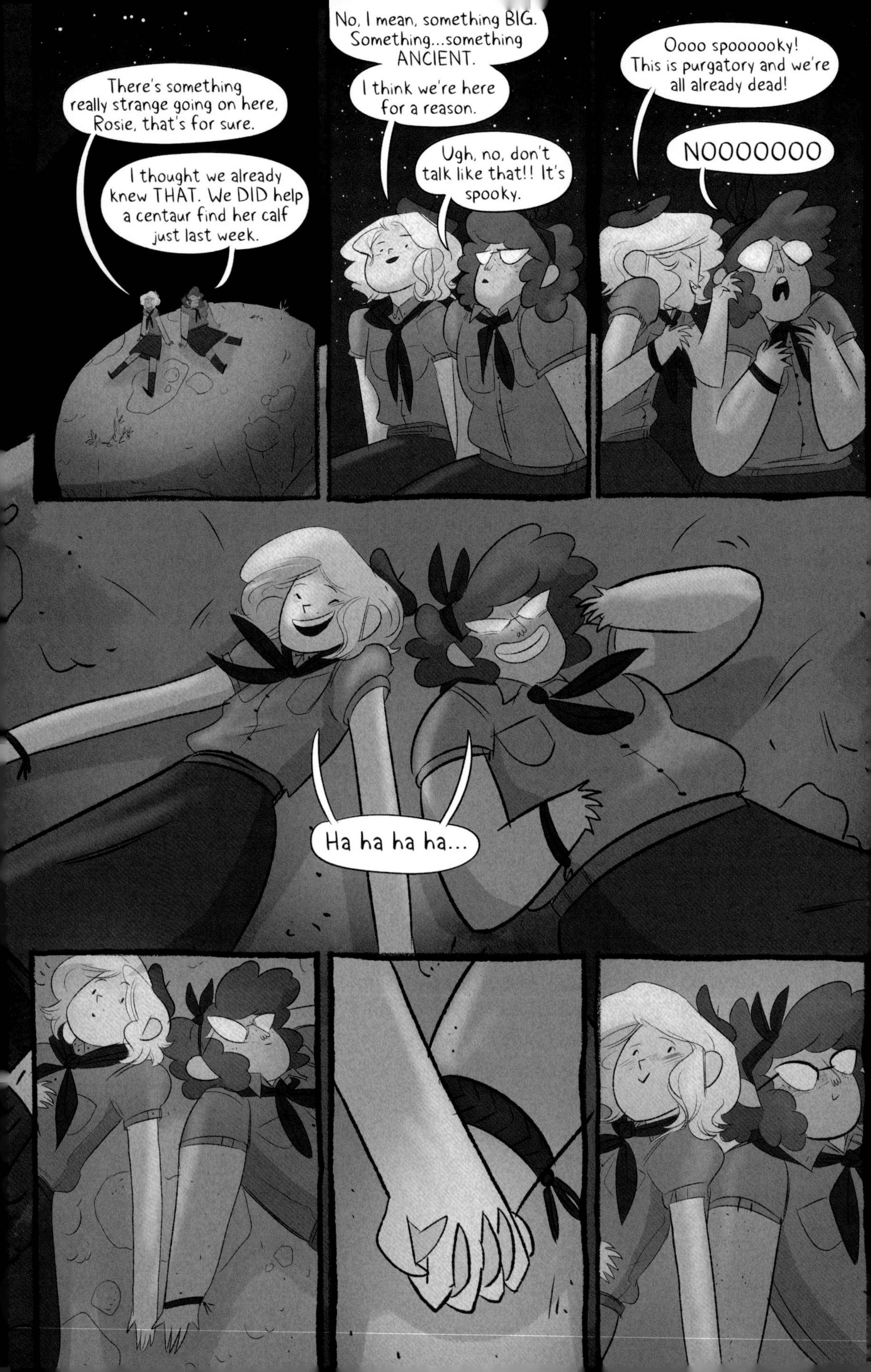
There's something really strange going on here, Rosie, that's for sure.
I thought we already knew THAT. We DID help a centaur find her calf just last week.
No, I mean, something BIG. Something...something ANCIENT.
I think we're here for a reason.
Ugh, no, don't talk like that!! It's spooky.
Oooo spooooooky! This is purgatory and we're all already dead!
NOOOOOOO
Ha ha ha ha...

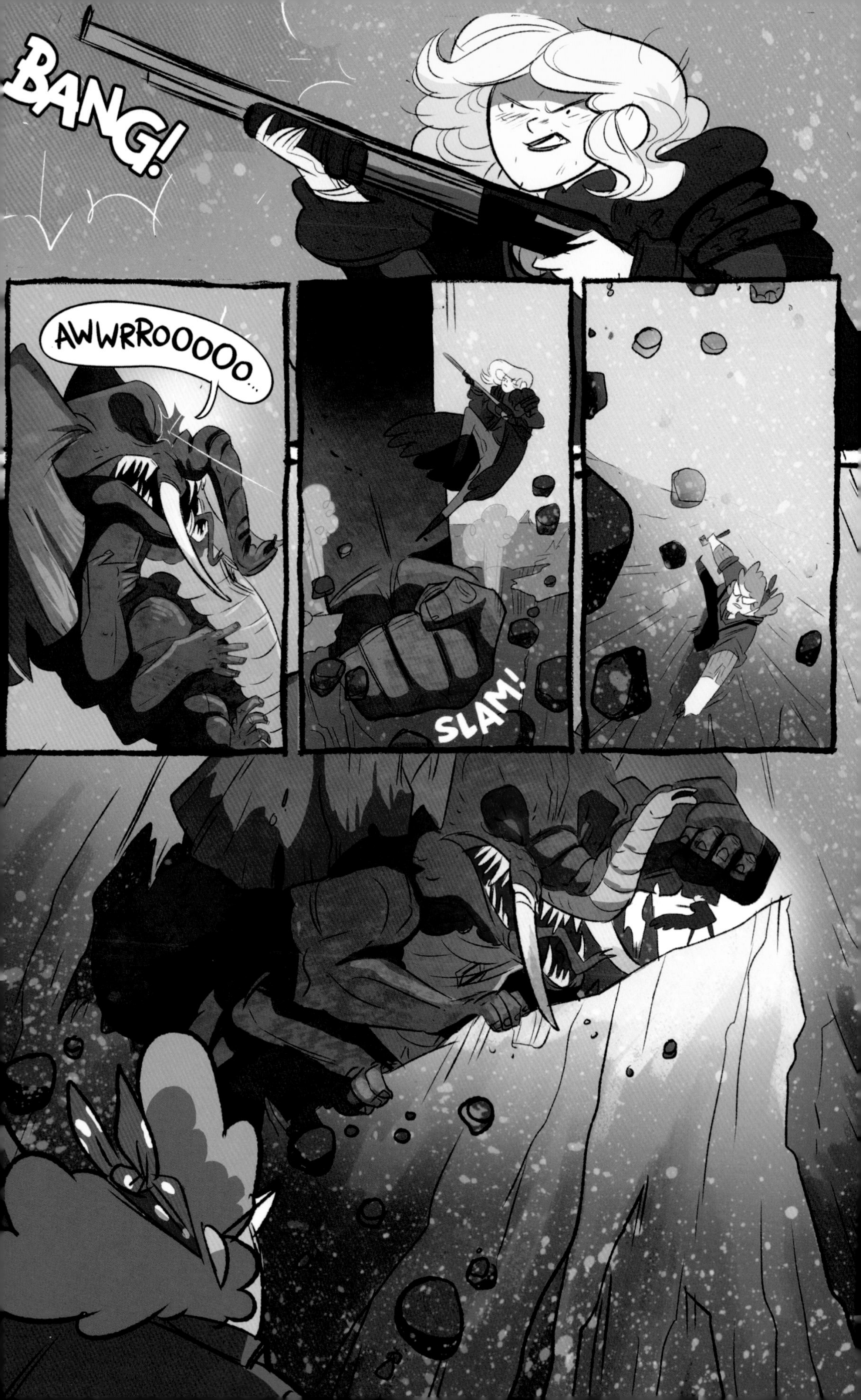
BANG!
AWWRROOOOOO...
SLAM!

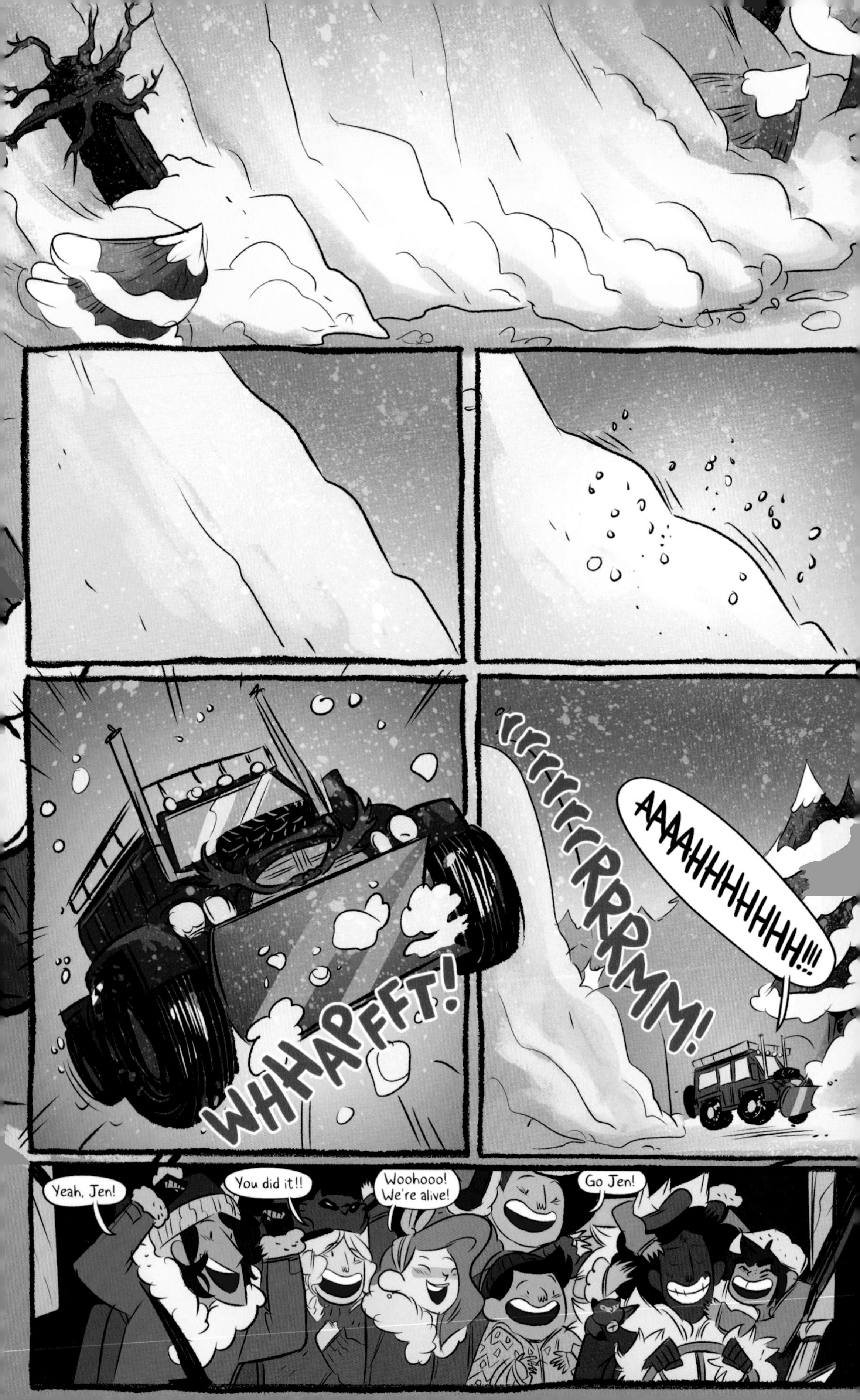
WHHAPFFT!
rrrrrrrrRRRMM!
AAAAHHHHHHHH!!!
Yeah, Jen!
You did it!!
Woohooo! We're alive!
Go Jen!

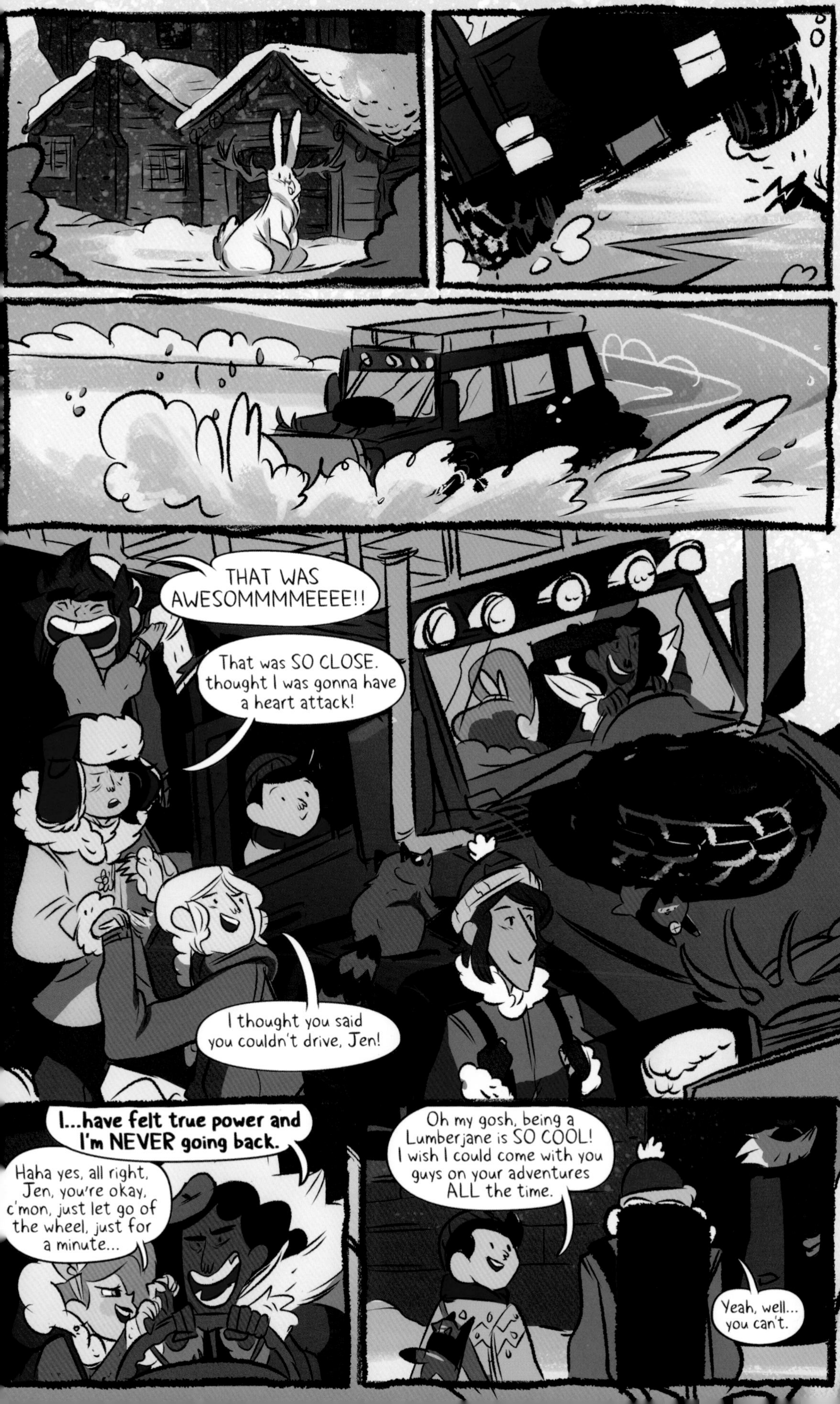
THAT WAS AWESOMMMMEEEE!!
That was SO CLOSE. thought I was gonna have a heart attack!
I thought you said you couldn't drive, Jen!
I...have felt true power and I'm NEVER going back.
Haha yes, all right, Jen, you're okay, c'mon, just let go of the wheel, just for a minute...
Oh my gosh, being a Lumberjane is SO COOL! I wish I could come with you guys on your adventures ALL the time.
Yeah, well... you can't.

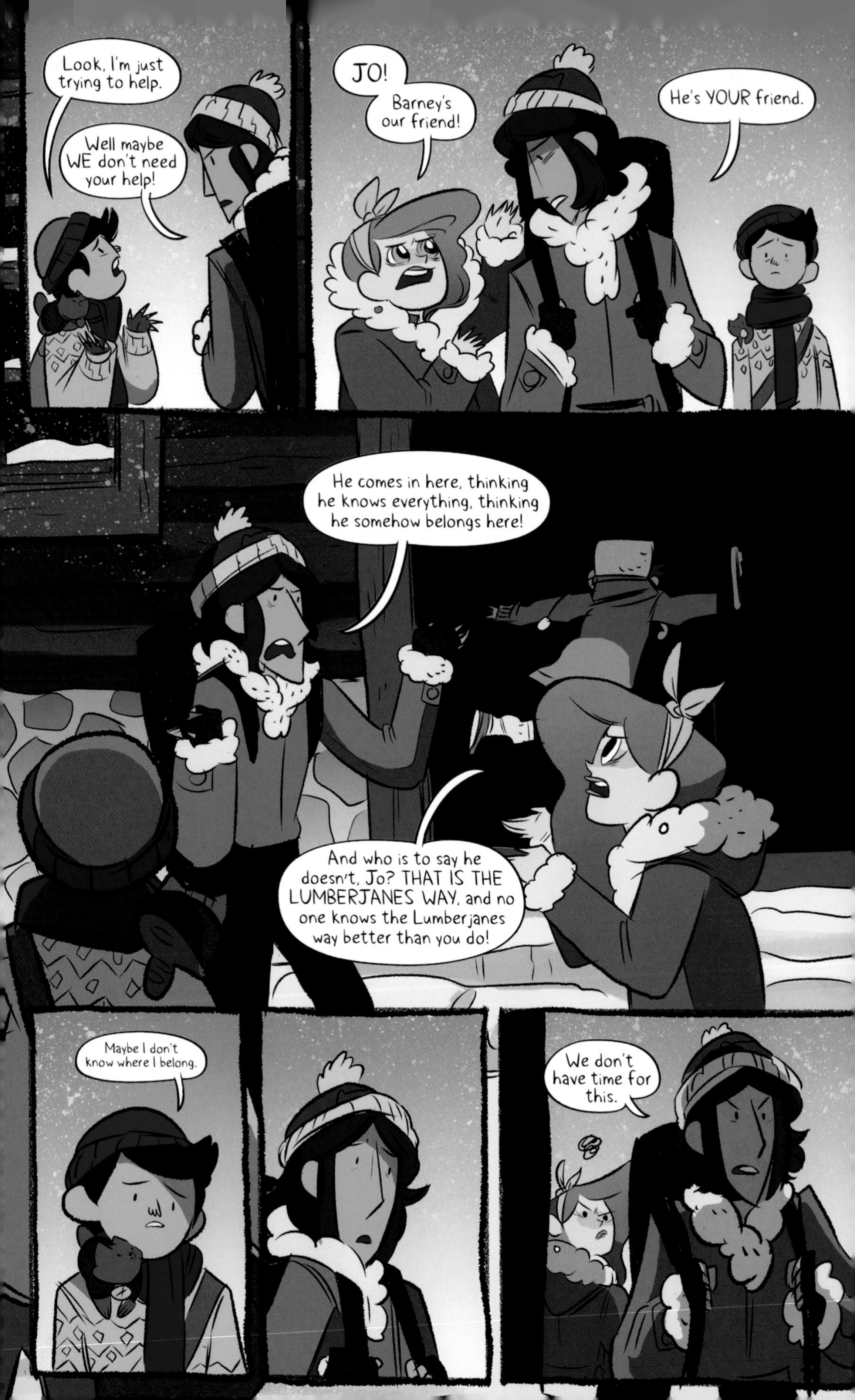
Look, I'm just trying to help.
Well maybe WE don't need your help!
JO! Barney's our friend!
He's YOUR friend.
He comes in here, thinking he knows everything, thinking he somehow belongs here!
And who is to say he doesn't, Jo? THAT IS THE LUMBERJANES WAY, and no one knows the Lumberjanes way better than you do!
Maybe I don't know where I belong.
We don't have time for this.

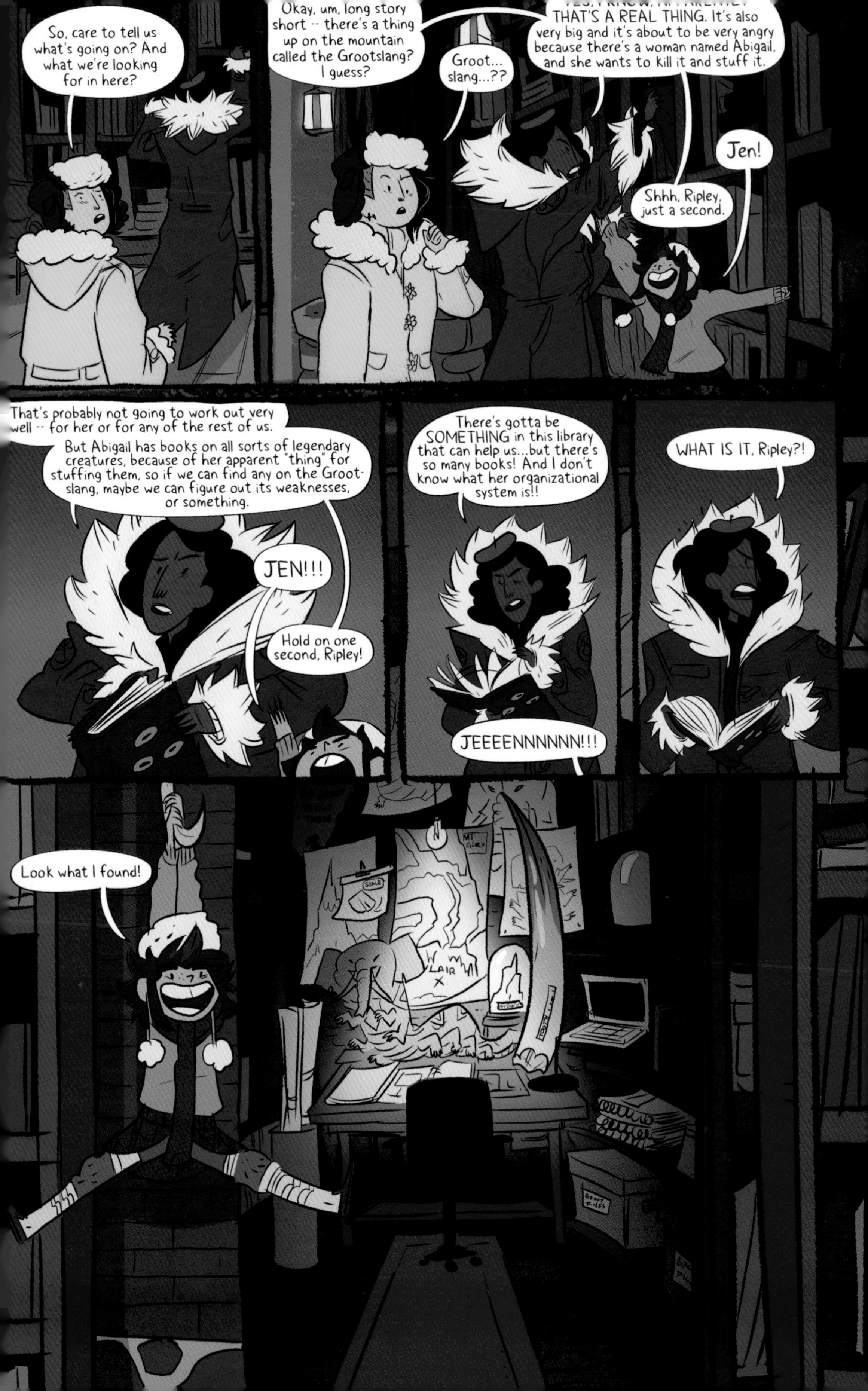

So, care to tell us what's going on? And what we're looking for in here?
Okay, um, long story short -- there's a thing up on the mountain called the Grootslang? I guess?
Groot... slang...??
THAT'S A REAL THING. It's also very big and it's about to be very angry because there's a woman named Abigail, and she wants to kill it and stuff it.
Jen!
Shhh, Ripley, just a second.
That's probably not going to work out very well -- for her or for any of the rest of us.
But Abigail has books on all sorts of legendary creatures, because of her apparent "thing" for stuffing them, so if we can find any on the Grootslang, maybe we can figure out its weaknesses, or something.
JEN!!!
Hold on one second, Ripley!
There's gotta be SOMETHING in this library that can help us...but there's so many books! And I don't know what her organizational system is!!
JEEEENNNNNN!!!
WHAT IS IT, Ripley?!
Look what I found!
LAIR

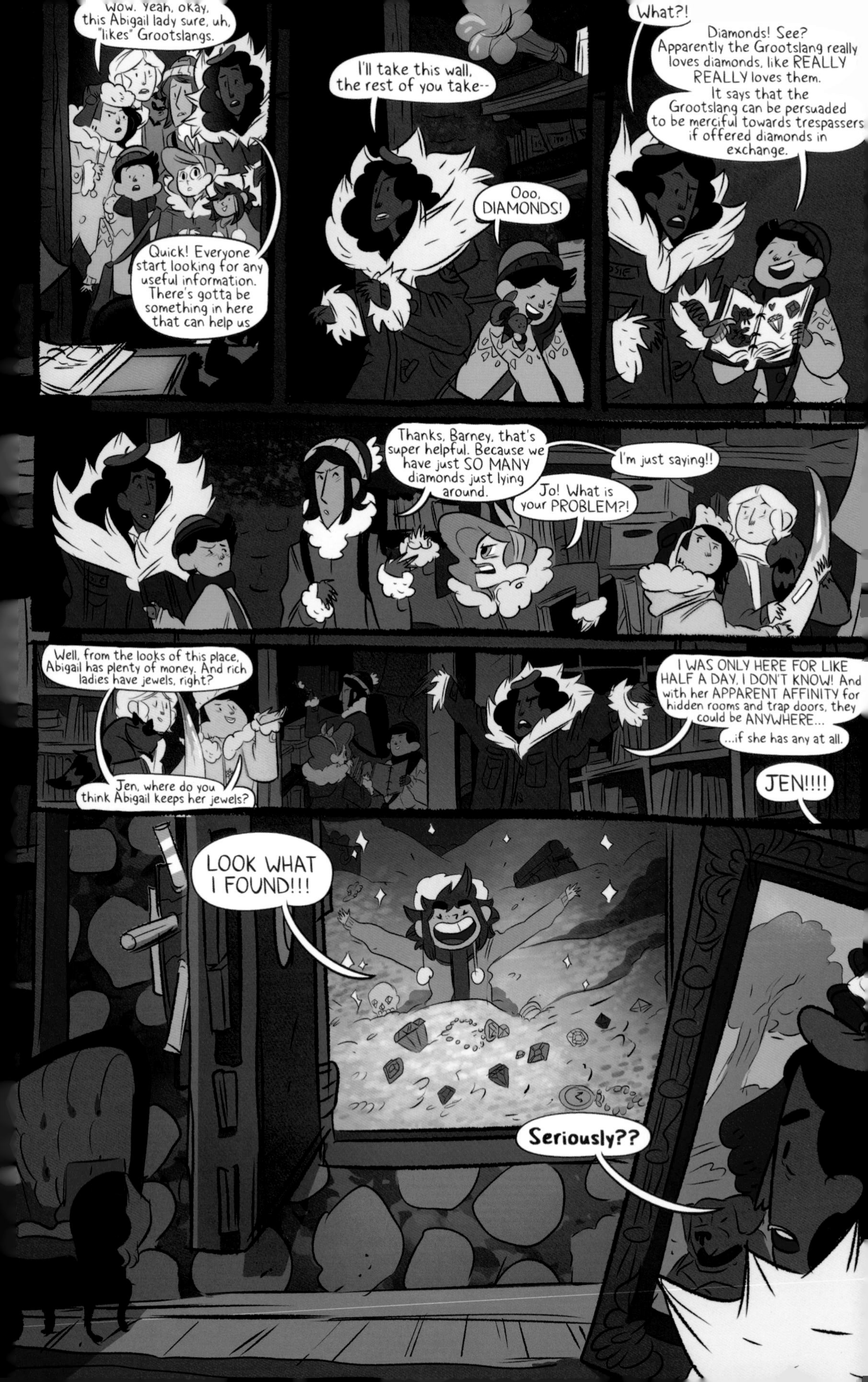
Wow. Yeah, okay, this Abigail lady sure, uh, "likes" Grootslangs.
Quick! Everyone start looking for any useful information. There's gotta be something in here that can help us
I'll take this wall, the rest of you take--
Ooo, DIAMONDS!
What?!
Diamonds! See? Apparently the Grootslang really loves diamonds, like REALLY REALLY loves them. It says that the Grootslang can be persuaded to be merciful towards trespassers if offered diamonds in exchange.
Thanks, Barney, that's super helpful. Because we have just SO MANY diamonds just lying around.
I'm just saying!!
Jo! What is your PROBLEM?!
Well, from the looks of this place, Abigail has plenty of money. And rich ladies have jewels, right?
Jen, where do you think Abigail keeps her jewels?
I WAS ONLY HERE FOR LIKE HALF A DAY, I DON'T KNOW! And with her APPARENT AFFINITY for hidden rooms and trap doors, they could be ANYWHERE...
...if she has any at all.
JEN!!!!
LOOK WHAT I FOUND!!!
Seriously??

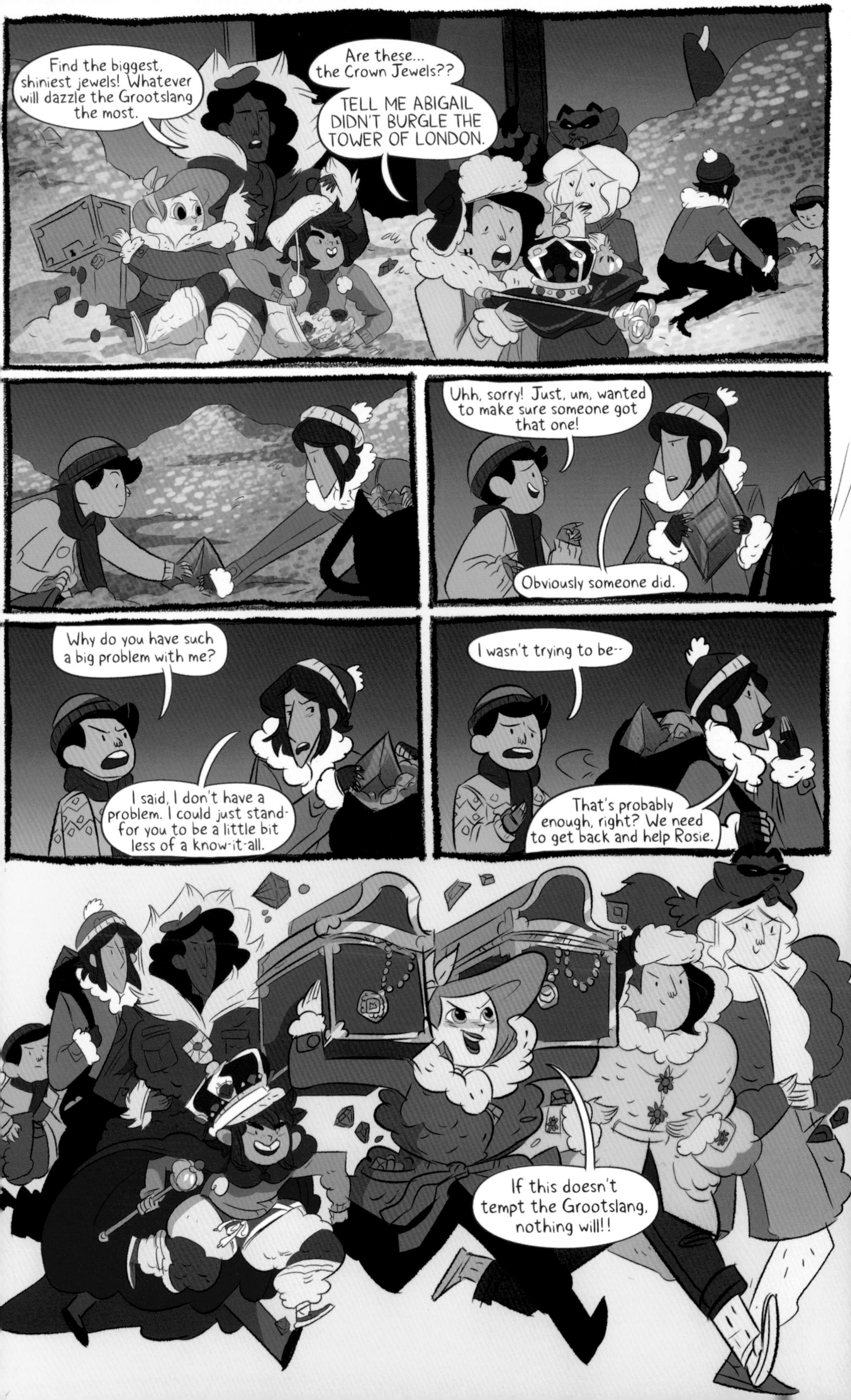
Find the biggest, shiniest jewels! Whatever will dazzle the Grootslang the most.
Are these... the Crown Jewels??
TELL ME ABIGAIL DIDN'T BURGLE THE TOWER OF LONDON.
Uhh, sorry! Just, um, wanted to make sure someone got that one!
Obviously someone did.
Why do you have such a big problem with me?
I said, I don't have a problem. I could just stand- for you to be a little bit less of a know-it-all.
I wasn't trying to be--
That's probably enough, right? We need to get back and help Rosie.
If this doesn't tempt the Grootslang, nothing will!!

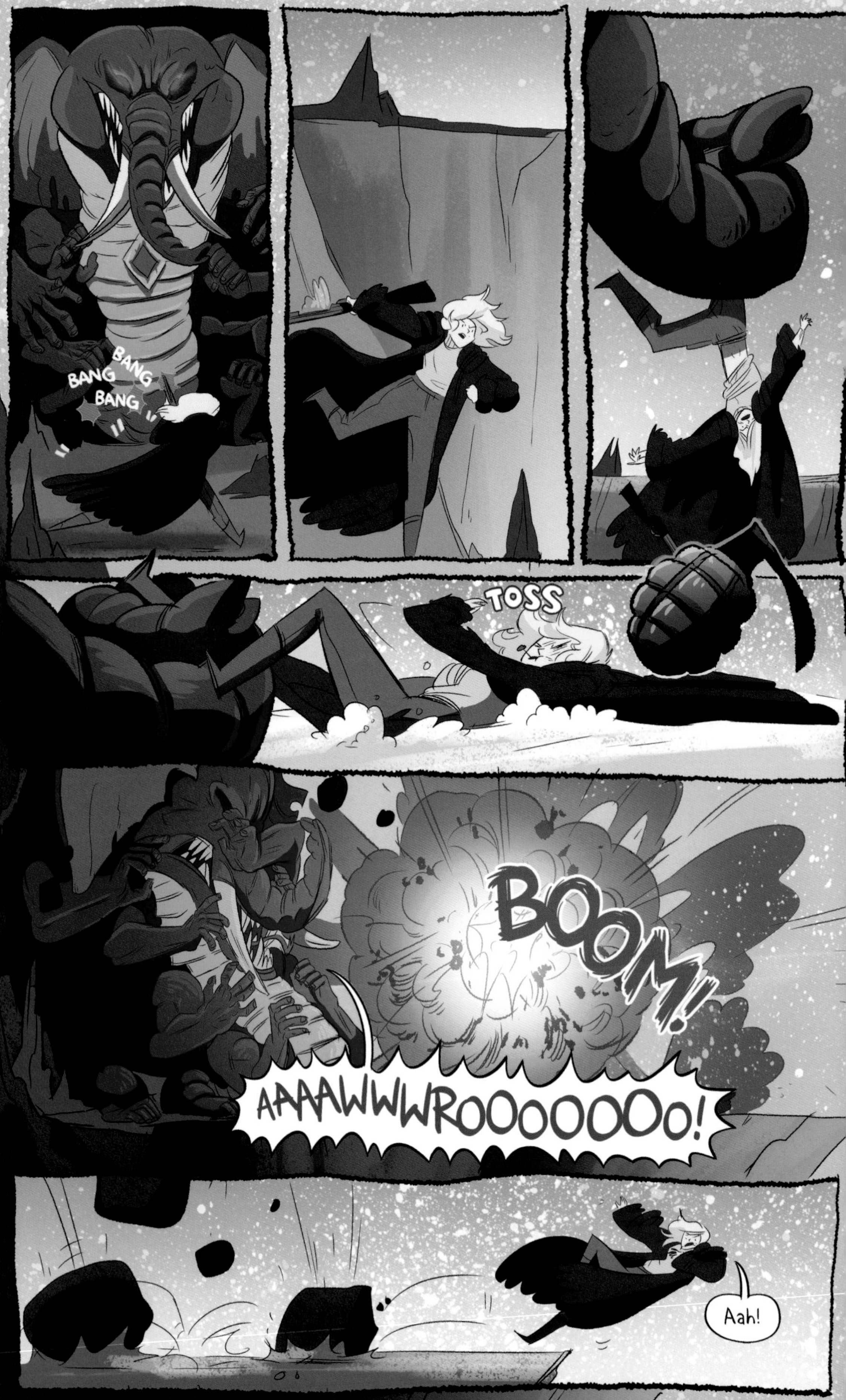
BANG
BANG
BANG
TOSS
BOOM!
AAAAWWWROOOOOOOo!
Aah!

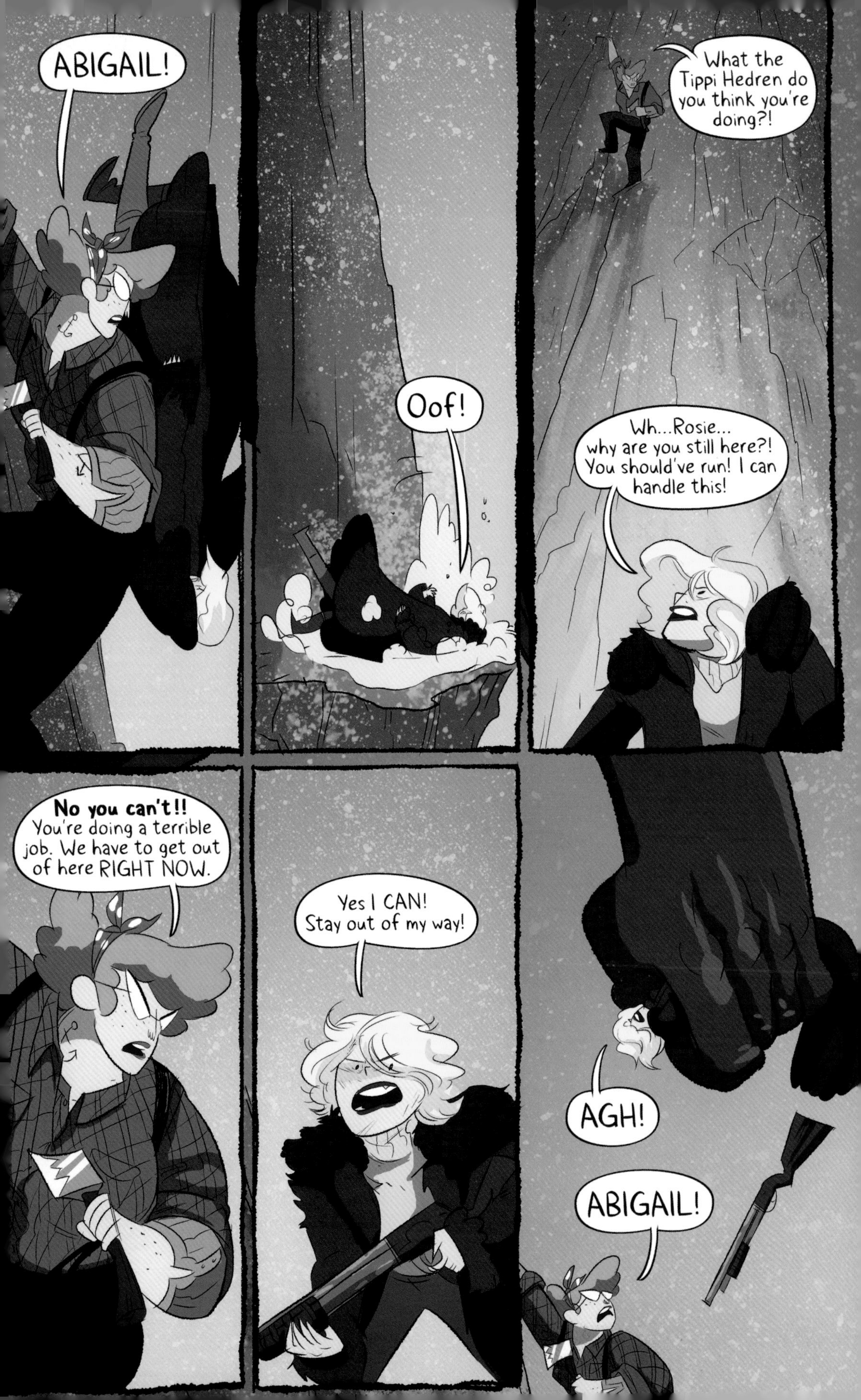
ABIGAIL!
Oof!
What the Tippi Hedren do you think you're doing?!
Wh...Rosie... why are you still here?! You should've run! I can handle this!
No you can't!! You're doing a terrible job. We have to get out of here RIGHT NOW.
Yes I CAN! Stay out of my way!
AGH!
ABIGAIL!

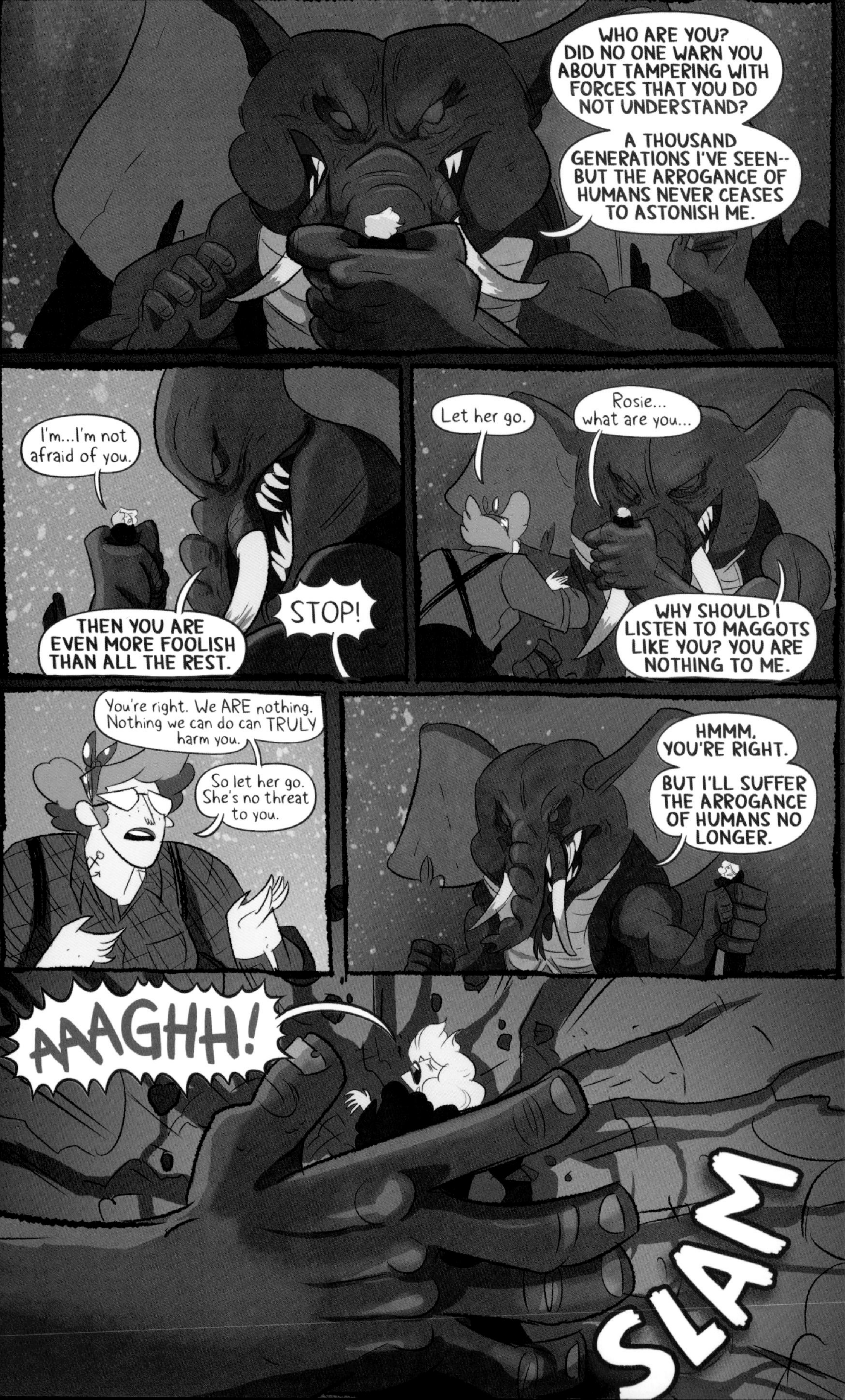
WHO ARE YOU? DID NO ONE WARN YOU ABOUT TAMPERING WITH FORCES THAT YOU DO NOT UNDERSTAND?
A THOUSAND GENERATIONS I'VE SEEN-- BUT THE ARROGANCE OF HUMANS NEVER CEASES TO ASTONISH ME.
I'm...I'm not afraid of you.
THEN YOU ARE EVEN MORE FOOLISH THAN ALL THE REST.
STOP!
Let her go.
Rosie... what are you...
WHY SHOULD I LISTEN TO MAGGOTS LIKE YOU? YOU ARE NOTHING TO ME.
You're right. We ARE nothing. Nothing we can do can TRULY harm you.
So let her go. She's no threat to you.
HMMM, YOU'RE RIGHT.
BUT I'LL SUFFER THE ARROGANCE OF HUMANS NO LONGER.
AAAGHH!
SLAM

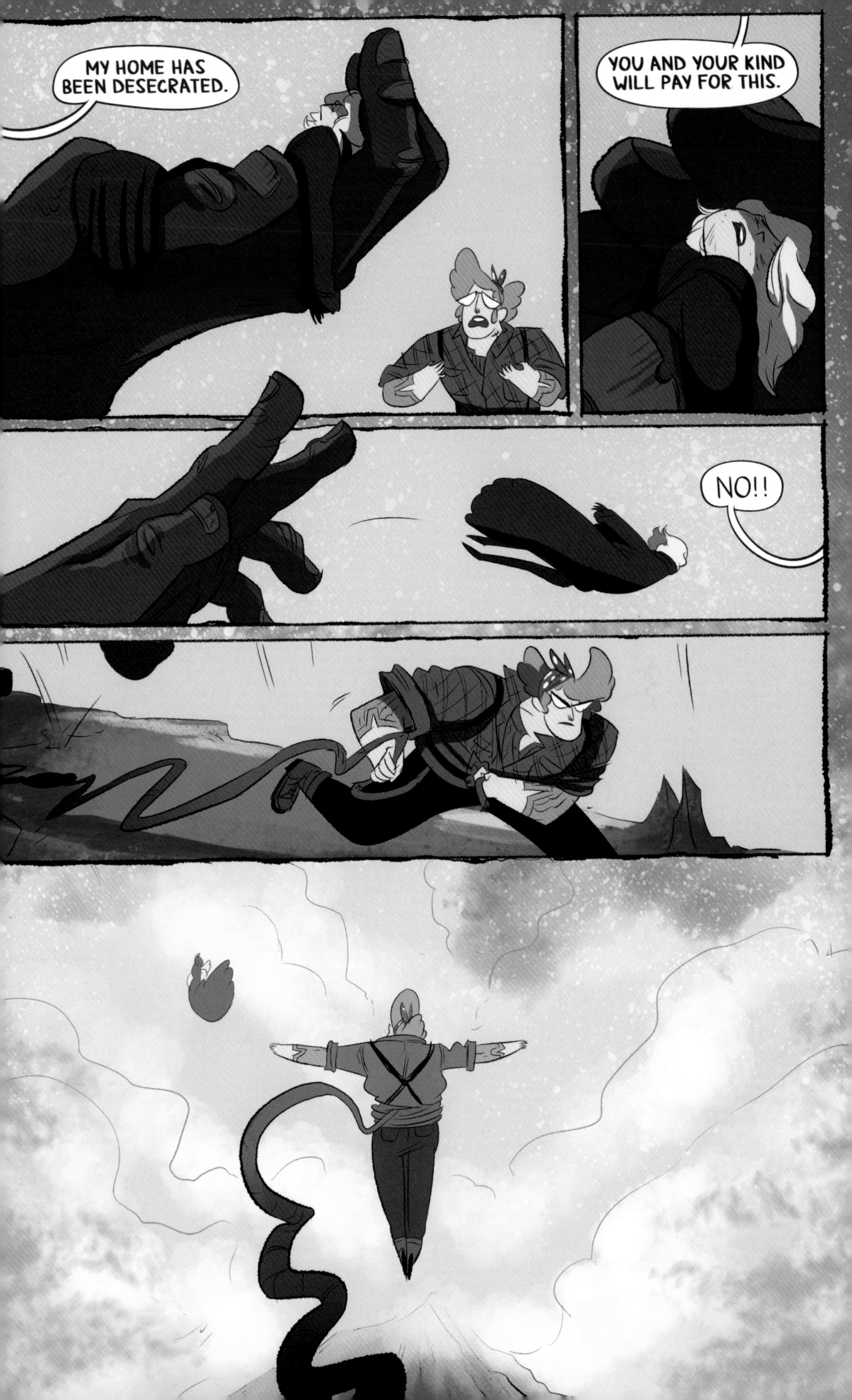
MY HOME HAS BEEN DESECRATED.
YOU AND YOUR KIND WILL PAY FOR THIS.
NO!!

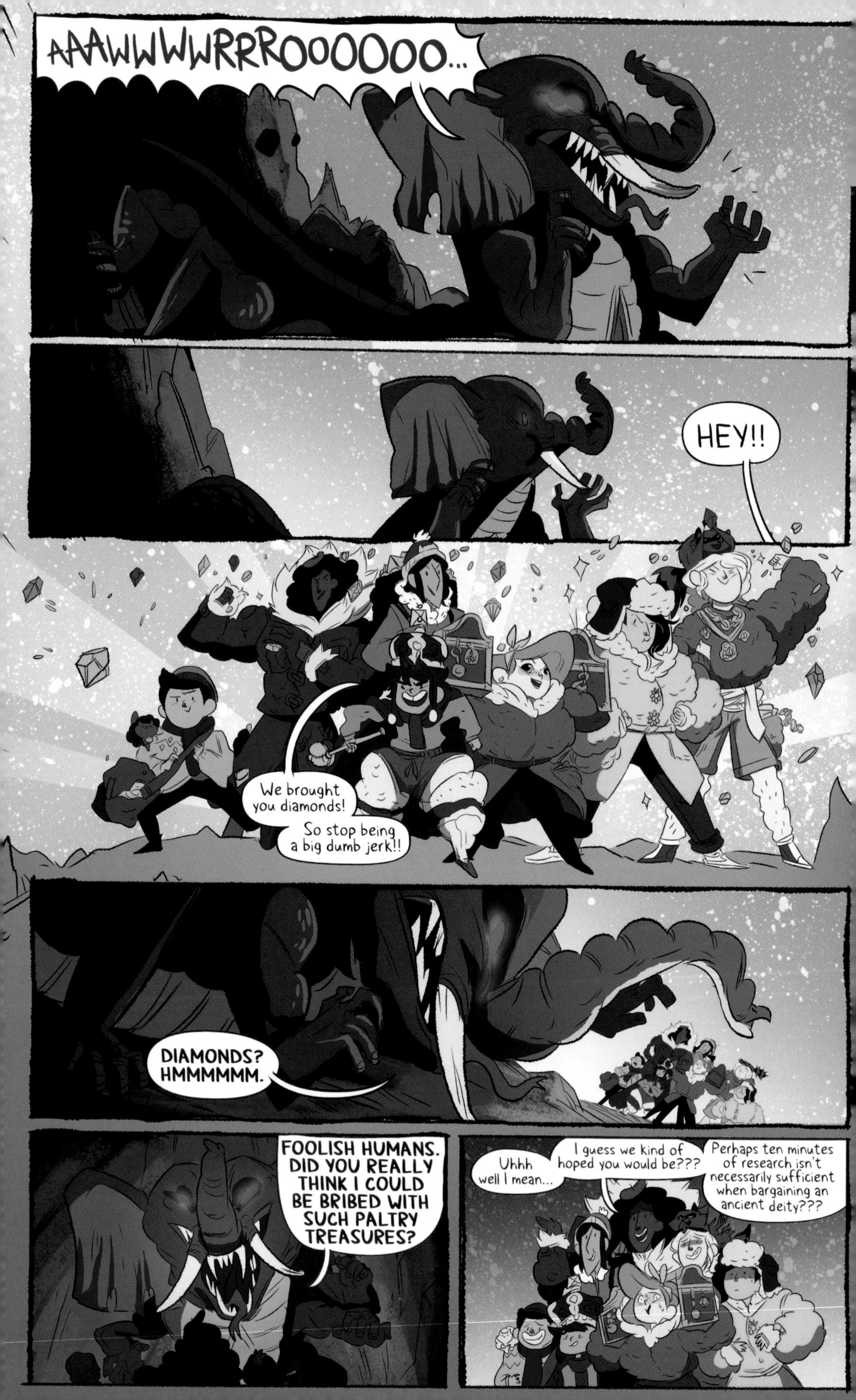

AAAWWWWRRROOOOOO...
HEY!!
We brought you diamonds!
So stop being a big dumb jerk!!
DIAMONDS? HMMMMMM.
FOOLISH HUMANS. DID YOU REALLY THINK I COULD BE BRIBED WITH SUCH PALTRY TREASURES?
Uhhh well I mean...
I guess we kind of hoped you would be???
Perhaps ten minutes of research isn't necessarily sufficient when bargaining an ancient deity???

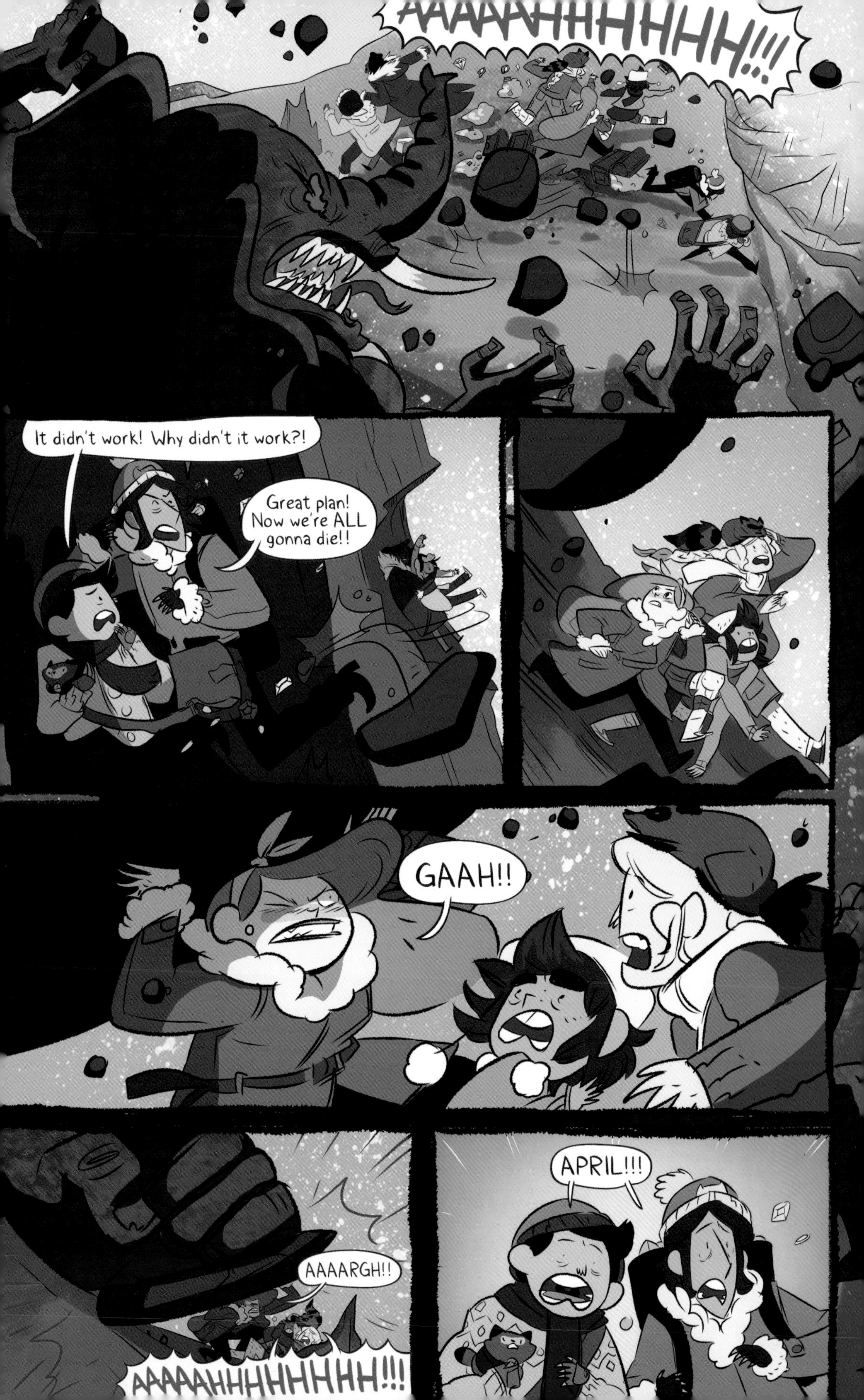
AAAAAHHHHHH!!!
It didn't work! Why didn't it work?!
Great plan! Now we're ALL gonna die!!
GAAH!!
AAAARGH!!
AAAAAHHHHHHHH!!!
APRIL!!!

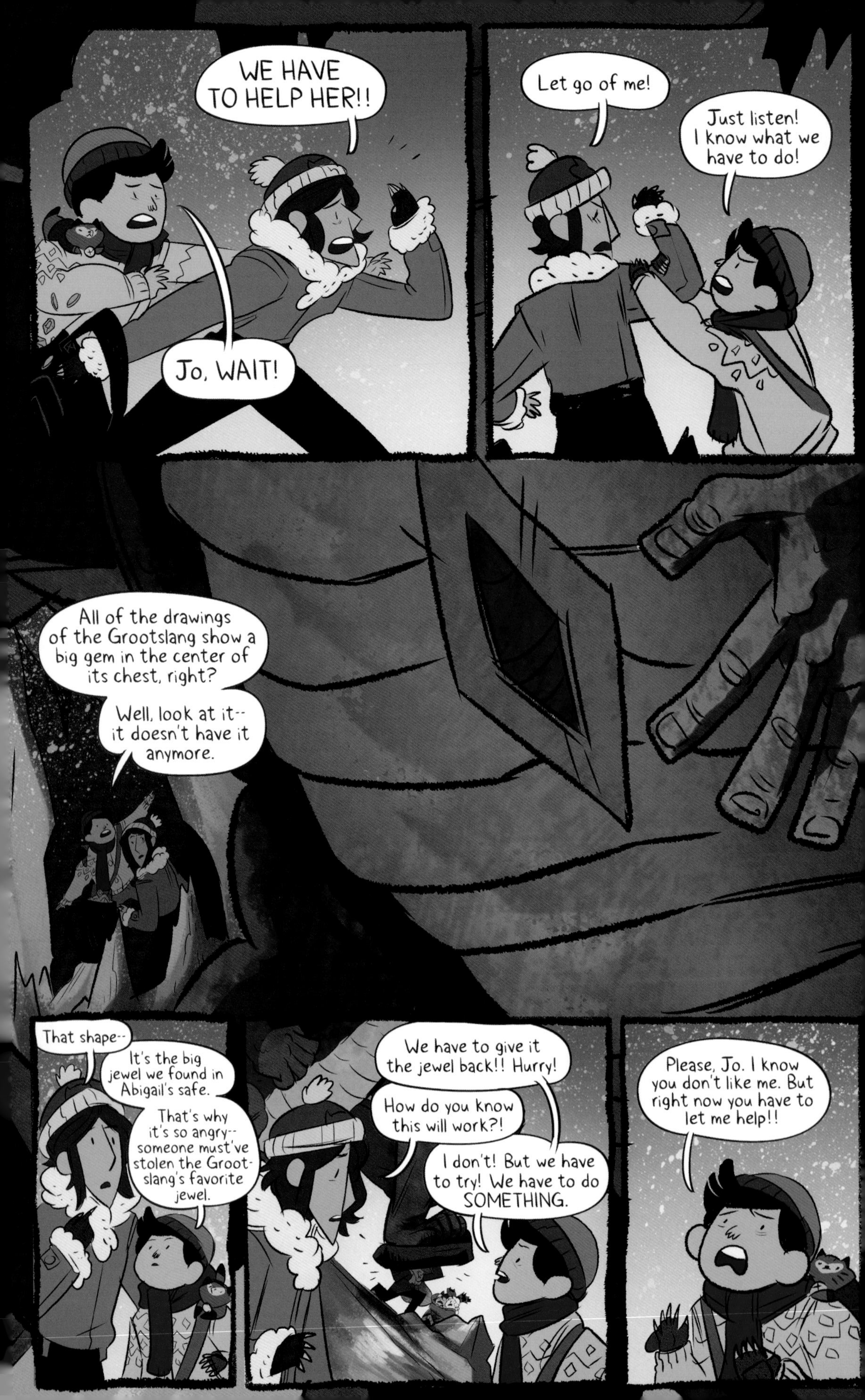
WE HAVE TO HELP HER!!
Jo, WAIT!
Let go of me!
Just listen! I know what we have to do!
All of the drawings of the Grootslang show a big gem in the center of its chest, right?
Well, look at it-- it doesn't have it anymore.
That shape--
It's the big jewel we found in Abigail's safe.
That's why it's so angry-- someone must've stolen the Grootslang's favorite jewel.
We have to give it the jewel back!! Hurry!
How do you know this will work?!
I don't! But we have to try! We have to do SOMETHING.
Please, Jo. I know you don't like me. But right now you have to let me help!!

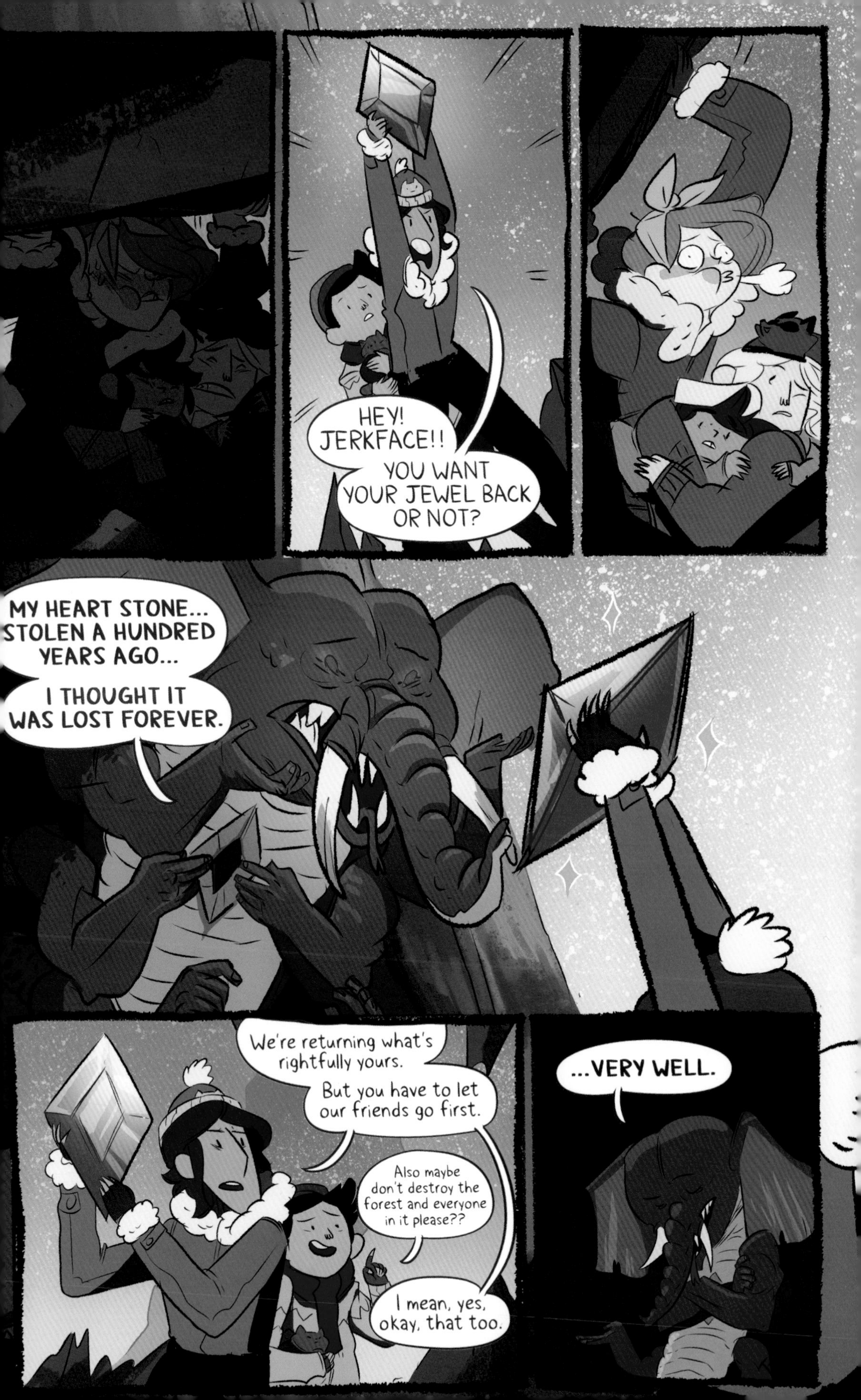
HEY! JERKFACE!!
YOU WANT YOUR JEWEL BACK OR NOT?
MY HEART STONE... STOLEN A HUNDRED YEARS AGO...
I THOUGHT IT WAS LOST FOREVER.
We're returning what's rightfully yours.
But you have to let our friends go first.
Also maybe don't destroy the forest and everyone in it please??
I mean, yes, okay, that too.
...VERY WELL.

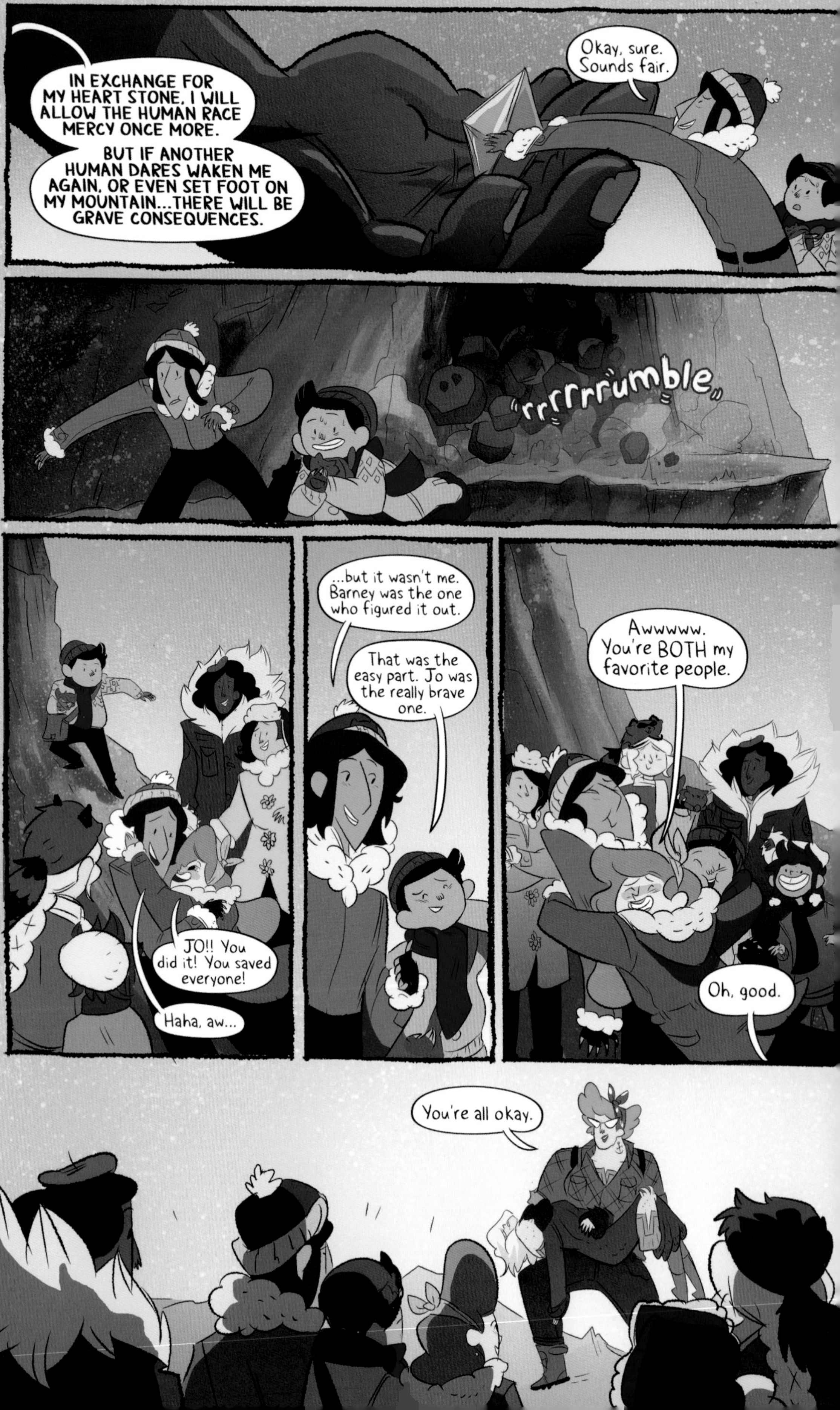

IN EXCHANGE FOR MY HEART STONE, I WILL ALLOW THE HUMAN RACE MERCY ONCE MORE.
BUT IF ANOTHER HUMAN DARES WAKEN ME AGAIN, OR EVEN SET FOOT ON MY MOUNTAIN...THERE WILL BE GRAVE CONSEQUENCES.
Okay, sure. Sounds fair.
"rrrrrrumble"
JO!! You did it! You saved everyone!
Haha, aw...
...but it wasn't me. Barney was the one who figured it out.
That was the easy part. Jo was the really brave one.
Awwwww. You're BOTH my favorite people.
Oh, good.
You're all okay.

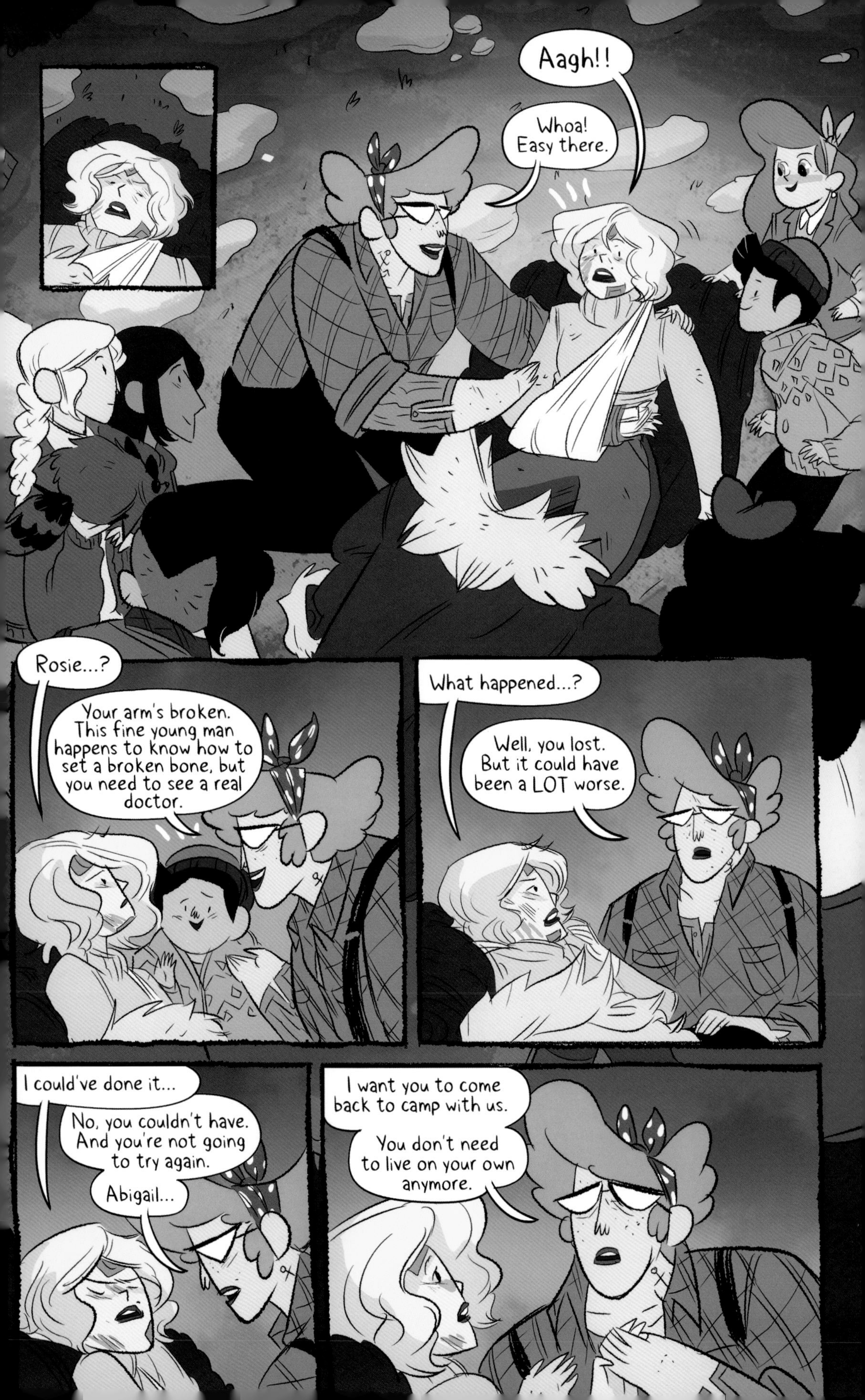
Aagh!!
Whoa! Easy there.
Rosie...?
Your arm's broken. This fine young man happens to know how to set a broken bone, but you need to see a real doctor.
What happened...?
Well, you lost. But it could have been a LOT worse.
I could've done it...
No, you couldn't have. And you're not going to try again.
Abigail...
I want you to come back to camp with us.
You don't need to live on your own anymore.

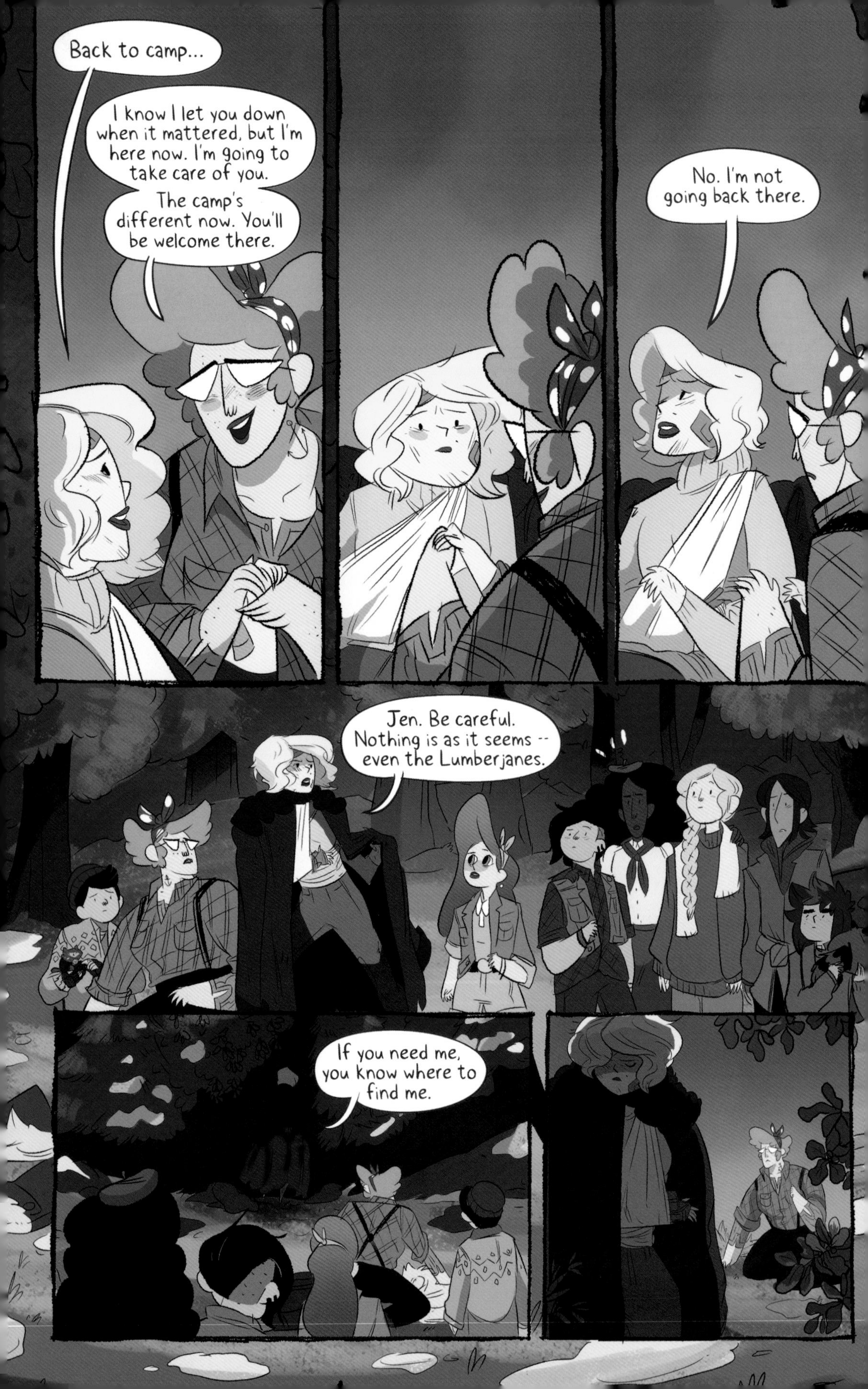
Back to camp...
I know I let you down when it mattered, but I'm here now. I'm going to take care of you.
The camp's different now. You'll be welcome there.
No. I'm not going back there.
Jen. Be careful. Nothing is as it seems -- even the Lumberjanes.
If you need me, you know where to find me.

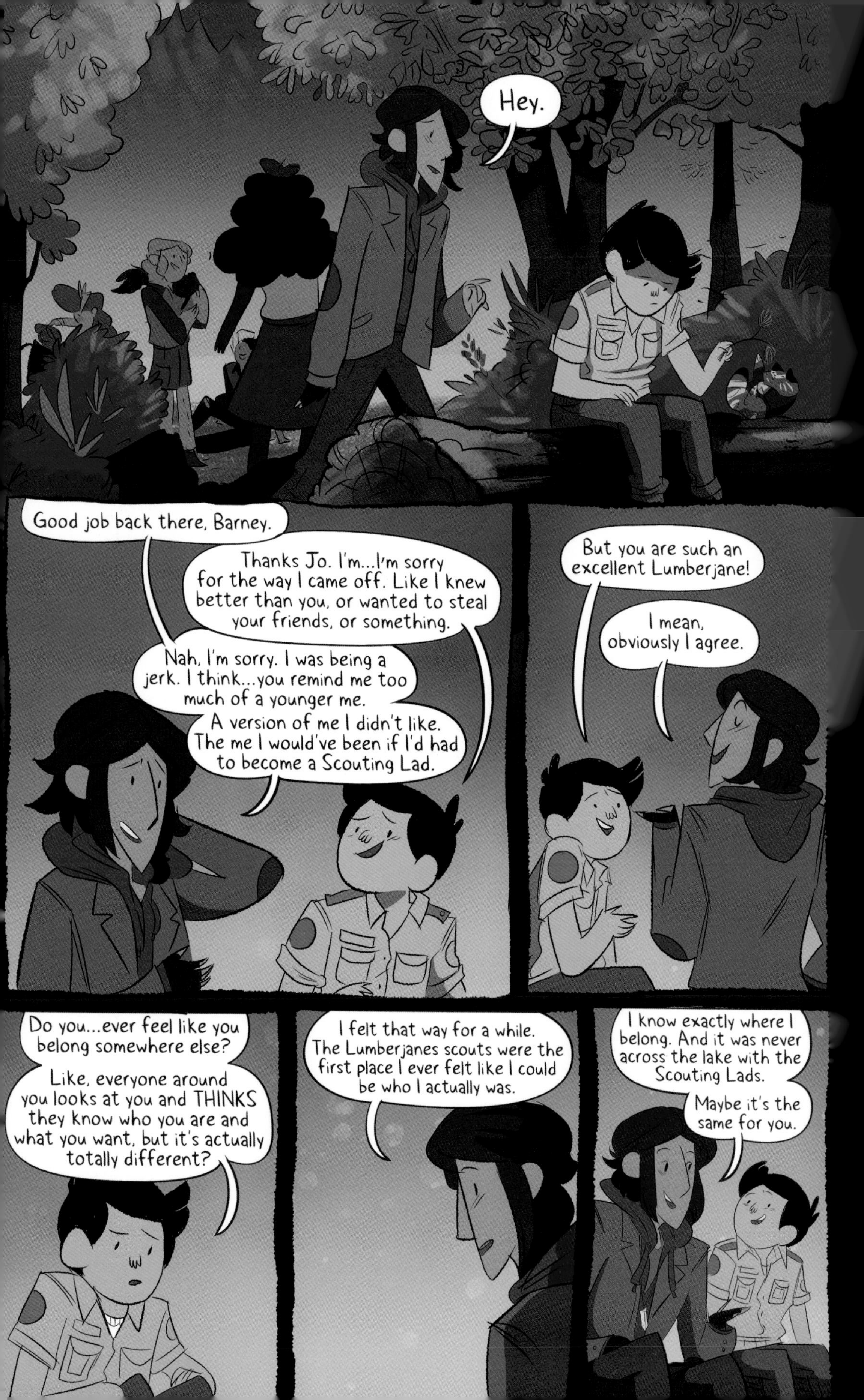
Hey.
Good job back there, Barney.
Thanks Jo. I'm...I'm sorry for the way I came off. Like I knew better than you, or wanted to steal your friends, or something.
Nah, I'm sorry. I was being a jerk. I think...you remind me too much of a younger me.
A version of me I didn't like. The me I would've been if I'd had to become a Scouting Lad.
But you are such an excellent Lumberjane!
I mean, obviously I agree.
Do you...ever feel like you belong somewhere else?
Like, everyone around you looks at you and THINKS they know who you are and what you want, but it's actually totally different?
I felt that way for a while. The Lumberjanes scouts were the first place I ever felt like I could be who I actually was.
I know exactly where I belong. And it was never across the lake with the Scouting Lads.
Maybe it's the same for you.

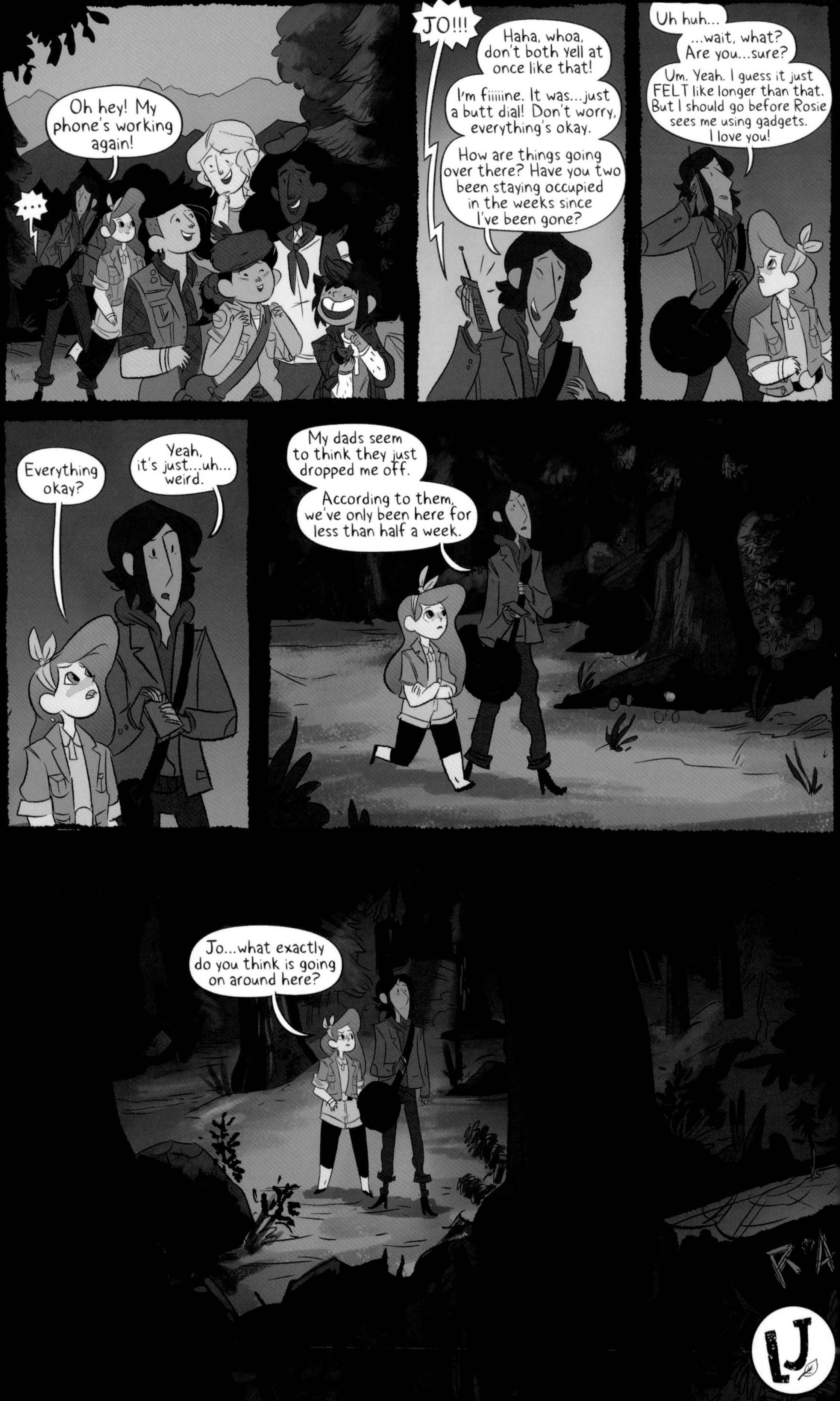
Oh hey! My phone's working again!
...
JO!!!
Haha, whoa, don't both yell at once like that!
I'm fiiiiine. It was...just a butt dial! Don't worry, everything's okay.
How are things going over there? Have you two been staying occupied in the weeks since I've been gone?
Uh huh...
...wait, what? Are you...sure?
Um. Yeah. I guess it just FELT like longer than that. But I should go before Rosie sees me using gadgets. I love you!
Everything okay?
Yeah, it's just...uh... weird.
My dads seem to think they just dropped me off.
According to them, we've only been here for less than half a week.
Jo...what exactly do you think is going on around here?

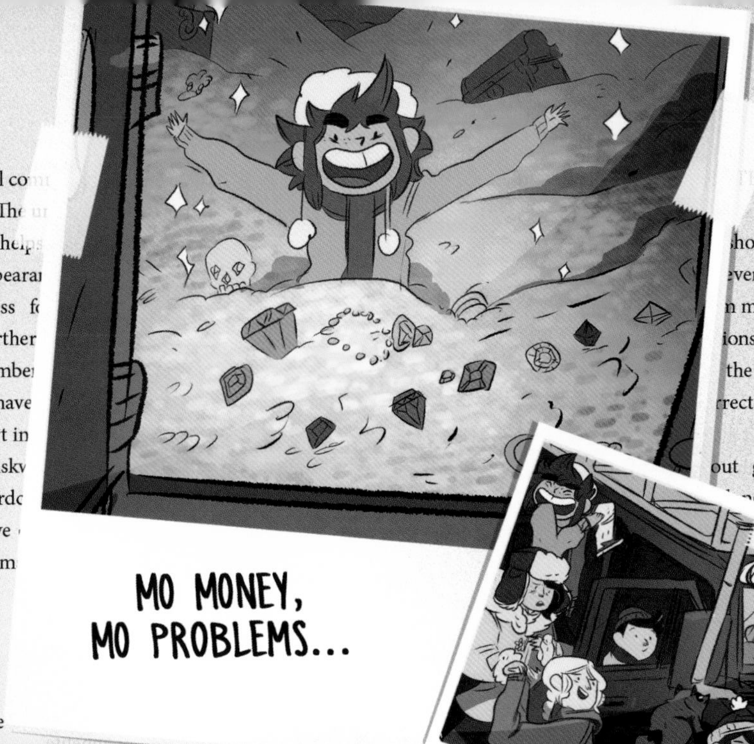
MO MONEY,
MO PROBLEMS...

will com

THE UNIFORM

The u

It help should be worn at camp appearan events when Lumberjanes dress f n may also be worn at other Further ions. It should be worn as a Lumbe the uniform dress with to have rrect shoes, and stocking or part in

Thiskv out grows her uniform or Hardc ter Lumberjane. have insignia she has them her her

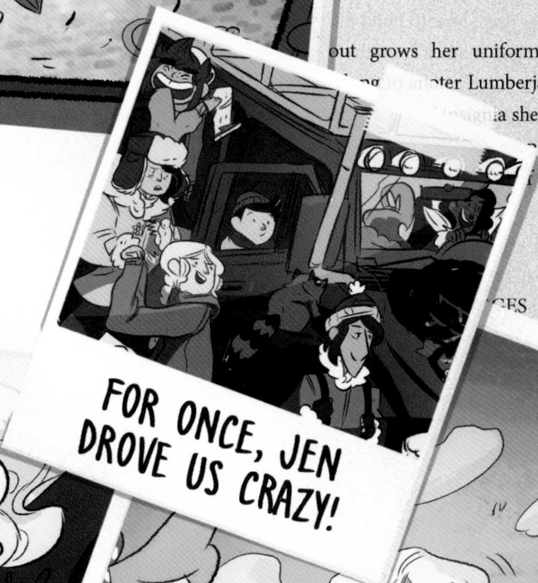
FOR ONCE, JEN
DROVE US CRAZY!

The yellow, short sle emb the w choose slacks, made o out-of-do green bere the colla Shoes may b heels, rou ngs or socks should ith the shoes or wi the uniform. Ne ces, bracelets, or other jewelry do belong with a Lumberjane uniform.

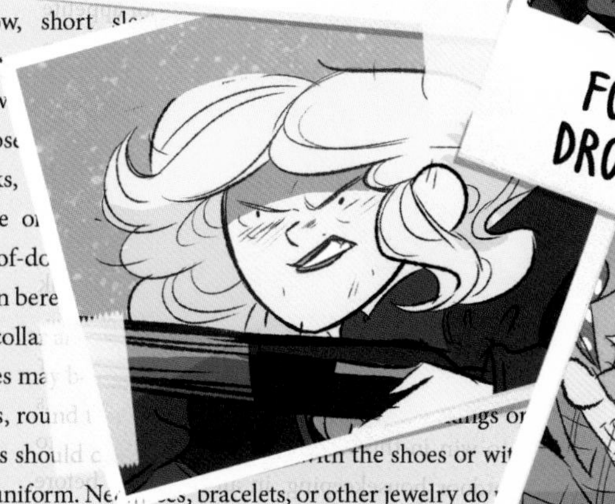

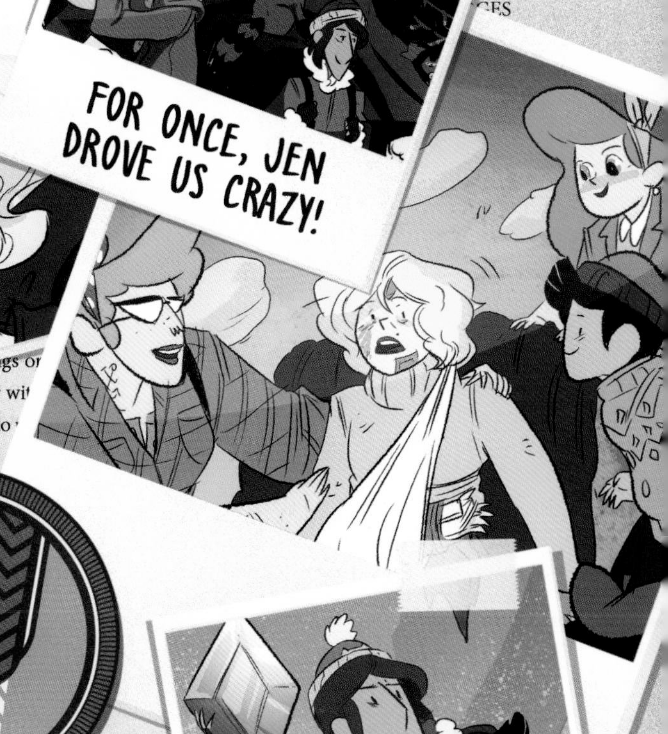

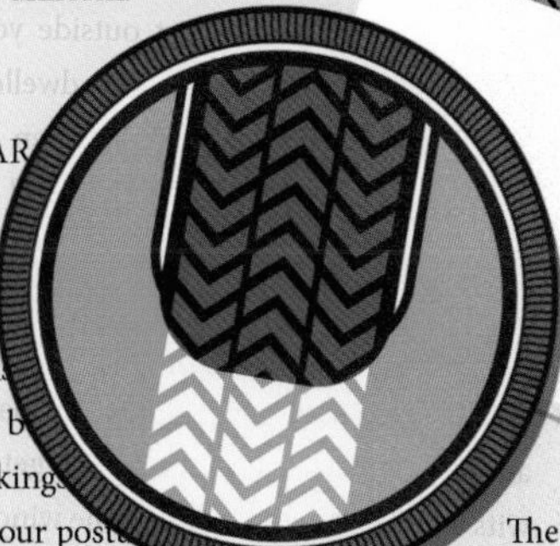

HOW TO WEAR

To look well in a uniform uniform be kept in goo pressed. See that the skirt i height and build, that the b that your shoes and stockings uniform, that you watch your post with dignity and grace. If the beret is removed indoors, be sure that your hair is neat and kept in place with an insonspicuous clip or ribbon. When you wear a Lumberjane uniform you are identified as a member of this organization and you should be doubly careful to conduct yourself in a way that will show everyone that courtesy and thoughtfullness are part of being a Lumberjane. People are likely to judge a whole nation by the selfishness of a few individuals, to criticize a whole family because of the misconduct of one member, and to feel unkindly toward and organization because of the

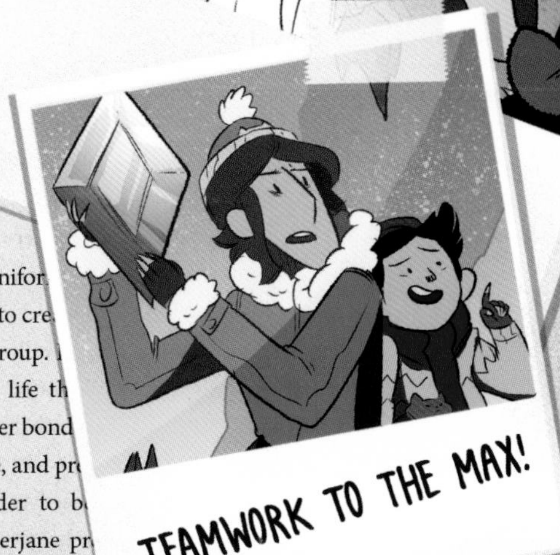
TEAMWORK TO THE MAX!

The unifor helps to cre in a group. active life th another bond future, and pr in order to b Lumberjane pr Penniquiqul Thi ore Lady Types, but m es will wish to have one. They can either bu the uniform, or make it themselves from materials available at the trading post.

COVER GALLERY

Lumberjanes "Wildlife" Program Field

BADGER OF HONOR BADGE

"The more the merrier."

A Lumberjanes success is not based solely on the badges that she earns, but it can be a lot of fun to collect them all. There are hundreds of badges that a Lumberjane is able to earn, from the *Pungeon Master* badge to the beloved *Dye Hard* badge, in which Lumberjanes learn how to create dye from nature around them. In our Lumberjanes camp, we want all the Lumberjanes to only take on the badges that they are able to fit into their time at the camp, and if that means someone is able to tackle the whole handbook and it's several other volumes, then we applaud this individual. It is up to the camper to find every counselor, every possible teacher, to find out what badges she can earn in the time frame she has allotted.

If a Lumberjane scout is able to collect all the badges available to them at the time that this badge becomes available, then they will get the *Badger of Honor* badge, as well as a lesson in how to extend their sash in a tasteful fashion. Though if they are already earning this badge then there is a good chance they they've already decides to extend their sash several times over. To the Lumberjane who decided to take on this challenge, keep in mind that competition is encouraged, as long as it remains happy, healthy, and non-detrimental to anyone else at the camp. The *Badger of Honor* badge is a badge earned because Lumberjanes never quit. Lumberjanes want to excel at everything they have the chance to. This is a badge earned by those who know what they want to accomplish and will be able to take on the challenge while most likely bringing their friends along for the ride.

To obtain the *Badger of Honor* badge, a Lumberjane must be persistent, she must keep her head up and tackle every obstacle that is thrown at her. She will go out of her way to find more badges for her to earn, and with the help of her friends, accomplish every task she sets forth

Issue Fourteen
JOY ANG

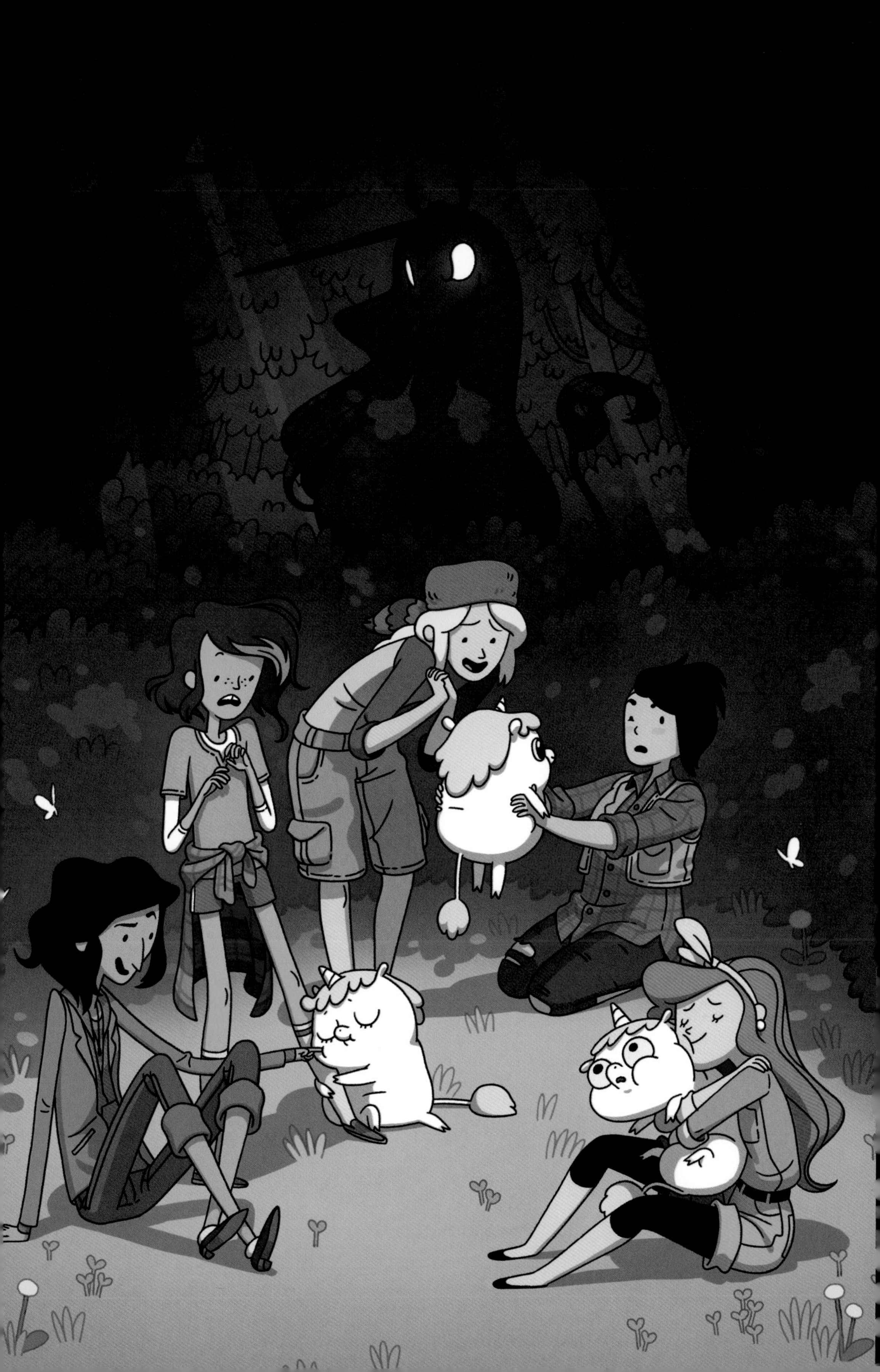

Issue Fourteen San Diego Comic-Con Exclusive
KASSANDRA HELLER

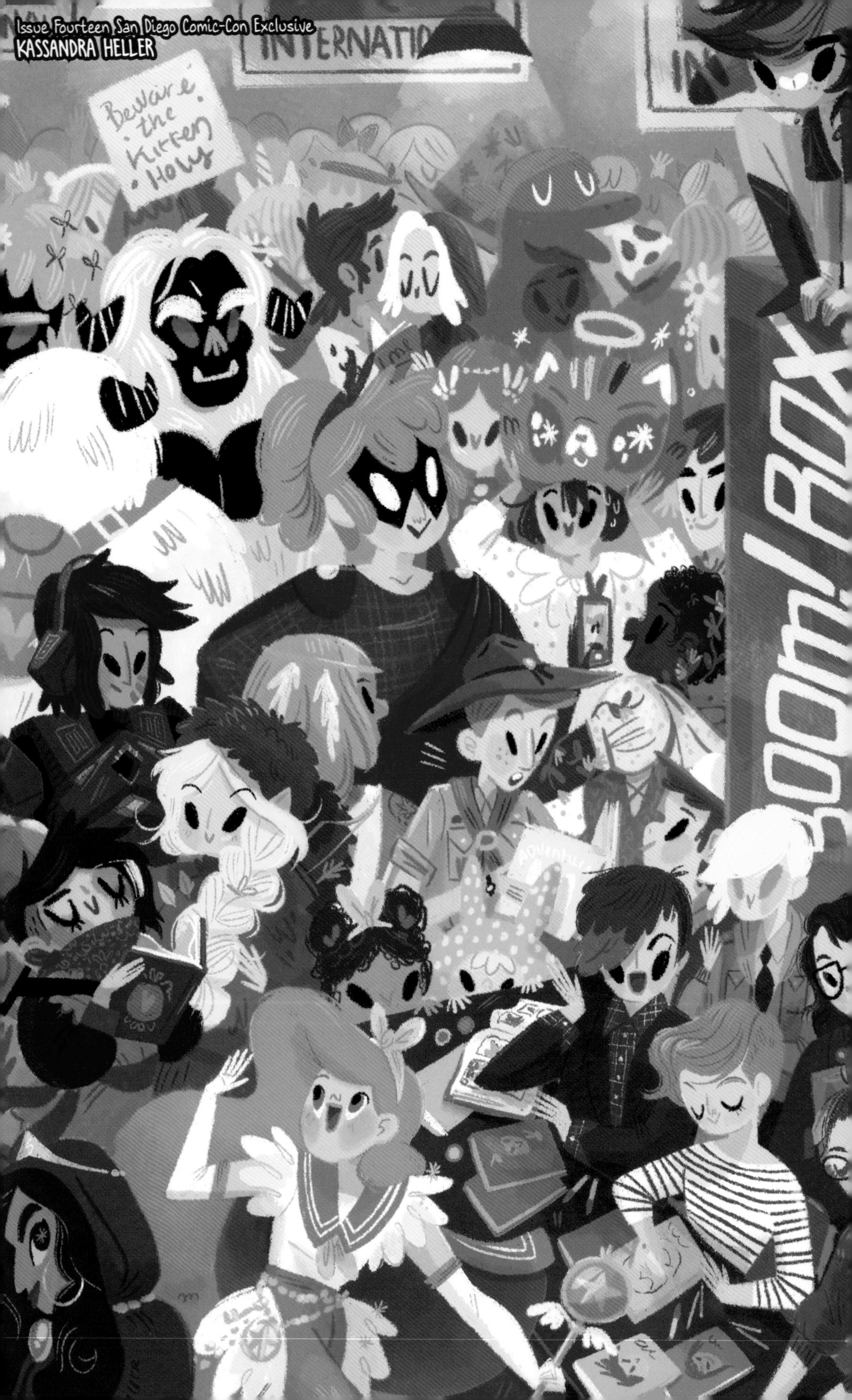
INTERNATIO
Beware the Kitten Holy
BOOM! BOX
Adventure

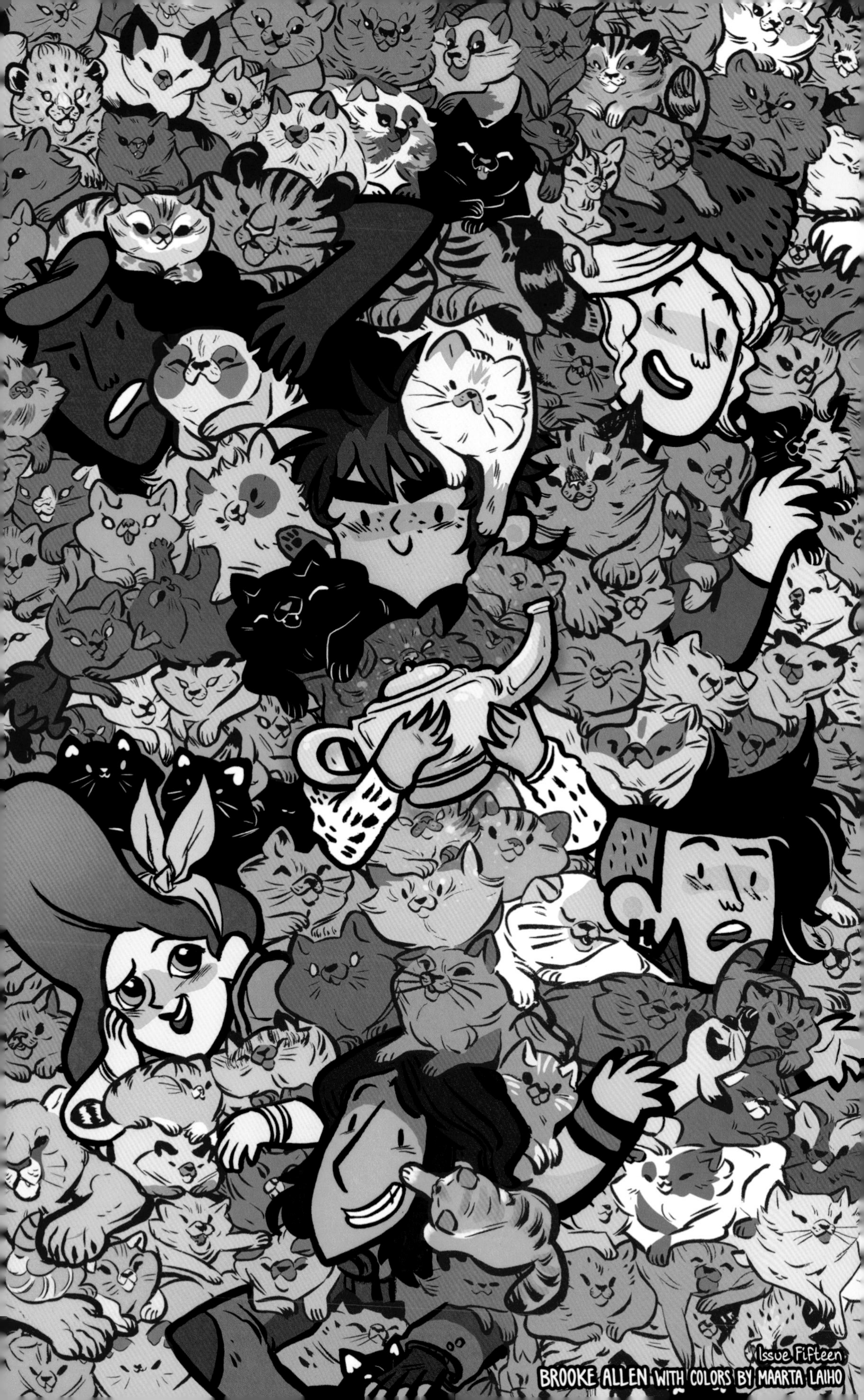
Issue Fifteen
BROOKE ALLEN WITH COLORS BY MAARTA LAIHO

Issue Fifteen Variant
RICARDO BESSA

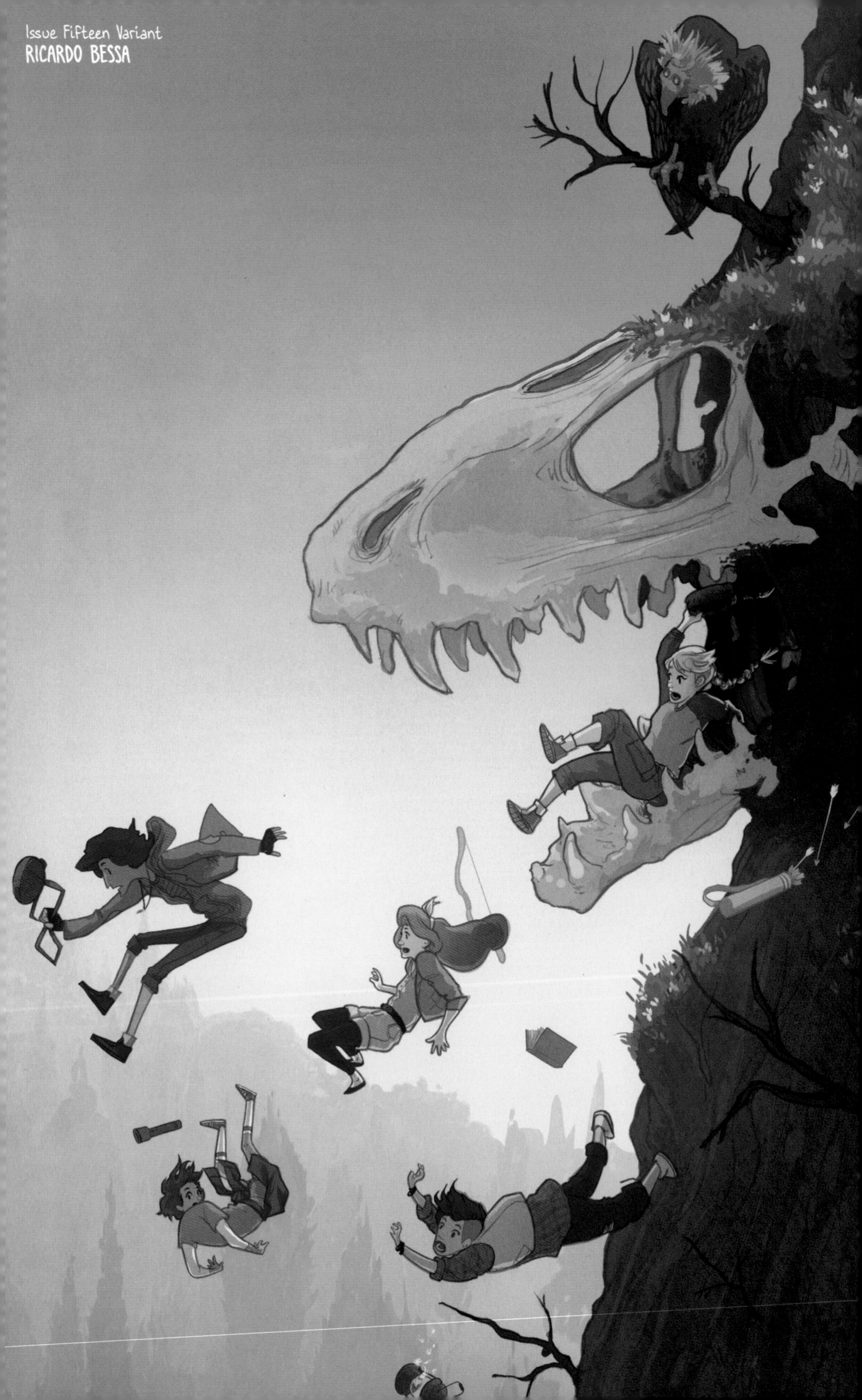

Issue Fifteen ComiXology Exclusive
HOPE LARSON WITH COLORS BY MAARTA LAIHO

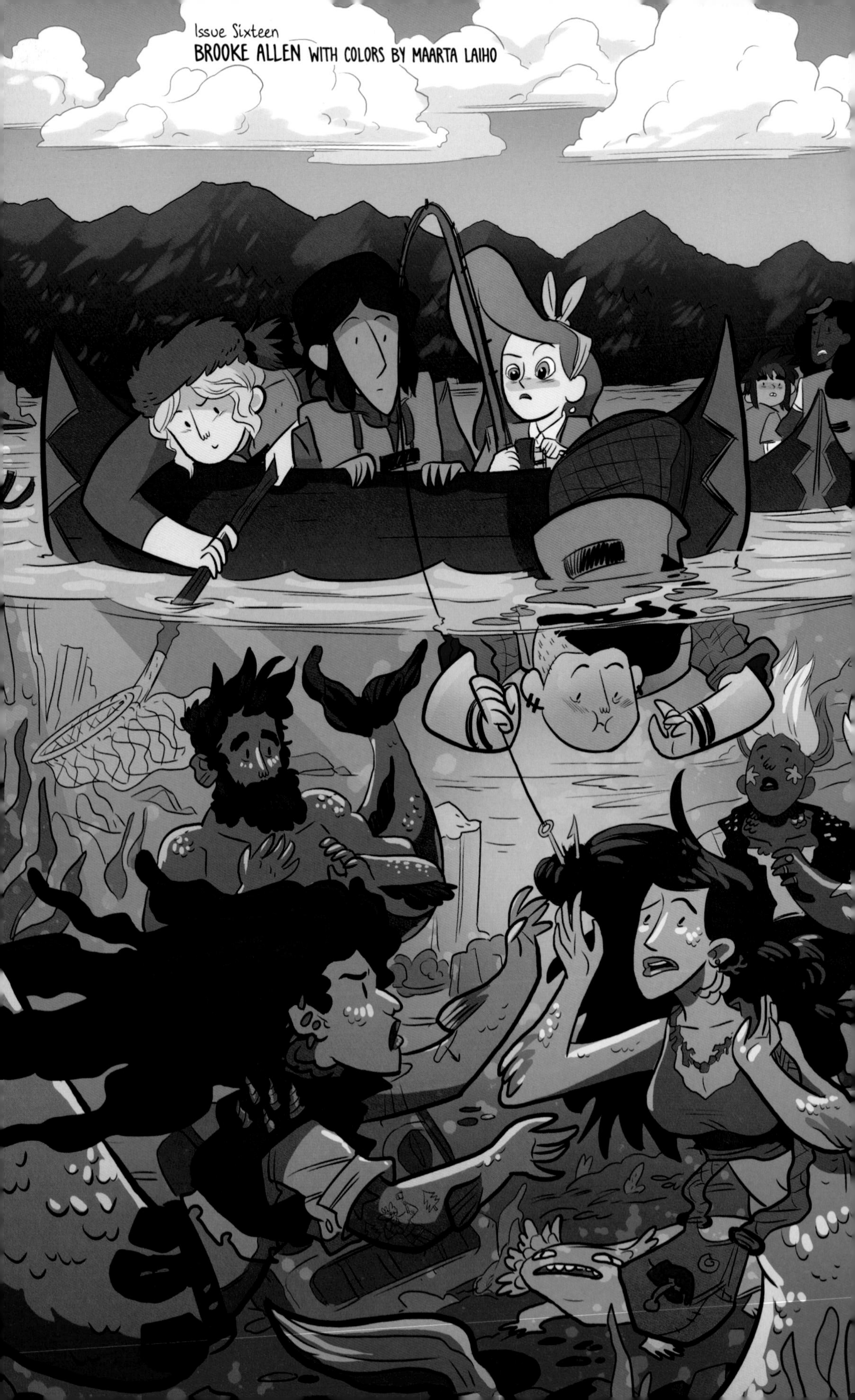
Issue Sixteen
BROOKE ALLEN WITH COLORS BY MAARTA LAIHO

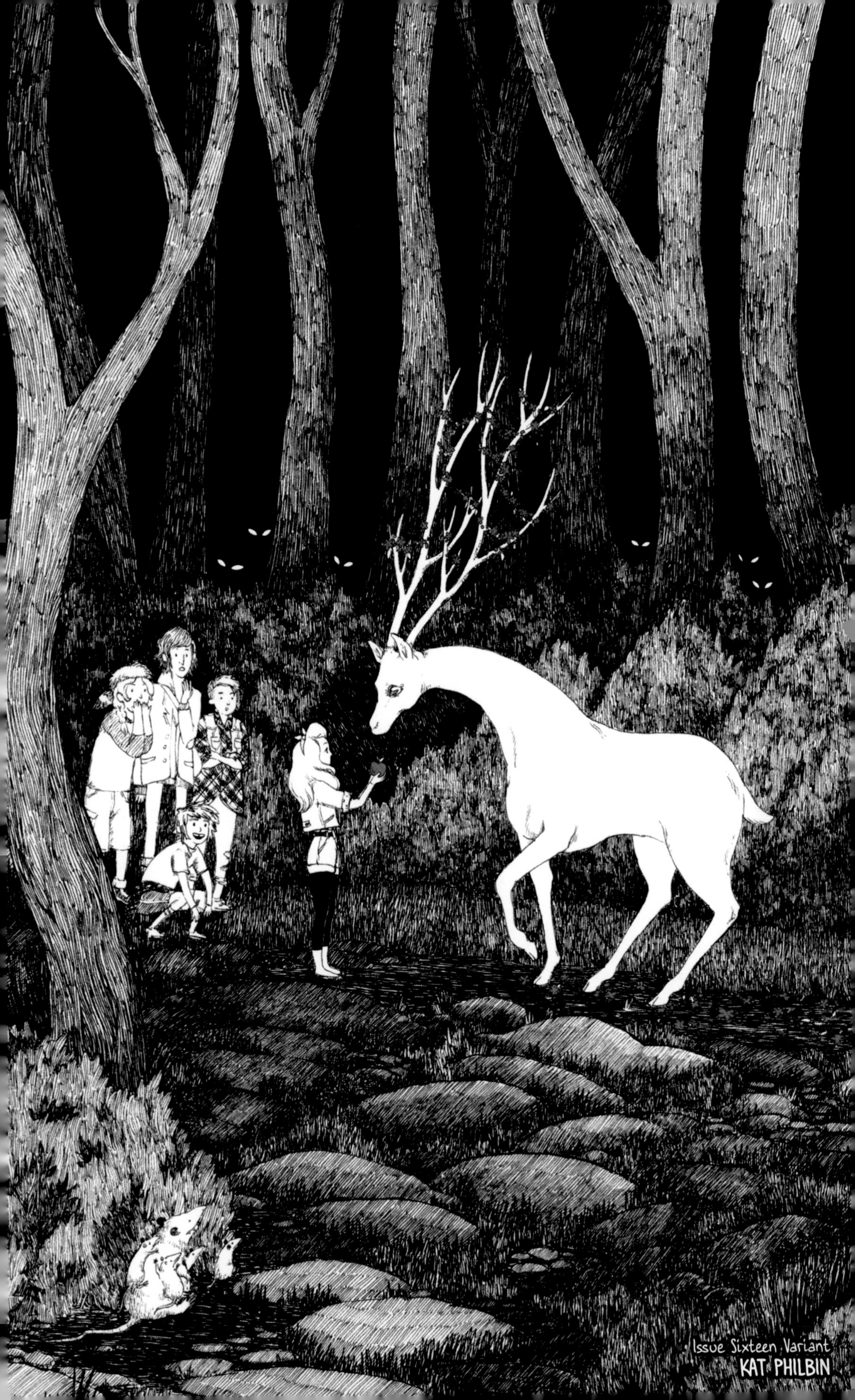
Issue Sixteen Variant
KAT PHILBIN

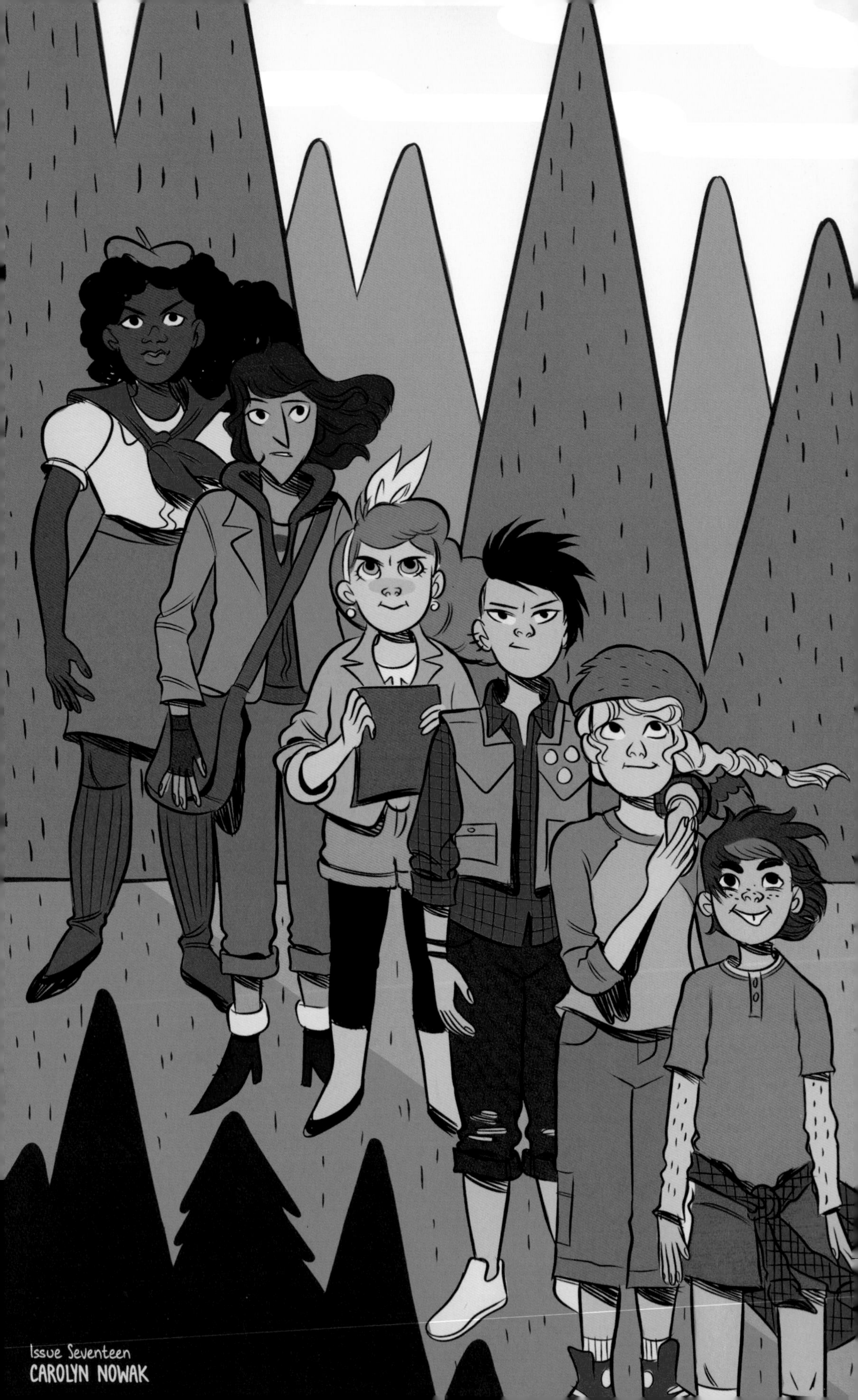

Issue Seventeen
CAROLYN NOWAK

Issue Seventeen Variant
JEN WANG

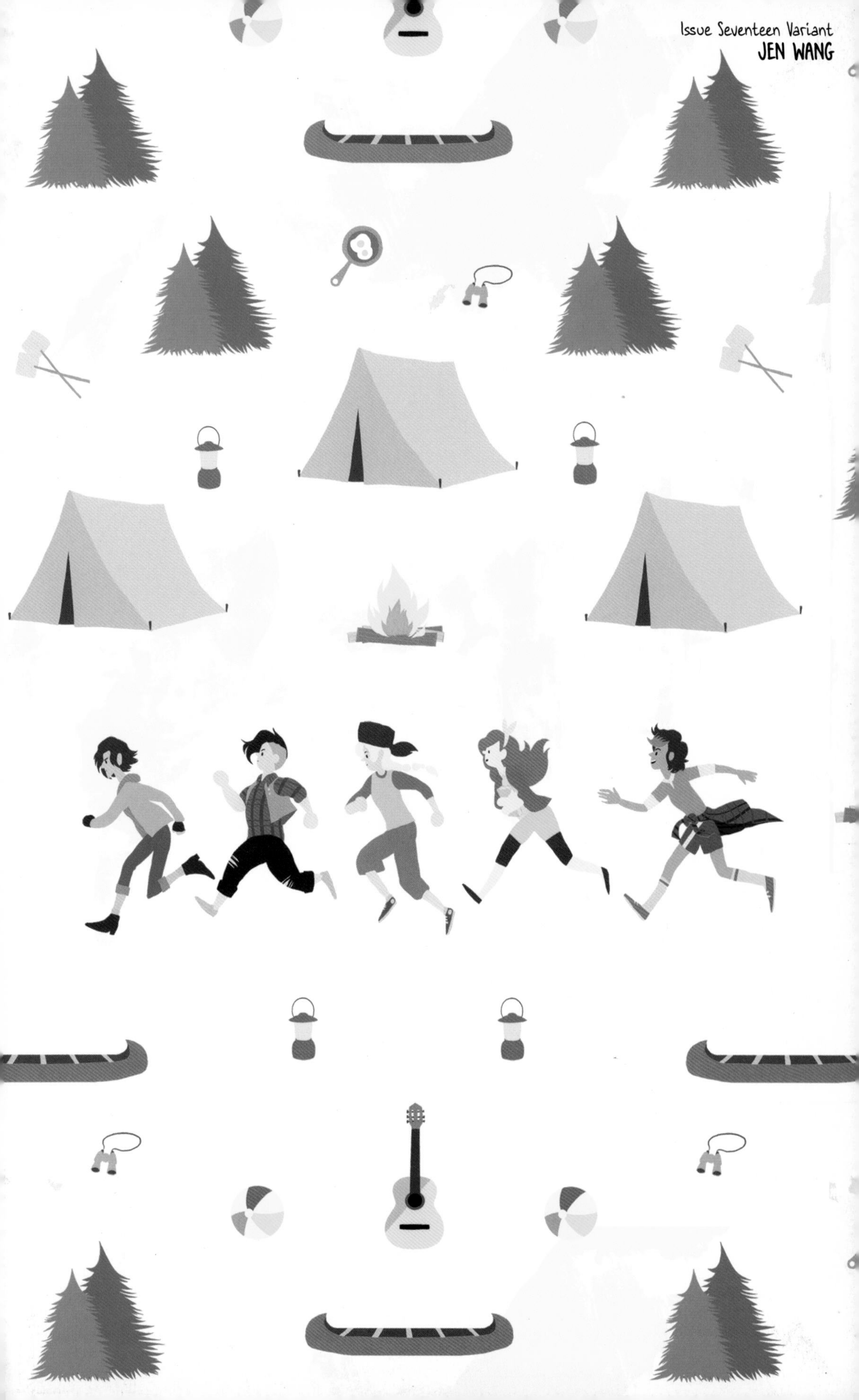

LJ

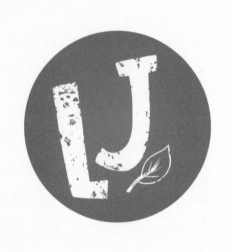